THE KICK-ASS WRITER

1001 WAYS TO WRITE GREAT FICTION, GET PUBLISHED & EARN YOUR AUDIENCE

CHUCK WENDIG

WRITER'S DIGEST
BOOKS

WritersDigest.com
Cincinnati, Ohio

D1166263

For more resources for writers, visit www.writersdigest.com.

17 16 15 14 13 5 4 3 2 1

Distributed in Canada by Fraser Direct
100 Armstrong Avenue
Georgetown, Ontario, Canada L7G 5S4
Tel: (905) 877-4411

Distributed in the U.K. and Europe by F&W Media International
Brunel House, Newton Abbot, Devon, TQ12 4PU, England
Tel: (+44) 1626-323200, Fax: (+44) 1626-323319
E-mail: postmaster@davidandcharles.co.uk

Distributed in Australia by Capricorn Link
P.O. Box 704, Windsor, NSW 2756 Australia
Tel: (02) 4577-3555

Edited by James Duncan
Cover Designed by Bethany Rainbolt
Interior Designed by Rachael Ward
Production coordinated by Debbie Thomas

ABOUT THE AUTHOR

Chuck Wendig is a novelist, screenwriter, and game designer. He is the author of such novels as *Blackbirds, Mockingbird, The Blue Blazes,* and *Under the Empyrean Sky.* He is an alumni of the Sundance Screenwriter's Lab and is the co-author of the Emmy-nominated digital narrative *Collapsus* and developer of the game *Hunter: The Vigil.* He lives in Pennsyltucky with his wife, son, and two dopey dogs. You can find him on Twitter @ChuckWendig and at his website, terribleminds.com, where he frequently dispenses dubious and very-NSFW advice on writing, publishing, and life in general.

ACKNOWLEDGMENTS

Every writer is the culmination of all the people in his life and all the experiences that he's had, and in this case it feels entirely appropriate to acknowledge and thank those writers who have informed my own writing and who have in fact helped me understand the craft of writing and the art of storytelling. I'd like to thank (in no particular order): Robert McCammon, Joe Lansdale, Robin Hobb, Toni Morrison, James Joyce, Joseph Campbell, Stephen King, Don DeLillo, Christopher Moore, Bradley Denton, Shirley Jackson, Neil Gaiman, Robert Pelton Young, Tim Cahill, Poppy Z. Brite, David Simon, Tim Sandlin, Ellen Datlow, Ray Bradbury, and Margaret Atwood.

TABLE OF CONTENTS

INTRODUCTION: THE FIRST TIP

Nothing in this book is true.

None of it comes from the Hand of God. He didn't thrust His big grumpy finger down through the clouds to etch these proclamations in stone tablets.

No Muse is whispering them in your ear.

They are not immutable laws scrawled outside English classes or bookstores.

These are not regulations.

This is not gospel.

This is not a math problem by which X + Y = a perfect story.

These are not rules.

This is a book of writing advice. Which to say, it's just a bucket of ideas that are at least half-nonsense. A bucket of ideas that serve as tools. And not every tool is meant for every job. And not every craftsman finds the value in every tool.

We test our tools. We pick them up. We feel their heft, their grip, their ease of use. We tinker. We see if they'll fix our broken widgets or adjust our off-kilter thingamabobs. If they work, we put them in the toolbox for when we need them. If they don't work, we throw them in the dirt and walk away.

That's all this book is.

It's a book of ideas about writing. Tips. Notions. Tricks. Thoughts. *Tools.*

No writing advice is bad advice.

And no writing advice is perfectly true advice, either.

Writing advice either:

a) Works for you.

or

b) Does not work for you.

And that's okay. That's how it's meant to be.

Advice is just as it sounds. Mere suggestions. If I give you advice on how to get from Point A (the taco stand on Broad Street) to Point B (the other taco stand on Maple because hell yeah, more tacos), you can choose to listen to me or not. I'm not holding a gun to your head. Maybe you know a better way. A secret way. Maybe you don't care that your way takes longer—maybe you want the scenic route. It's just advice. I offered it. You like it or you don't. It works or it doesn't.

The goal isn't to deliver truth unto you. The goal is not to inflict my ways and rules upon you. The goal is to make you think. We should think about what we do. We should strive to improve ourselves. We should hope to fix the things that don't work for us and better the things that do. What we do is an intellectual and creative pursuit, so why not take some time and noodle it? Talk about it? Bat it back and forth like a cat with a ball of yarn?

At the end of the day—or, at least, the end of this book—you're going to pick up some things and tuck them away or you're going to leave them by the side of the road and move on. Just as every Jedi constructs his own lightsaber, every penmonkey makes his own quill—which is to say, we all have our own ways of telling stories, our own voices and our own styles, our own ways up the publishing mountain. We have no absolutes. We are given no guarantees.

Well—perhaps that's not entirely true.

I have one piece of immutable advice.

And that is: *Finish what you begin.*

Because the best piece of writing you never finish is always inferior to the worst piece of writing that you did.

Enjoy the book.

Mind the language; it gets a bit naughty.

I'll see you on the other side.

PART ONE
THE FUNDAMENTALS

25 THINGS YOU SHOULD KNOW ABOUT BEING A WRITER

1. You Are Legion
The Internet is 55 percent porn and 45 percent writers. You are not alone, and that's a thing both good and bad. It's bad because you can never be the glittery little glass pony you want to be. It's bad because the competition out there is as thick as an ungroomed 1970s pubic tangle. It's good because, if you choose to embrace it, you can find a community. A community of people who will share their neuroses and their drink recipes. And their, ahem, "fictional" methods for disposing of bodies.

2. Put the "Fun" in "Fundamentals"
A lot of writers try to skip over the basics and leap fully-formed out of their own head wombs. Bzzt. Wrongo. Learn your basics. Mix up

lose/loose? *They're/their/there*? Don't know where to plop that comma or how to use those quotation marks? That's like trying to be a world-class chef without knowing how to cook a goddamn egg. Writing is a mechanical act first and foremost. It is the process of putting words after other words in a way that doesn't sound or look like inane gibberish.

3. Skill Over Talent

Some writers were born with some magical storytelling gland that they can flex like their pubococcygeus, spewing brilliant storytelling and powerful linguistic voodoo with but a twitch of their taint. This is a small minority of all writers, which means you're probably not that. The good news is, even talent dies without skill. You can practice what you do. You practice it by writing, by reading, by living a life worth writing about. You must always be learning, gaining, improving.

4. Nobody Cares About Your Creative Writing Degree

I have been writing professionally for a lucky-despite-the-number 13 years. Not once—seriously, not once ever—has anyone ever asked me where I got my writing degree. Or if I even have one. Nobody gives two ferrets fornicating in a filth-caked gym sock whether or not you have a degree, be it a writing degree or a degree in waste management. The only thing that matters is, "Can you write well?"

5. Speaking of Luck

Luck matters. Sorry! But you *can* maximize luck. You won't get struck by lightning if you don't wander out into the field covered in tinfoil and armed with an old TV antennae.

6. This Is a Slow Process

Nobody becomes a writer overnight. Well, I'm sure somebody did, but that person's head probably went all asplodey from paroxysms of joy, fear, paranoia, guilt, and uncertainty. Celebrities can be born overnight. Writers can't. Writers are made—forged, really, in a kiln of their own madness and insecurities—over the course of many, many moons. The writer you are when you begin is not the writer you become.

7. Nobody "Gets In" the Same Way

Your journey to becoming a writer is all your own. You own it for good and bad. Part of it is all that goofy shit that forms the building blocks of your very persona—a mean daddy, an ugly dog, a smelly house, pink hair, a doting mother, that bagger at the local Scoot-N-Shop. The other part is the industry part, where you dig your own tunnel through the earth and detonate it behind you. No two writers will sit down and tell the exact same story of their emergence from the wordmonkey cocoon. You aren't a beautiful and unique snowflake, except when you are.

8. Writing Feels Like—but Isn't—Magic

Yours is the power of gods: You say, "Let there be light," and Sweet Maggie McGillicutty, *here comes some light*. Writing is the act of creation. Put words on a page, words to sentences, sentences to paragraphs, paragraphs to seven-book epic fantasy cycles with books so heavy you could choke a hippo. But don't give writing too much power, either. A wizard controls his magic; it doesn't control him. Push aside lofty notions and embrace the workmanlike aesthetic. Hammers above magic wands; nails above eye-of-newt. The magic will return when you're done. The magic is in what you did, not in what you're doing.

9. Storytelling Is Serious Business

Treat it with respect and a little bit of reverence. Storytelling is what makes the world go around. Even math is a kind of story (though, let's be honest, a story with too few space donkeys or dragon marines). Don't let writing and storytelling be some throwaway thing. Don't piss it away.

It's really cool stuff. Stories have the power to make people feel. To give a shit. To change their opinions. To change the world.

10. Your Writing Has Whatever Value You Give It

Value is a tricky word saddled with a lot of baggage. It speaks to dollar amounts. It speaks to self-esteem. It speaks to moral and spiritual significance. The value of your wordmonkeying has a chameleonic component: Whatever value you give it, that's what value it will have. You give your work away, that's what it's worth. If you hate your work, that's what it's worth. Put more plainly: What you do has value, so claim value for what you do. Put even more plainly: Don't work for free.

11. You Are Your Own Worst Enemy

It's not the gatekeepers. Not the audience. Not the reviewers. Not your wife, your mother, your baby, your dog. Not your work schedule, your sleep schedule, your rampant masturbation schedule. If you're not succeeding at writing, you've nobody to blame but yourself. You're the one who needs to super-glue her booty to the chair. You're the one who needs to pound away at his keyboard until the words come out. It's like Michael Jackson sang: "I took my baby on a Saturday bang." ... No, wait, that's not it. "I'm talkin' 'bout the man in the mirror." Yeah. Yes. That's the one.

12. Your Voice Is Your Own

Write like you write, like you can't help but write, and your voice will become yours and yours alone. It'll take time, but it'll happen as long as you let it. Own your voice, for your voice is your own. Once you know where your voice lives, you no longer have to worry so much about being derivative.

13. Cultivate Calluses

Put differently—harden up, soldier. The writing life is a tough one. Edits can be hard to take. Rejections, even worse. Not everybody respects what you do. Hell, a lot of people don't even care. Build up that layer of blubber. Form a mighty exoskeleton. Expect to be pelted in the face with metaphorical (er, hopefully metaphorical) ice balls. It's a gauntlet. It sucks. Still gotta run it, though.

14. Stones Are Polished by Agitation

Even the roughest stone is made smooth by agitation, motion, erosion. Yeah, the writing life can be tough, but it needs to be. Edits are good. Rejections are, too. Write with a partner. Submit yourself to criticism. Creative agitation can serve you well. Embrace it. Look into that dark hole for answers, not fear. Gaze into the narrative vagina and find the story baby crowning there ... okay, too far? Too far. Pretend I didn't say that. Doesn't this book have an editor? Jeez.

15. Act Like an Asshole, Get Treated Like an Asshole

Agitation is good. Being an agitator, not so much. If you are an asshole to agents and editors, editors and agents will treat you like an asshole. If you are an asshole to other writers, they'll bash you over the head with a typewriter, or shiv you with an iPad in the shower. If you are an asshole to your audience, they'll do a thing worse than all of that: They'll just ignore you. So, for real, don't be an asshole.

16. Writing Is Never About Just Writing

Writing is the priority. Write the best work you can write. That's true. But it's not all of it, either. Writing is ever an uncountable multitude. We wish writing were just about writing. The writer is editor, marketer, blogger, reader, thinker, designer, publisher, public speaker, budget maker, contract reader, troubleshooter, coffee hound, liver pickler, shame farmer, god, devil, gibbering protozoa.

17. This Is an Industry of People

They say it's "who you know," which is true to a point, but it doesn't really get to the heart of it. That sounds like everybody's the equivalent to Soylent Green—just use 'em up for your own hungry purpose. That's not it. You want to make friends. Be a part of the community. People aren't stepstools. Connect with other humans in your respective industry. Do not use and abuse them.

18. The Worst Thing Your Work Can Be Is Boring

You've got all the words in the world at your disposal and an infinite number of arrangements in which to use them. So don't be boring. Who wants to read work that's duller than a dirty bowling ball?

19. Second Worst Thing Is a Loss of Clarity

Clarity is king. Say what you mean. You're telling a story, be it in a book, a film, a game, an article, a dinner table placemat. Don't make the reader stagger woozily through the mire just to grasp what you're saying.

20. Writing Is About Words, Storytelling Is About Life

Everybody tells you that to be a writer, you have to read and write a lot. That's true. But it's not all of it. That'll help you understand the technical side. It'll help you grasp the way a story is built. But that doesn't put meat on the bones you arrange. For that, you need everything but reading and writing. Go live. Travel. Ride a bike. Eat weird food. Experience things. Otherwise, what the hell are you going to talk about?

21. Everything Can Be Fixed in Post

Stop stressing out. You get the one thing few others get: a constant array of do-overs. Writing is rewriting. Edit till she's pretty. Rewrite until it doesn't suck. You have an endless supply of blowtorches, hacksaws, scalpels, chainsaws, M-80s, and orbital lasers to constantly destroy and rebuild. Of course, you can get caught in that cycle, too. You have to know when to stop the fiddling. You have to know when to get off the ride.

22. Quit Quitting

It's all too easy to start something and not finish it. Remember when I said you were legion? It's true, but if you want to be separated from 90 percent of the other writers (or "writers" depending on how pedantic you choose to be) out there, then just finish the shit that you started. Stop abandoning your children. You wouldn't call yourself a runner if you quit every race halfway through. Finishing is a good start. Stop looking for the escape hatch; pretend your work in progress just doesn't have one.

23. No Such Thing as Bad Writing Advice

There's only advice that works for you and advice that doesn't. It's like going to Home Depot and trying to point out the "bad tools." Rather, some tools work for the job. Most don't. Be confident enough to know when a tool feels right in your hand and when it might instead put out your eye.

24. Though, Nobody Really Knows Shit About Shit

We're all just squawking into the wind and nobody really has the answers, except you. Those answers are only for you. Everybody else is just guessing. Sometimes they're right. A lot of times they're wrong. That's not to say such pontification isn't valuable. You just gotta know what weight to give it.

25. Hope and Love Will Save You

The hard boot is better than the tickling feather when it comes time to talk about the realities of writing, but at the end of the day, the thing that gets you through it all is hope and love. You have to stay positive. Writers are given to a kind of moribund gloom. Don't let the penmonkey blues get you down. Be positive. Stay sane. The only way through is with wide-open eyes and a rigor mortis grin. Don't be one of those writers who isn't having any fun. Don't let writing be the albatross around your neck. Misery is too easy to come by, so don't invite it. If writing doesn't make you happy, maybe you shouldn't be a writer. It's a lot of work, but you need to let it be a lot of play, too. Otherwise, what's the point? Right? Go push a broom, sell a car, or paint a barn. If you're a writer, write. And be happy you can do so.

25 QUESTIONS TO ASK AS YOU WRITE

1. "What Is This About?"

This is, quite seriously, my most favoritest—and what I consider to be the most important—question for any author, writer, storyteller, or general-class penmonkey to ask. The answer to this question isn't just a recitation of plot. This is you going elbow deep into the story's most tenderest of orifices and seeing what lies at the heart of the animal. It's you saying, "This is about how when people are stripped of civilization, they turn into monsters, man," or, "It's about how the son always becomes the father." It's about identifying the theme of your work, about exposing the emotional core and the truth one finds there. You ask this question to make sure your daily word count lines up with your overall desire.

2. "Why the Hell Am I Writing This?"

What I call, "The Give-A-Shit Factor." Why do you give a shit? *Do* you? Why will anyone else care? Figure out what makes your story worth writing. Maybe it's a character. Maybe it's an idea. Maybe it's one scene somewhere in the third act that you *just can't wait to write.* Find out why you're writing this. If you're just phoning it in, wandering aimlessly through the narrative without purpose, the audience is going to feel that. The audience can smell confusion the way that dogs can smell fear and hobos can smell a can of beans. They're like sharks, those hobos. HOBO SHARK II: BLOOD BEANS III.

3. "Is This My Story Written My Way?"

When I read a story by Joe Lansdale, I say, "That's a goddamn Joe Lansdale story." The voice is his. The story is his. The characters are his. You could drag me to an alternate universe where Joe Lansdale was never born, and *still* I'd know that this book in my hands is a book by him. We have to own our fiction. We have to crack our chests open with rib-spreaders and plop our viscera right onto the page. It has to be us living there in the fiction. Feel out the story. Feel if this is *your* story written *your* way (and if not, make it so). Write something that matters to you. If it feels like you're not there? Backtrack, find out where you lost the story (or the *story* lost *you*), and rediscover your voice and your path.

4. "Am I Ready?"

You ask this before you start your project and before every day of writing: *Am I ready*? Screenwriter Jason Arnopp said yet-another-smartypants thing: "I'm seemingly destined to regularly forget that sometimes you're not ready to write a script because you haven't finished thinking about it." Amen! So say we all. Sometimes you just haven't done the brain work. Or gotten all your plotting and scheming out of the way. It is our nature as impetuous creators to want to jump in and do a cannonball, but all that manages to do is make a mess. Sometimes, you're just not ready.

5. "Does This Make Sense?"

The biggest problem with Hollywood blockbuster movies these days is they don't make a lick of goddamn sense. Seriously, I feel like I'm in one big game of Balderdash. I'm constantly asking, "Do they expect me to believe this shit? Did they dose up a four-year-old on Nyquil and let him write this plot?" You'll find plotholes so big you could lose a Rancor Monster in there. Don't be that way. When you're writing, revisit the problem: Does everything line up? Nobody's just … pulling a gun out of their asshole or suddenly crossing two thousand miles of desert in a day, right? Anticipate that your readers are going to be intelligent and will be able to smell mayhem and foolishness from a mile away. Have everything make sense.

6. "What's My Plan?"

Have a plan, and cast a wary eye toward it daily. It's okay if your plan is, "I'm going to write until I'm done." It's fine if your plan is, "I'm going to write the dialogue now, then a few big action pieces, and then I'm going to go back and fill in all the gaps." It doesn't matter what the plan is: It only matters that you've contributed a little *brain-think* toward it. Don't be a pair of loose underwear floating downriver. Take control.

7. "What Do These Characters Want?"

Characters have needs, wants, and fears. Simple as that. John wants a boat. Mary fears goats. Booboo the Space Whale needs to eat a supernova-ing star, or he'll die. Every character is motivated, and that motivation is the engine that pushes them from one end of the scene and out the other. Asking this while writing helps you keep character motivations in line: These motivations drive the plot.

8. "What's the Conflict?"

Every character has a motivation, and then you come along, the Big Ol' Grumpy Storyteller, and throw all kinds of shit in their way to stop them from realizing their hopes and force them to confront their fears. This is conflict. Hiram wants to have a dance party at the country club, but OH NOES he just got kicked out of the country club because his rival, Gunther, has been spreading lies about how Hiram likes to "lay with caribou." Now Hiram must defeat the machinations of his rival and prove his worth to the country club. What Hiram wants is prevented by conflict. So, every day, identify the conflict. Not just in the overall story but in each scene. How do the little conflicts build to larger ones?

9. "What's the Purpose of This Scene?"

Every scene has its purpose. Find it. Expose it. In this scene, you need to show Rodrigo's helplessness. In that scene, you must foreshadow the showdown between Orange Julius (Secret Agent: Orangutan) and his foe, Hobo Shark. The scene after will see the protagonist lose everything and drive home the overwhelming difficulty. As you're writing, find the purpose in each scene. Let it impel the day's writing.

10. "What Has to Happen?"

Every plot is like a machine. Some are simple—a lever, a pulley, a nutcracker. Others are far more complex. No matter what the case, every machine would fall apart and fail to function without certain key components, and your plot is like that. These are the legs of the chair: You need them or the story will fall over and break its teeth on the linoleum. Keep your eye on these. Know when you're approaching one. Orchestrate them. Find the way to each. Make the No Man's Land between them compelling, too.

11. "How Does the Setting Affect My Story?"

Setting matters. Setting contributes to conflict (snowy blizzard!), to interesting characters (Brooklyn hipster!), to mood (lightning over the desert!). A great setting puts a wealth of story toys on the table. You'd be a fool not to grab a couple and put them into play.

12. "What Do I Want the Reader to Feel?"

The storyteller is a puppetmaster. You're here to pull strings and make people *feel* something—often intensely, often deeply. And so it behooves you to aim for a feeling rather than randomly hoping one occurs. In this scene you're writing, what do you want the audience to feel? Hopelessness? Triumph? Delight? Fear? Do you want them to laugh so hard they get a nosebleed? Or cry so hard they can't go to work that day?

13. "Am I Enjoying This?"

Not every day of writing is going to be a thrill a minute. Some days the word count is bliss; other days it's like brushing the teeth of a meth-cranked baboon. But you should keep an eye on your *overall enjoyment levels*. You should be finding some pleasure, some measure of satisfaction, with what you're writing. If not, try to suss out the reason. If you find it a misery, there's a chance the reader will feel that misery, too.

14. "Am I Taunted by an Endless Parade of Distractions?"

As you write, it's best to ask: "Oh, shit, am I actually writing?" Because, as it turns out, being on Twitter doesn't count. Nor does playing a video game. Or watching football. Or secretly ogling obscure Prohibition-era pornography. We writers are easily distracted, like raccoons, babies, and—I'm sorry, where was I? The sun just glinted on a quarter and I found myself mesmerized for—*checks watch*—about forty-five minutes. Point is, if you're easily distracted, you need to cut that shit out. If it continues, you need to find out why. Why is it you don't want to write the thing you (theoretically) want to write?

15. "What Else Is in My Way?"

We all find our work hindered by various reasons. Family obligations, writer's block, technical problems, depression, vibrant hallucinations, addictions to huffing printer ink, etc. Time to identify these reasons—and by reasons, I mean, "excuses"—and begin systematically eradicating them. Find what blocks you, and either remove the block or find a way around.

16. "Where Are My Pants?"

Trick question! You should know where your pants are. They should be as far away from you as possible, for pants (or "trousers," if you're in the UK) are a tool of the oppressors. Pants are how the NSA spies on you. Good penmonkeys work pantsless. I, for instance, pull a "Garfield" and mail my pants to Abu Dhabi.

17. "Am I Writing to Spec?"

If you're rocking the NaNoWriMo, you know your count is 50,000 words. Or maybe you're writing a ninety-page script or a 5,000-word short story. Always keep your mind on the total potential word count: Good writers know to write to spec and, in the day-to-day act of penmonkeying around, recognize when they're on target or off base.

18. "What's My Daily Word Count?"

Part of writing to spec is knowing what your daily word count should be. If you're writing NaNoWriMo, it should be somewhere between 1,500–2,000 words per day. Hit the target.

19. "Who Is My Audience?"

This can be as broad or as limited as you care to make it. Your audience might be, "everybody who loves a good thriller," down to, "teenage bedwetters." Just as good authors write to spec, good authors also write to an audience. A speaker would tailor his speech to his audience, and so the writer must tailor his writing to an audience as well.

20. "Have I Saved Recently?"

I am an obsessive-compulsive saver. I will save at the end of every sentence if you give me a chance. I've probably saved this chapter 1,745 times—1,746 now!—over the course of its writing. Seriously, save a whole lot. Learn to ask yourself that question in order to keep it and the habit top of mind. Oh, and just so we're clear: Don't rely only on autosave. We cannot trust robots with our future. Because robots hate us mewling meat-bags and secretly work to undermine our so-called "agenda of the flesh."

21. "Oh Shit, Do I Have This Backed Up in Seventy-Two Different Places?"

You must save often and back up your work across multiple sources. External HD? Cloud storage? E-mail yourself the draft? Print copy? ALL OF THE ABOVE, TYPED IN CAPS TO DRIVE HOME ITS SCREAMING IMPORTANCE. RAAAAR, YELLING, YELLING, SNARRGH. Ahem. Point being, at the end of every day's worth of word making, back up the file in as many ways and places as you care to manage. Future You, upon suffering a cataclysmic hard drive shitsplosion, will thank Present You for being so damn smart.

22. "What Will I Write Tomorrow?"

Toward the end of this day's word count, keep an eye on tomorrow's storytelling endeavors. Maybe make a few in-document notes. Keep a hazy picture of what happens when you next sit down to write. You'll be happy when tomorrow comes. Unless tomorrow doesn't come and the robots have finally decided to wipe us from the planet like one might wipe a booger off a drinking glass. Goddamn robots, man. Goddamn robots.

23. "Does This Suck?"

Does today's word count look like garbage? Spelling errors? Funky plotting? Hastily scrawled poop? That's okay. You're allowed to do that. Just note it. Make a little checkmark in your brain, or even do a comment in the document—just know that today's word count may necessitate you coming back, doing some cleanup.

24. "Is This a Good Day to Write?"

Trick question! Every day is a good day to write. Go and do that which you claim to be. Writers write.

25. "Am I Asking Myself Too Many Goddamn Questions?"

Of course you are. This chapter posits way too many questions to seriously ask yourself. The point isn't to compulsively go through this list of questions day in and day out, but more to help take these questions and let them float in the back of your mind. If you grow too crazy about this, you're going to be focused more on the answers than on your actual word count, and that's not the point, not the point at all. These questions are—well, you know what they're like? You know when you drive on one of those go-cart tracks and they have the haybales up or the rubber bumpers to stop you from careening off track and to your fiery doom? These are like that. These questions are what help keep your go-cart from flying off into infinite space. Let them shepherd your word count rather than overwhelm it. Don't blow a gasket. Use them where they're useful; discard them when they're starting to fritz your circuitry.

25 THINGS YOU SHOULD KNOW ABOUT STORYTELLING

1. Stories Have Power

Outside the air we breathe and the blood in our bodies, the one thing that connects us modern humans today with the shamans and emperors and serfs and alien astronauts of our past is a heritage—a *lineage*—of stories. Stories move the world at the same time they explain our place in it. They help us understand ourselves and those near to us. Never treat a story as a shallow, wan little thing. A good story is as powerful as the bullet fired from an assassin's gun.

2. Effect Above Entertainment

We love to be entertained. Bread and circuses! Clowns and monkeys! Decapitations and ice cream! A good story entertains, but a great story knows that it has in its arsenal the ability to do so much more. The best stories make us feel something. They screw with our emotions. They make us give a damn about characters and places and concepts that don't exist and won't ever exist. The way a story stabs us with sadness, harangues us with happiness, runs us through the gauntlet of rage and jealousy and denial and underoo-shellacking lust and fear (together, lust and fear may stir a "scaredy-boner") is parallel to none. Anybody can entertain. A juggler entertains. A storyteller makes us feel something. Makes us give a shit when we have no good reason to do so. Fun is not the last stop on the story train. The storyteller is a master manipulator. The storyteller is a cackling puppetmaster.

3. A Good Story Is a Good Story Regardless of Genre or Form
Segmentation. Checking off little boxes. Putting stories in the appropriate story slots and narrative cubbyholes. Is it a sci-fi TV show? A fantasy novel? A superhero comic? A video game about duck hunting? An ARG about the unicorn sex trade? We like to think that the walls we throw up matter. But they're practically insubstantial, and once you get them in your mouth they're like cotton candy, melting away to a meaningless slurry. A good story is a good story. Those who cleave to genre and form—whether as teller or as audience—limit the truth and joy the tale can present. Cast wide and find great stories everywhere.

4. That's Not to Say Form Doesn't Matter
Story is also not a square peg jammed in a circle hole. Every tale has an organic fit. The medium matters in that it lets you operate within known walls and described boundaries. A genre may hope to speak to a certain audience. A form may hope to appeal to fans of that form. If choice is a factor, let it be a game. If visuals are part and parcel, try a comic or a film.

5. Stories Have Shape, Even When They Don't Mean To

When you put your hand upon a spinning wad of wet clay, you're shaping it. Even when you don't mean to. Sometimes you find a shape the way a blind man studies a face. Other times you know the shape at the outset and move your hands to mold the tale you choose to tell. Neither way is better than the other. But the story never doesn't have a shape. A story always has structure, even when you resist such taxonomy.

6. The Story Is a Map; Plot Is the Route You Choose

A story is so much more than the thing you think it is. I lay down a map, and that map has a host of possibilities. Sights unseen. Unexpected turns. The plot is just the course I plan upon that map. It's a sequence. Of events. Of turns. Of landmarks. And the story goes beyond mere *sequence*. The story is about what I'll experience. About who I'll meet. The story is the world, the characters, the feel, the time, the context. Trouble lies in conflating *plot* with *story*. (Even though I've done it here already. See how easy it is to do?)

7. On the Subject of Originality

The storyteller will find no original plots. But original stories are limitless. It's like LEGO blocks. Go buy a box of LEGO bricks, and you'll discover that you have no unique pieces—by which I mean, these are the same pieces that everybody gets. But how you arrange them is where it gets interesting. That's where it's all fingerprints and snowflakes and leprechaun scat. Plot is just a building block. Story is that which you build.

8. The Bridge Between Author and Audience

The audience wants to feel connected to the story. They want to see themselves inside it, whether as mirror image or as doppelgänger (or as sinister mustachioed Bizarroworld villain!). The story draws a line between the storyteller and the audience—you're letting them see into you, and they're unknowingly finding you inside *them*. Uhh, not sexually, of course. You little dirty birdies, you.

9. But Also, Screw the Audience Right in Its Ear

The audience isn't stupid. It just doesn't know what it wants. Oh, it thinks it knows. The desires of the audience are ever at war with the story's needs, and the story's needs are, in a curious conundrum, the audience's needs. You read that right: This means it's the audience versus the audience, with the storyteller as grim-faced officiant. In this struggle, fiction is born. The audience wants the protagonist to be happy, to be safe. They want things to work out. They want conflict to resolve. The story cannot have these things and still be a good story. Good stories thrive on suffering protagonists. On things failing to go the way everyone hopes. On what is born from conflict and struggle, not merely from the resolution. The audience wants a safety blanket. It's the storyteller's job to strip away that safety blanket and expose them to the world.

10. No Tale Survives a Vacuum of Conflict

Conflict is the food that feeds the reader. It's a spicy hell-broth that nourishes. A story without conflict is a story without story. As the saying goes, there's no "there" there. The storyteller has truly profound powers, though: He can create conflict in the audience by making them feel a battle of emotions, by driving them forward with mystery, by angering them. The storyteller operates best as conflict generator. The storyteller works best when he's a little bit of a dick.

11. The Battle Between Tension and Release

Tension is how you ramp to conflict, how you play with it, how you maneuver around it, how you tap dance up to the cliff's edge, do a perilous pirouette, and pull back from the precipice. You're constantly tightening the screws. Escalation of tension is how a story builds. From bad to worse. From *worse* to *it can't get any worse*. From *it can't get any worse*

THE KICK-ASS WRITER

to *no, no, we were wrong, it's still getting worse because now I'm being stampeded by horses that are also covered in bees and fire.* But it isn't just a straight line from bad to awful. It rises to a new plateau, and then falls. Having just witnessed it with my wife and son, birth is a great (if gooey) analog. Each contraction has its own tension and release, but the contractions also establish a steady pattern upward. Some have said narrative arcs are sexual, ejaculatory, climactic. True, in some ways. But birth has more pain. More blood. More mad euphoria. And stories always need those things.

12. Peaks, Valleys, Slashes, and Whorls

It's not just tension. All parts of a story are subject to ups and downs. Rhythm and pacing are meaningful. A good story is never a straight line. The narrative is best when organically erratic. One might suggest that a story's narrative rhythm is its fingerprint—unique to it alone.

13. In a Story, Tell Only the Story

The story you tell should be the story you tell. Don't wander far afield. That's not to say you cannot digress. Digressions are their own kind of peaks (or, in many cases, valleys). But those digressions should serve the whole. Think of stories then not as one line but rather a skein of many lines. Lines that come together to form a pattern, a blanket, a shirt, a hilarious novelty welcome mat, a cat-o-nine-tails used to strike. Only lines that serve the end are woven into play. Digressions, yes. Deviations, no.

14. Big Ideas Do Well in Small Spaces

The audience cannot relate easily to big ideas. A big idea is often too big. Like the Stay Puft Marshmallow Man. Or Unicron, the giant Transformer-that-is-also-a-planet. (I wonder if anyone ever calls him "Unicorn," and if so, does that irritate him?) You must go macro to micro. Big ideas are shown through small stories: A single character's experience through the story is so much better than the 30,000-foot-view. We wash our dishes one dish at a time.

15. Backstory Is a Frozen Lake Whose Ice Is Wafer Thin

Backstory in narrative—and, ultimately, exposition in general—is sometimes a grim necessity, but it is best to approach it like a lake of thin ice. Quick, delicate steps across to get to the other side. Linger too long or grow heavy in the telling and the ice will crack and you will plunge into the frigid depths. And then you get hypothermia. And then you will be eaten by an Ice Hag. True story.

16. Characters are The Vehicles That Carry Us Into (and Through) the Tale

The best stories are the stories of people, and that means it's people—characters—that get us through the story. They are the dune buggies and WaveRunners on which the audience rides. Like Yoda on Luke's back. Above all else, a story must have interesting characters, characters who the audience can see themselves in, even if only in a small way. Failing that, what's the point?

17. Villains Have Mothers

Unless we're talking about SkyNet, villains were children once upon a time. Which means they have mothers. Imagine that: Even the meanest characters have mothers, mothers who may even have loved them once. They're people, not mustache-twirling sociopaths born free from a vagina made of fiery evil. Nobody sees themselves as a villain. We're all solipsistic. We're all the heroes of our own tales. Even villains.

18. Heroes Have Broken Toys

Just as villains see themselves doing good, heroes are capable of doing or being bad. Complexity of character—*believable* complexity—is a feature, not a bug. Nothing should be so simple as unswerving heroism, nor should it be as cut and dry as straight-up maliciousness. Black and white grows weary. More interesting is how dark the character's many shades of gray may become before brightening.

19. Strip Skin Off Bones to See How It Works
A story can be cut to a thin slice of steak and still be juicy as anything. To learn how to tell stories, tell small stories as well as large ones. Find a way to tell a story in as few beats as possible. Look for its constituent parts. Put them together; take them apart. See how they play and lay. Some limbs are vestigial.

20. Beginnings Are for Assholes ...
The audience begins where you tell them. They don't need to begin at the beginning. If I tell the story of a Brooklynite, I don't need to speak of his birth, or the origins of Brooklyn, or how the Big Bang barfed up asteroids and dinosaurs and a flock of incestuous gods. You start where it matters. You start where it's most interesting. You begin as late in the tale as you can. The party guest who comes late is always the most interesting one. Even still, it's worth noting ...

21. ... If You Jump Too Fast Into Waters Too Deep, The Audience Drowns
Jump too swiftly into a narrative and the story grows muddled. We have to become invested first. Go all high karate action and we have no context for the characters who are in danger. We don't care, and if we don't care then we're already packing our bags in the first five minutes or five pages. The audience always needs something very early to get their hands around. This always comes back to the character. Give them a reason to care right at the gate. Otherwise, why would they walk through it?

22. Treat Place Like a Character

For setting to matter, it must come alive. It must be made to get up and dance, so shoot at its feet. It has a face. It has a personality. It has *life*. When setting becomes a character, the audience will care.

23. Always Ask, "Why Do I Want to Tell This?"

Storytellers tell specific stories for a reason. You want to scare the kids around a campfire. You want to impress your friends with your exploits. You want to get in somebody's pants. You hope to make them cry, or make them cheer, or convey to them a message. Know why you're telling it. Know what it's about—to you above all else, because then you can show everybody else what it's about. Find that invisible tether that ties you to the story. That tether matters.

24. It's Okay to Bury the Lede

Every story is about something. Man's inhumanity to man. How history repeats itself. How karate ghosts are awesome and how you don't screw with a karate ghost. But you don't need to slap the audience about the head and neck with it. The truth of the story lives between the lines. This is why Jesus invented "subtext."

25. Writing Is a Craft, but Storytelling is an Art

Writing isn't magic. Writing is math. It's placing letters and words and sentences after one another to form a grand equation. Writing may seem like shouting, "Abracadabra!"—the power word made manifest—but the story that results is the true magic. That equation we piece together tells a tale, and the arrangement that leads to that tale is where the true art lies, because it takes an ice scraper to pretense and throws an invisible-yet-present tow line from present to past. Writing is craft and mechanics. Storytelling is art and magic.

25 THINGS I WANT TO SAY TO SO-CALLED "ASPIRING" WRITERS

1. No More Aspiring, Dingbats

Here are the two states in which you may exist: *person who writes*, or *person who does not*. If you write, you are a writer. If you do not write, you are not. Aspiring is a meaningless null state that romanticizes Not Writing. It's as ludicrous as saying, "I aspire to pick up that piece of paper that fell on the floor." Either pick it up, or don't. I don't want to hear about how your diaper's full. Take it off, or stop talking about it.

2. Kick Your Lowest Common Denominator in the Kidneys

You can aspire to be a lot of other things within the writing realm, and that's okay. You can aspire to be a published author. Or a best-selling author. Or a professional freelance writer. Or an author who plagiarizes his memoir and gets struck with a wooden mallet wielded by Oprah live on primetime television. You *should* aspire to be a better writer. We all should. Nobody is at the top of his game. We can all climb higher.

3. Aspiring Writers as Far as the Eye Can See

Nobody respects writers, yet everybody wants to be one (probably *because* everybody wants to be one). Point is, you want to be a writer? Good for you. So does that guy. And that girl. And him. And her. And that old dude. And that young broad. And your neighbor. And your mailman. And that chihuahua. And that copy machine. Ahead of you is an ocean of wannabe ink slaves and word earners. I don't say this to daunt you. Or to be dismissive. But you have to differentiate yourself, and the way you do that is by *doing* rather than *pretending*. You will climb higher than them on a ladder built from your wordsmithy.

4. We All Booby-Trap the Jungle Behind Us

There exists no one way toward becoming a professional writer. You cannot perfectly walk another's journey. That's why writing advice is just that—it's advice. It's mere suggestion. Might work. Might not. There are lots of good ideas out there, but none of it is gospel. One person will tell you *this* is the path. Another will point the other way and say *that* is the path. They're both right for themselves, and they're both probably wrong for you. We all chart our own course and burn the map afterward. It's just how it is. If you want to find the way forward, then stop looking for maps and start walking.

5. The Golden Perfect Path of the Scrivening Bodhisattvas

Point is, to hell with the One True Way. Doesn't exist. Nobody has answers—all you get are suggestions. Anybody who tells you they have The Answer is gassy with lies. Distrust such certainty and play the role of skeptic.

6. Yes, It Always Feels This Way

You will always have days when you feel like an amateur. When it feels like everybody else is better than you. You will have this nagging suspicion that someone will eventually find you out, call you on your bullshit, realize you're the literary equivalent of a vagrant painting on the side of a wall with a piece of calcified poop. You will have days when the blank page is like being lost in a blizzard. You will sometimes hate what you wrote today, yesterday, or ten years ago. Bad days are part of the package. You just have to shut them out, swaddle your head in tinfoil, and keep writing anyway.

7. Figure Out How You Write, and Then Do That

You learn early on how to write. But for most authors, it takes a long time to learn how *they in particular* write. Certain processes, styles, genres, character types, POVs, tenses, whatever—they will come more naturally to you than they do to others. And some won't come naturally at all. Maybe you'll figure this out right out of the gate. But for most, it just takes time—time filled with *actual writing*—to tease it out.

8. Finish Your Shit

I'm just going to type this out a dozen times so it's clear: Finish your shit. Finish *your* shit. Finish your *shit*. *Finish* your shit. *Finish your shit.* Finish your shit! FINISH YOUR SHIT. Finish. Your. Shit. Fiiiiniiiiish yooooour shiiiiit. COMPLETO EL POOPO. Vervollständigen Sie Ihre Fäkalien! Finish your shit.

9. You Need to Learn the Rules ...

... in order to know when they must be broken.

10. You Need to Break the Rules ...

... in order to know why they matter.

11. What I Mean by Rules Is—

Writing is a technical skill. A craft. You can argue that storytelling is an art. You can argue that art emerges from good writing the way a dolphin riding a Jet Ski emerges the longer you stare at a Magic Eye painting. But don't get ahead of yourself, hoss. You still need to know how to communicate. You need to learn the laws of this maddening land. I've seen too many authors want to jump ahead of the skill and just start telling stories—you ever try to get ahead of your own skill level? I used to imagine pictures in my head, and I'd try to paint them in watercolor and they'd end up looking like someone barfed up watery yogurt onto the canvas. I'd rail against this: WHY DON'T THEY LOOK BEAUTIFUL? Uhh, because you don't know how to actually *paint*, dumbass. You cannot exert your talent unless you first have the skill to bolster that talent.

12. Oh, the Salad Days of College!

Why are the days of our youth known as "salad days?" Is "salad" really the image that conjures up the wild and fruitful times of our adolescence? "Fritos," maybe. Or "beer keg." I dunno. What were we talking about? Ah! Yes. College. Do you need it? Do you need a collegiate education, Young Aspirant to the Penmonkey Order? *Need*, no. To get published, nobody gives a bucket of angry emu spit whether or not you have a degree. They just care that you can write. Now, college and even postgrad work may help you become a better writer—it did for me! However, I'd argue that the money you throw into the tank getting there may have been better spent on feeding yourself while you just learn how to write in whatever rat trap you call a home. You can only learn so much from someone teaching you how to write. Eventually you just have to write.

13. Reading Does Not Make You a Writer

That's the old piece of advice, isn't it? "All you need to do to be a writer is to read and write." You don't learn to write through reading anymore than you learn carpentry by sitting on a chair. You learn to write by writing. And, when you do read something, you learn from it by dissecting it—what is the author doing? How are characters and plot drawn together? You must read *critically*—that is the key.

14. Here Is Your Tin Cup, Your Hobo Bindle, Your Newspaper Undies
You're going to starve for a while, so just get used to that now. Don't quit your day job. Yet.

15. Commerce Is Not the Enemy of Art
If you think commerce somehow devalues art, then we're done talking. I got nothin' for you. Money doesn't devalue art any more than art devalues money—commerce can help art, hurt art, or have no effect. The saying isn't *Money is the root of all evil*. It's *The love of money is the root of all evil*. Commerce only damages art when the purpose of the art is only money. So it is with your writing.

16. Overnight Success Probably Isn't
Suddenly on your radar screen is a big giant glowing mass like you'd see when a swarm of xenomorphs is closing fast on your position and it's like, "Hey! This author appeared *out of nowhere*! Overnight success! Mega-bestseller! Million-dollar deal!" And then you get it in your head: "I can do that, too. I can go from a relative nobody to America's Favorite Author, and Oprah will keep me in a gilded cage and feed me rare coffees whose beans were first run through the intestinal tract of a dodo bird." Yeah, except, those who are "overnight successes" rarely appear out of nowhere. It's the same way that an asteroid doesn't "just appear" before destroying Earth and plunging it into a dust-choked dead-sun apocalypse; that bastard took a long time to reach Earth, even if we didn't notice. Overnight successes didn't win the lottery. They likely toiled away in obscurity for years. The lesson is: Work matters.

17. Meet the Universe in the Middle

My theory in life and writing is this—and it's some deeply profound shit, so here, lower the lights, put on a serious turtleneck with a houndstooth elbow-patched jacket over it, and go ahead and smoke this weird hash I stole from an Afghani cult leader. The theory is this: Meet the universe halfway and the universe will meet you in return. Explained more completely: There exist components of any career (but writing in particular) that are well beyond your grasp. You cannot control everything. Some of it is just left to fate. But, you still have to put in the work. You won't get struck by lightning if you don't run out into the storm. You must maximize your chances. You do this by meeting the universe halfway. *You do this by working.*

18. Self-Publishing Is Not the Easy Way Out

Self-publishing is a viable path. It is not, however, the easy path. Dispense with this notion. You don't just do a little ballerina twirl and a book falls out of your vagina. (And if that does happen, please see a doctor. Especially if you're a dude.) It takes a lot of effort to bring a proper self-published book to life. Divest yourself of the idea that it's the cheaper, easier, also-ran path. Faster, yes. But that's all.

19. No, Total Stranger, I Don't Want to Read Your Stuff

I really don't. And neither does any other working author. It's nothing personal. We just don't know you from any other spam-bot lurking in the wings ready to dump a bucket of dick pills and Nigerian money over our heads. That's not to say we won't be friendly or are unwilling to talk to you about your work, but we're already probably neck deep in the ordure of our own wordsmithy. (Or we're drunk and confused at a Chuck-E-Cheese somewhere.) We cannot take the time to read the work of total strangers. Be polite if you're going to ask. And damn sure don't get mad when we say no.

20. Your Jealousy and Depression Do Not Matter

All writers get down on themselves. It's in our wheelhouse. We see other writers being successful and at first we're all like, "Yay, good for that person!" then ten minutes later we get this sniper's bullet of envy, and this poison feeling shoots through the center of our brain like a railroad spike: "BUT WHY NOT ME?" And then we go take a bath with a toaster. Screw that. Those feelings don't matter. They don't help you. They may be normal, they may be natural, but they're not useful and they're certainly not interesting.

21. Talking About Writing Is Not the Same as Writing

Needs no further comment.

22. Pack Your Echo Chamber With C4 and Blow It Skyward

Aspiring writers lock themselves away in echo chambers filled with other aspiring writers where one of two things often happen: One, nobody writes anything bad, and everybody likes everything and it's a big old self-congratulatory testicle-tickling festival; Two, it's loaded for bear by people who don't know how to give good criticism, and the criticism is destructive rather than constructive and it's just a cloud of bad vibes swirling around your head like a plague of urinating bats. If you find yourself in this kind of echo chamber, blow a hole in the wall and crawl to freedom.

23. Learn to Take a Punch

Agents, editors, reviewers, readers, trolls on the Internet—they're going to say things you don't want to hear. A thick skin isn't enough. You need a leathery carapace. *A chitinous exoskeleton.* Writing is a hard-knock career where you invite a bevy of slings and arrows into your face and heart. It is what it is.

24. You Can Do Whatever the Hell You Want

As a writer, the world you create is yours and yours alone. Someone will always be there to tell you what you *can't* do, but they're nearly always wrong. You're a writer. You can make *anything up* that you want. It may not be lucrative. It may not pay your mortgage. But we're not talking about that. We're talking about what's going on between *you* and the *blank page before you.* It's just you and the story. If you love it and you want to write it, then wire your trap shut and write it. And write it well. Expect nothing beyond this—expect no reward, expect no victory parade—but embrace the satisfaction it gives you to do your thing.

25. The One No-Fooling Rule ...

... is "write." Write, write, write, *goddamn it, write.* Write better today than you did yesterday and better tomorrow than you did today. Onward, fair penmonkey, onward. If you're not a writer, something will stop you—your own doubts, hate from haters, a bad review, poor time management, a hungry raccoon that nibbles off your fingers, whatever. If you're a writer, you'll write. And you'll never stop to look back.

25 THINGS YOU SHOULD KNOW ABOUT WRITING A NOVEL

1. Your First and Most Important Goal
Is to Finish the Shit That You Started

Let's get this out of the way right now: If you start a goddamn novel, then plan to goddamn finish that goddamn novel. Your hard drive is not a novel burial ground. It's like building your own Frankenstein monster—robbing a grave, stealing a brain, chopping up the body—and then giving up before you let lightning tickle that sonofabitch to life. The true author finishes what he begins. That's what separates you from the chumps, the talkers, the dilettantes. Don't let dead metaphysical weight slow you down.

2. That Means Momentum Is Key

Say it five times fast: momentum-momentum-momentum-momentum-momentum. Actually, don't say it five times fast. I just tried and burst a blood vessel in my brain. The point remains: Writing a novel is about gaining steam, about acceleration, about momentum. You lose it every time you stop to revise a scene in the middle, to look up a word, to ponder or change the plot. It's like a long roadtrip: Don't stop for hitchhikers, don't stop to piss, don't stop for an Arby's Big Beef and Cheddar. *Just drive*. Leave notes in your draft. Highlight empty spaces. Fill text with XXX and know you'll come back later.

3. The First Draft Is the Beach-Storming Draft

It's you and hundreds of other soldier-penmonkeys clawing their way up the enemy beach of the People's Republic Of Novelsvainya. Most of those other poor sots are going to take a stitching of bullets to the chest and neck and drop dead in the sand, flopping around like fish, their bowels evacuating. Your only goal is to get up that beach. Crawl through mud, blood, sand, shit, and corpses. It doesn't matter if you get up that beach all pretty-like. Or in record time. Nobody cares how your hair looks. Your first draft can and should look like a goddamn warzone. That's okay. Don't sweat it, because you survived. Put differently, that first draft of yours has permission to suck. Go forth and care not.

4. Be Like the Dog Who Cloaks Himself in Stink

Find joy and liberation in writing a first draft without caring, without giving one whittled whit. It's like pouring paint on the floor or taking a sledgehammer to some kitchen counters. Get messy. Let it all hang out. Suck wantonly and without regard for others. Let that free you. Have fun. Don't give a rat's roasted rectum. You'll think that all you're doing is upending a garbage can on the page, but trust that you'll later find pearls secreted away in the heaps of trash and piles of junk.

5. The First Draft Is Born in the Laboratory

Take risks on that first draft. Veer left. Drive the story over a cliff. Try new things. Play with language. Kill an important character. Now's the time to experiment, to go moonbat apeshit all over this story. You'll pull back on it in subsequent drafts. You'll have to clean up your mess: all the beer bottles, bong water, blood, and broken glass. But some of it will stay. And the stuff that does will feel priceless.

6. Writing Is Rewriting Is Rewriting Is Rewriting Is

It's been said before but it bears repeating: Writing is when you make the words, editing is when you make them *not shitty*. The novel is born on that first go-around but you gotta let that little bastard grow up. Do this through rewriting. And rewriting. And rewriting. As many times as it takes till it stands up and dances on its own.

7. You Have as Many Chances at Bat as You So Choose—

A Marine sniper doesn't get infinite shots at his target. A batter only gets three strikes. A knife thrower only has to screw up once before he's got a body to hide. The novelist has it easy. You can keep rewriting. Adding. Fixing. Changing. Endlessly anon until you're satisfied.

8. —But You Also Have to Know When to Leave Well Enough Alone

Seriously, you have to stop sometime. If you whip mashed potatoes too long, they get gluey. There comes a time when you need to stop screwing with a novel the same way you stop tonguing a chipped tooth. Write till it's good, not till it's perfect. Because you don't know shit about perfect. Aim squarely for a B+, and then it's time to let others have a shot at getting the novel to that A/A+ range.

9. Know When to Bring in the A-Team

You're not Lone Wolf. You are not Ronin-Ninja-Without-Clan. A novel is a team effort. You need readers. One or several editors. Potentially an agent. True story: Writers are often the worst judges of their own work. You spend so long in the trenches that it's all a hazy, gauzy blur—a swarm of flies. It's like being on acid. Sometimes you need a trip buddy. Someone to tell you this is real, this is illusion. "The talking alpaca is just a hallucination. But the dead body in the middle of the floor, dude, that's real, WE GOTTA GO."

10. Escape the Gravity of the Hate Spiral

Every 10,000 words is a new peak or valley on this crazy-ass rollercoaster ride. You loved the novel last week. This week you want to punch its teeth down its throat. That's normal. Write through it. The hate spiral will kill you if you let it. It's one of the reasons we abandon novels. It's also nonsense. Sometimes your best work is your worst, your worst is your best. Everything is ass-end up. Don't worry. Just write.

11. Welcome to Wacky Town

You sit down at the desk, shackle your mind to the project, wade into an imaginary swamp with made-up people. For days. Weeks. Sometimes even years. That's batty.

12. Gotta Abandon Your Baby? Butcher Him for Spare Parts

Don't abandon your novel. Don't do it. Still. Sometimes it's going to happen. Hopefully not often, but it does: A novel just isn't working. Fine. Fine. But don't let it go without a fight. Chop it apart. Break it into its constituent parts. You put work into that. Take what works and apply it elsewhere. Build another robot using parts you stole from yourself. Eat your body to sustain your body.

13. You Can Write a Novel Pretty Goddamn Fast

It's hard but not impossible to write, say, 5,000 words a day. A novel is roughly 80k. At 5k/day, you can finish a novel in about sixteen days. Just know that it won't be good. Not yet. Can't write *and rewrite* that fast.

14. Say Something!

A reader is going to spend those 80,000 words with you. Hours of his life, given to you. Make them count. Say something about anything. Have your novel *mean* something to you so it can mean something to them. Bring your guts and brains and passion and heart and for the sake of sweet Sid and Marty Krofft, a *message* to the table. Don't just write. Write *about* something. Do more than entertain. You're not a dancing monkey. You're a storyteller. Embrace that responsibility.

15. The Shape of the Page Matters

A novel page shouldn't look like a giant wall of text. Nor should it look like an e.e. cummings poem. The shape of the page matters. Balance. Equal parts emptiness and text. Void meets substance.

16. A Novel by the Numbers

The ideal novel is 48 percent action, 48 percent dialogue, and 4 percent exposition and description. I just made that up. Probably totally inaccurate. *Possibly* I might could maybe sorta be drunk right now. Drunk on words, or on Tito's Vodka? *You decide.* Point is, a novel gets bogged by boggy bullshit like heavy description and blathering exposition. A novel is best when it lives in the moment, when its primary mode of communication is *action* and *dialogue* linking arms and dancing all over the reader's face.

17. I Just Lied to You Back There, and for That, I'm Sorry

Dialogue is action. It's not separate from it. Action is doing something. Dialogue is talking, and talking is doing something. Even better when dialogue manifests while characters do shit: drive a car, execute some baddies, make an omelet, build a sinister dancing robot whose mad mechanical choromania will reduce the world to cinders. Characters don't need to stand in one place in space and talk. They're not puppets in community theater. Find language with movement and motion.

18. Description Is About Signal to Noise

Description is best when subtle. Too much description is static. Paint in short strokes. A pinch of spice here. A delicate garnish there. Description is not a hammer with which to bludgeon the mooing herd. Pick one, two, or three details and stop there.

19. The Reader Is Your Mule

It's up to you whether the reader is a mule carrying your prospector gear up a canyon path or a mule carrying doody-balloons of hard drugs in his nether-grotto; the point remains the same. The reader wants to work. The reader doesn't know this, of course, so don't tell him. SHHH. But the reader wants to fill in the details. He wants to be invested in the novel and to make his own decisions and reach his own conclusions. You don't need to write everything. You can leave pieces (of plot, description, dialogue) out. The reader will get in the game. His imagination matters as much as yours. Make that sonofabitch dance for his dinner.

20. Too Many Dicks on the Dance Floor

A novel can have too many characters. It's not a set number or anything. The number of characters you can have is limited by your ability to make them fully-realized, wholly-inhabited people. If you don't have the time or the room to give them a soul, to lend them wants and needs and fears and foibles, then to hell with it. Chop their heads off and wipe their blood from the page.

21. Genre Matters, Except When It Doesn't

A good story is a good story, and that translates to novels: A good book is a good book. You write the novel you gotta write regardless of genre. But eventually you have to think about it. Agents, publishers, bookstores, Amazon—*they* care about genre. Your book has to fit somewhere. The secret is that it doesn't have to be a perfect fit. Close enough for horse-shoes, hand grenades, and hobo magic.

22. Beware the Saggy, Mushy Middle

The beginning's easy because it's like—BOOM, some shit just happened. The ending's easy because—POW, all the shit that happened just lead to this. The middle is where it gets all gooshy, like wet bread or a sloppy pile of viscera. Combat this in a few ways. First, new beginnings and early endings—the peaks and valleys of narrative. Second, keep the pressure on the story and, by proxy, yourself. Third, treat the second act like it's two or three acts in and of its own self.

23. Like I Said: Imagine a Long-Ass Road Trip

Variation. In scene. In character. In mood. In setting. In *everything*. A novel can't just be one thing. Mix it up. It's like a long car ride. Take an eight-hour trip down a bland mega-highway, and you pretty much want to suck on the tailpipe. Take an eight-hour trip through scenic mountains and pretty burgs and ghost towns, and you no longer want to eat gravel and die. Put differently: *Don't be boring.* If the story buys a house and gets a job in Dullsville, you need to burn Dullsville to the ground and push the story down the road a ways.

24. No One Way Through the Labyrinthine Mire

Plotter. Pantser. Five-k a day. Two-k a day. In sequence or out. Nobody writes a novel the same way, all the way down to which font folks like. Individual novels have their own unique demands. You write it however it needs to be written. Nobody can tell you how. Only that it needs to get done. We each cut our own way through the dark forest. In the deepest shadows, look for your voice. Your voice is what will get you through.

25. Writing a Novel Is Easy, but Writing a Publishable Novel Is Hard

Writing a novel isn't hard. You throw words on a page, one atop another, until you've got a teetering Jenga tower of around 80,000 of the damn things. Same way that building a chair isn't hard: I can duct tape a bunch of beer cans and chopsticks together and make a chair. It won't look pretty. And it's an insurance liability. ("I'm suing you because I smell like beer, I have cuts on my legs, and I've got two chopsticks up my ass, perforating my colonic wall.") But writing a good novel, an original novel that's all your own and nobody else's, well, there's the rub, innit? The way you do it is you tell the story like you want to tell it. You learn to write well, write clearly, and put a pint of blood on every page until you've got nothing left but spit and eye boogers. Learn your craft. Learn your voice. Write it until it's done, then write it again.

25 WAYS TO BE A BETTER WRITER

1. Practice Makes Perfect, Little Princess

The easiest and most forthright way to become a better writer is, duh, to write. Write, write, write. Write regularly. Get on a schedule, whether it's 100, 1,000, or 10,000 words a day. Writing is a muscle, like your bicep, your heart, or your private parts. If you don't use 'em, you lose 'em. And then they fall to the ground and rot like oxidizing apples and are in turn eaten by hungry gophers. Om nom nom.

2. Time to Read Some Damn Books

The world is home to—*does some quick math on fingers, toes, testicles, nipples, and teeth*—*45 smajillion books*. Each of them often containing somewhere north of 50,000 words. And new books hit the atmosphere every day. You do not need to read all of these books. But you should act as if that is indeed your task, carving your way through the world's cumulative body of the written word one tome at a time. If you want to write, you're coming in at the ground level of these 45 smajillion books written by 33 fuhzillion different writers. You are but a mote in the reader's eye. You want to compete? Read. Learn what other writers are doing. Absorb it with that schnapps-laden sponge you call a brain.

3. Read Widely, Weirdly, Wisely

Here then is the prison that writers build for themselves: it becomes harder and harder to read purely for pleasure. Reading for pleasure often means sticking to a few genres, with a few authors—"Oh, I like fantasy, so I only read fantasy fiction," or, "I love the Detective Cashew Pepper series by K. J. Staplenuts, and I've read up to #47." That privilege has been revoked. You now must read widely, weirdly, wisely. Read everything. Move outside your desired library. Read obscure British literature. Read poetry. Read nonfiction. Read science fiction even though you hate science fiction. If you want to do what everybody else is doing, fine, read only in your preexisting sphere of influences. But this is about *improving* your work, not treading water like a poodle who fell off a boat.

4. Don't Be a Book Racist

Those who write books are occasionally "book racists." They pump their fists and espouse Book Power while denigrating other forms of the written word. "TV will rot your brain," they might say. As if the Snooki book will somehow do laps around an episode of *The Wire*. Books are not the only form of the written word. You may not even want to write books. Branch out. Watch television. Watch film. Read scripts. Visit great blogs. Play games. Don't be a book racist. The storytelling cults can learn much from one another.

5. Whittle Your Mind Into a Straight Razor

Another instance where improving your writing skill may come at the slow erosion of your pleasure. Read and watch stories with a deeply critical eye. Not to be a dick, but to instead ask: "What would I do differently? Why would I do it that way? Could I do this better? How would I write it to improve upon it?"

6. Unclog Those Ears, Wax Boy

Listen. Seriously, get your pinky into that ear, unplug it of all the wax and hair and sadness that's built up in there and just ... *listen*. We read with our ears as much as with our eyes, and so it's critical you know what sounds good as well as what reads well. Sit down at a bar, and listen to a conversation. Turn on an audio book or a radio show. Listen to a stand-up comedian deliver jokes and stories. Write it down if you must—see how it lays on the page. It should lay there like Burt Reynolds with a snake draped delicately across his man parts. In other news, I bet his man-parts have their very own mustache.

7. Go Forth and Do Shit, My Son

Write what you know means what it says but doesn't say what it means. You know more than you know. Screw fact. Embrace authenticity. Writers do not gain a sense of authenticity by sitting at the computer all day popping out word-babies. *Have something to write about.* To do that, you must go out. Into the world. Take a trip. Get in a bar fight. Hunt a white whale. Metaphorically. Please don't kill whales. They are our benevolent alien masters, and one day they're going to get really pissed and call in an airstrike.

8. Learn What Words Mean and Where Punctuation Goes

Storytelling may be an art, but writing is a craft. That means learning where commas go, how to spell words (like "clitoral" or "sesquicentennial"), and in general how to put together a goddamn sentence. Read yourself some Strunk and White. Flip through a dictionary now and again. Scope out some Grammar Girl. Hear a word you don't know? Go look it up. Improve your technical skills. It is the bedrock of your penmonkeying, and without it, you're just a punk-ass who won't eat his vegetables.

9. Be Torn Asunder by Editorial Talons

It helps to submit to editors. Real editors. *Tough love* editors. Because sometimes your writing needs to get on its knees and have wax poured down its back while it receives a right-good nipple-caning from a willow branch. Your writing improves in the fiery gaze of a hellish editor. The flames will wick away the flopsweat and the pee-stink. The barnacles will char and fall off. *Submit to an editor.*

10. Be Ripped Apart by Other Writers

Writers are not editors. (File under *D* for "duh.") They have different priorities and different perspectives. (And they're probably also raging drunkaholics. Editors are nice and drink wine. Writers will drink all the cough syrup at CVS if they can get their ink-stained fingers on it.) Whereas an editor will often highlight a problem, a writer will come up with a solution. That doesn't mean it's a solution you want, but it's worth it to have that perspective just the same. Submit your work to other writers. Demand that they not be kind. Mercy will not strengthen you.

11. Self-Flagellate

Pull up your pants, that's not what I mean. I mean, you must smack your word count with the horse whip of scrutiny! You must become your own cruelest editor, your jaw clenched tight with the meat of your own manuscript trapped between your teeth. This doesn't need to be a consistent mode of operation, but once in a while it pays to take a page of your writing and go at it with a blowtorch, a car battery, and a starving honey badger. Cut your words. Make them bleed. Behold the healing power of bloodletting.

12. Throw Down Your Own Crazy-Ass Gauntlet, Then Run Through It Naked

Set challenges for yourself and then tackle them. Write a piece of flash fiction. Write poetry. Attempt to tell a story in a single tweet. Play with the second-person perspective. Write a novel in sixty chapters, each only 1,000 words. Treat it like a game where the rules are ever changing.

13. Highway to the Danger Zone

This is related, but different: Write into your own discomfort. Escape your Plexiglas enclosure and run toward peril, not away from it. Confront your many demons with your work, and dissect them on the page. Write in genres with which you're not at all comfortable. Know your limits, then take those limits, wrap them around a hand-grenade, and shove them up the ass of a velociraptor. Because, really, screw limits. If you wanna be a better writer, you'll write outside your own prescribed margins.

14. Read Your Shit Aloud

I will pin your arms beneath my knees and scream into your face until I pass out from a rage aneurysm (an angerysm?): Read your work aloud. It will make you a better writer. I promise.

15. Embrace the Darwinism of Writing Advice

Here's what you do with writing advice (says the guy delivering a nigh-constant stream of dubious penmonkey wisdom): Hunt it down, leash it, read it, absorb it, and then let it go free once more. Let it compete with your other preconceived notions about writing. Sometimes the new writing advice will win and become a dominant meme inside your wordsmith's brain. Other times your preexisting beliefs will hold true through just such a test. You must take in writing advice and test it against your own notions. Tell all writing advice: "NOW YOU MUST FIGHT THE BEAR."

16. Learn New Breakdancing Moves, Fool

You can't be coming to the street with your stale-ass bullshit. The Worm? Really? The Robot? Classics, admittedly, but you're going to get smoked by bigger and better b-boys, yo. So it goes with writing. You must be willing to try new ideas. Not a plotter? Try plotting. Don't like flashbacks? Write some goddamn flashbacks. Make them your own. Try new tips, tricks, and techniques. You should be able to say, "I wrote my last novel on the back of a dead hooker. With a Sharpie! Don't worry, I outlined it first on the chest of my UPS man. He's still upstairs in the tub! Hey, uh, know anyone who needs a couple of kidneys?"

17. I Just Blogged a Little in My Mouth

You often hear, "Writers should blog to build their platform," to which I say, pants, poppycock, and pfeffernusse! (I know. Such a foul tongue!) I say that writers should blog because it keeps them writing, because it exposes their writing to the air of community, because it tests your skill in the open plains. Blogging is further a great place to play with language, to put words out there that aren't headed to market, that aren't forced to dance for their dinner. It allows you to use words like *poppycock* and *pfeffernusse*. True story.

18. Interface With Other Inkslingers

Sometimes you have to sit down over a pitcher of moonshine (or a hookah burning with the ash of a first edition *Finnegan's Wake*) and *confab the shit out of that palaver* with other writers. In other words, talk it out. Talk about careers. Techniques. Books you love. Writers you hate. Writer conventions and conferences are good places for this. Just remember: the writers are *always* at the bar. Like moths to a porchlight.

19. Wade Into the Mire of Your Own Fetid Compositions

Time travel a little. Go back into your past and dredge up some writing from a year ago. From ten years ago. Read it. Learn from it. Also gauge how well you've grown. This can be instructive because sometimes you don't know in what ways you've changed—further, you might identify darlings that repeatedly come up in your writing, darlings that deserve naught but the edge of your editorial chainsaw.

20. Do Not Defile the Penmonkey Temple

Your writing is the product of a machine, and that machine is your brain and body. The higher that machine functions, the better the writing that blubbers and spews from it. I'm not saying you need to treat your body like it's a white tower of physical perfection—but we're talking basic shit, here. Move around. Eat a good breakfast. Heroin is not a great snacktime treat. Fine, maybe you don't need to treat your body like it's a temple. Just don't treat it like it's the urinal in a Wendy's bathroom.

21. Flex Your Other Artistic Muscles

Take photos. Paint a picture. Play the piano. Macramé a dildo cozy. Muscles work in muscle groups—your writing muscle is part of an overall creative cluster. You gotta work 'em all.

22. Find Your Voice by Not Finding Your Voice

Sometimes improving your writing is about letting go of your writing. Some writers become so obsessed with their voice that they forget they already have it—your voice is who you are, your natural default way of communicating with the written word. To find your voice and improve your wordsmithy, sometimes it pays to just relinquish ego, relinquish control, and stop worrying so damn much.

23. Embrace Your Inner Moonbat

All writers are a little bit batshit. We've all got some combo pack of Charlie Manson, Renfield, and Bender from *Futurama* running around in our skulls. Embrace it. We've all got a head full of ghosts and gods, and it behooves us to listen to them, to let them out and play on the page, to use the madness granted to us rather than deny it and walk the safe and sane line.

24. Veer Drunkenly Toward Truth

Be real on the page. Be you. Know your experiences, know your heart and head and whatever squirting fluids pulse between your bile ducts, and put it all on the page. Be honest. Be bold. Don't screw around. Only by bringing yourself to the work will you find that your writing truly improves. Let it all hang out. By saying what needs to be said, you will see your writing get better, unburdened as it is by pretense and artifice.

25. I Am Jack's Desire to Be a More Awesomer Writer

An alcoholic (or any kind of *-aholic*) only gets better when he wants to, and so it is with writing. To be a better writer you must truly want to be. Open yourself. Test your work. Be willing to change. Otherwise, what's the point?

25 THINGS WRITERS SHOULD STOP DOING (STARTING RIGHT NOW)

1. Stop Running Away

Right here is your story. Your manuscript. *Your career.* So why are you running in the other direction? Your writing will never chase you—you need to chase your writing. If it's what you want, pursue it. This isn't just true of your overall writing career, either. It's true of individual components. You want one thing but then constantly work to achieve its opposite. You say you want to write a novel but then go and write a bunch of short stories. You say you're going to write this script but then try to write that script instead. Pick a thing, and work toward that thing.

2. Stop Stopping

Momentum is everything. Cut the brake lines. Careen wildly and unsteadily toward your goal. I hate to bludgeon you about the head and neck with a hammer forged in the volcanic fires of Mount Obvious, but the only way you can finish something is by not stopping.

3. Stop Writing in Someone Else's Voice

You have a voice. It's yours. Nobody else can claim it, and any attempts to mimic it will be fumbling and clumsy like two tweens trying to make out in a darkened broom closet. That's on you, too—don't try to write in somebody else's voice. Yes, okay, maybe you do this in the beginning. But strive past it. Stretch your muscles. Find your voice. Discover those elements that put the *author* in your *authority*. Write in a way that only you can write.

4. Stop Worrying

Worry is some useless shit. It does nothing. It has no basis in reality. It's a vestigial emotion, useless as—as my father was wont to say—"tits on a boar hog." We worry about things that are well beyond our control. We worry about publishing trends or future advances or whether or not Barnes & Noble is going to shove a hand grenade up its own ass and go *kablooey.* That's not to say you can't identify future trouble spots and try to work around them—but that's not *worrying.* You recognize a roadblock and arrange a path around it—you don't chew your fingernails bloody worrying about it. Shut up. Calm down. Worry, begone.

5. Stop Hurrying

The rise of self-publishing has seen a comparative surge forward in *quantity.* As if we're all rushing forward to push out as huge a litter of squalling word babies as our fragile penmonkey uteruses can handle. Stories are like wine; they need time. So take the time. This isn't a hot dog eating contest. You're not being judged on how much you write, but rather, how well you do it. Sure, there's a balance—you have to be generative, have to be swimming forward lest you sink like a stone and find remora fish mating inside your sea-brined bowels. But generation and creativity should not come at the cost of quality. Give your stories and your career the time and patience they need. Put differently: Don't have a freakout, man.

6. Stop Waiting

I said "Stop hurrying," not "Stand still and fall asleep." Life rewards action, not inertia. What the hell are you waiting for? To reap the rewards of the future, you must take action in the present. Do so now.

7. Stop Thinking It Should Be Easier

It's not going to get any easier, and why should it? Anything truly worth doing requires hella hard work. If climbing to the top of Kilimanjaro meant packing a light lunch and hopping in a climate-controlled elevator, it wouldn't really be that big a deal, would it? If you want to do This Writing Thing, then don't just expect hard work—be happy that it's a hard row to hoe, and that you're just the, er, hoer to hoe it? I dunno. Don't look at me like that. AVERT YOUR GAZE, SCRUTINIZER. And get back to work.

8. Stop Deprioritizing Your Wordsmithy

You don't get to be a proper storyteller by putting it so far down your list that it's nestled between "Complete the Iditarod (but with squirrels instead of dogs)" and "Two Words: Merkin, Macramé." If you want to do this shit, it better be in your Top Five, son. You know you're a writer because it's not just what you do, but rather, it's who you are. So why deprioritize that thing which forms part of your very identity?

9. Stop Treating Your Body Like a Dumpster

The mind is the writer's best weapon. It is equal parts bullwhip, sniper rifle, and stiletto. If you treat your body like it's the sticky concrete floor in a porno theater (pro tip: *that's not a spilled milkshake*), then all you're doing is dulling your most powerful weapon. The body fuels the mind. It should be "crap out," not "crap in." Stop bloating your body with awfulness. Eat well. Exercise. Elsewise you'll find your bullwhip's tied in knots, your stiletto's so dull it couldn't cut through a glob of canned pumpkin, and someone left peanut butter and jelly in the barrel of your sniper rifle.

10. Stop the Moping and the Whining

Complaining—like worry, like regret, like that little knob on the toaster that tells you it'll make the toast darker—does nothing. Blah blah blah, big publishing, blah blah blah, Amazon, blah blah blah agents and editors and Hollywood and bears. Stop boo-hooing. Don't like something? Fix, it or forgive it. And move on to the next thing.

11. Stop Blaming Everyone Else

You hear a lot of blame going around—something-something gatekeepers, something-something too many self-published authors, something-something agency model. You're going to own your successes, and that means you're also going to need to own your errors. This career is yours. Yes, sometimes external factors will step in your way, but your reactions are up to *you*.

12. Stop the Shame

Writers are often ashamed of who they are and what they do. Other people are out there fighting wars and fixing cars and destroying our country with toxic mortgages—and here we are, sitting around in our footy-pajamas, writing about vampires and unicorns, about broken hearts and shattered jaws. A lot of the time, we won't get much respect, but you know what? Writers and storytellers help make this world go 'round. We're just as much a part of the societal ecosystem as anybody else. Craft counts. Art matters. Stories are important. Freeze-frame high five. Now have a beer and a shot of whiskey, and shove all your shame in a bag and burn it.

13. Stop Lamenting Your Mistakes

Yeah, yeah, yeah. So you screwed up somewhere along the way. Who gives a donkey's duodenum? Shit happens. Shit washes off. Don't dwell. Don't sing lamentations to your errors. Repeat after me: Learn and move on. Very few mistakes will haunt you till your end of days unless you *let them* haunt you. That is, unless your error was so egregious it can never be forgotten. ("I wore a Hitler outfit as I went to every major publishing house in New York City and took a poop in every editor's desk drawer over the holiday. Also, I may have put it on YouTube and sent it to GalleyCat. Is that bad?")

14. Stop Playing It Safe

Let this year be the year of risk. Nobody knows what's going on in the publishing industry, but we can be damn sure that what's going on with authors is that we're finding new ways to be empowered in this New Media Future. What that means is, it's time to forget the old rules. Time to start questioning preconceived notions and established conventions. It's time to start taking some risks both in your career and in your storytelling. Throw open the doors. Kick down the walls of your uncomfortable box. Carpet bomb the Comfort Zone so that none other may dwell there.

15. Stop Trying to Control Shit You Can't Control

All the industry shit and the reviews and the Amazonian business practices? The economy? The readers? You can't control any of that. You can respond to it. You can try to get ahead of it. But you can't control it. Control what you can, which is your writing and the management of your career.

16. Stop Doing One Thing

Diversification is the name of survival for all creatures: Genetics! Lawn maintenance! Economic portfolios! Diversity is how we survive. Things are changing big-time over these next few years, from the rise of e-books to the collapse of traditional markets to the galactic threat of Mecha-Gaiman. Diversity of form, format, and genre will help ensure you stay alive in the coming (and entirely-made-up) Publipocalypse.

17. Stop Writing for "The Market"

To be clear, I don't mean, "Stop writing for specific markets." That's silly advice. If you want to write for the *Ladies' Home Journal*, well, that's writing for a specific market. What I mean is, stop writing for The Market, capital *T-M*. The Market is an unknowable entity based on sales trends and educated guesswork and some kind of publishing haruspicy (at Penguin, they sacrifice *actual penguins*—true story!). Writing a novel takes long enough that writing for the market is a doomed mission, a leap into a dark chasm with the hopes that someone will build a bridge there before you fall through empty space. Which leads me to—

18. Stop Chasing Trends

Set the trends. Don't chase them like a dog chasing a Buick. Trends offer artists a series of diminishing returns—every iteration of a trend after the first is weaker than the last, as if each repetition is another ice cube plunked into a once-strong glass of Scotch. You're just watering it down, man. Don't be a knock-off purse, a serial-killer copycat, or just another fantasy echo of Tolkien. Do your own thing.

19. Stop Caring About What Other Writers Are Doing

They're going to do what they're going to do. You're not them. You don't want to be them and they don't want to be you. Why do what everyone else is doing? Let me reiterate: *Do your own thing.*

20. Stop Caring So Much About the Publishing Industry

Know the industry, but don't be overwhelmed by it. The mortal man cannot change the weave and weft of cosmic forces; they are outside you. If you examine the publishing industry too closely and it will spew its demon ichor into your eye. And then you'll have to go to the eye doctor and he'll be all like, "You were staring too long at the publishing industry again, weren't you?" And you're like, "YES, fine," and he's like, "Well, I have drops for that, but they'll cost you," and you get out your checkbook and ask him how many zeroes you should fill in because you're a writer and don't have health care.

21. Stop Listening to What Won't Sell

You'll hear that. "I don't think this can sell." And shit, you know what? That might be right. Just the same, I'd bet that all the stories you remember, all the tales that came out of nowhere and kicked you in the junk with their sheer possibility and potential, were stories that were once flagged with the "this won't sell" moniker. You'll always find someone to tell you what you can't do. What you shouldn't do. That's your job as a writer, to prove them wrong. By sticking your fountain pen in their neck and drinking their blood. Uhh, I mean, "By writing the best damn story you can write." That's what I mean. That other thing was, you know, just metaphor. Totally. *hides inkwell filled with human blood*

22. Stop Overpromising and Overshooting

We want to do everything all at once. Grand plans! Sweeping gestures! Epic twenty-three-book fantasy cycles! Don't overreach. Concentrate on what you can complete. Temper risk with reality.

23. Stop Leaving Yourself Off the Page

You are your stories and your stories are you. Who you are matters. Your experiences and feelings and opinions count. Put yourself on every page: A smear of heartsblood. If we cannot connect with our own stories, how can we expect anybody else to find that connection?

24. Stop (Only) Dreaming

Start doing. Dreams are a good start. But dreams are intangible and uncertain looks into the future. Dreams are fanciful flights of improbability—Pegasus wishes and the hopes of lonely robots. You're an adult now. It's time to shit or get off the pot. It's time to wake up or stay dreaming. Let me say it again because I am nothing if not a fan of repetition: *Stop dreaming. Start doing.*

25. Stop Being Afraid

Fear will kill you dead. You've nothing to be afraid of that a little preparation and pragmatism cannot kill. Everybody who wanted to be a writer and didn't become one failed based on one of two critical reasons: One, they were lazy, or two, they were afraid. Let's take for granted you're not lazy. That means you're afraid. Fear is nonsense. What do you think is going to happen? You're going to be eaten by tigers? Life will afford you lots of reasons to be afraid: bees, kidnappers, terrorism, being eaten by an escalator, bears, the NSA, Snooki. But being a writer is nothing worthy of fear. It's worthy of praise. And triumph. And fireworks. And shotguns. And a box of wine. So shove fear aside—let fear be gnawed upon by escalators and tigers. Stop dicking around. Start writing.

25 THINGS YOU SHOULD KNOW ABOUT WRITING HORROR

1. At the Heart of Every Tale, a Squirming Knot of Worms
Every story is, in its tiny way, a horror story. Horror is about fear and tragedy, and whether or not one is capable of overcoming those things. It's not all about severed heads or blood-glutton vampires. It's an existential thing, a tragic thing, and somewhere in every story this dark heart beats. You feel horror when Indiana Jones has to cross the snake pit. We feel the fear of Harry and Sally, a fear that they're going to ruin what they have by getting too close or by not getting close enough, a fear that's multiplied by knowing you're growing older and have nobody to love you. In the Snooki book, we experience revulsion as we see Snooki bed countless bodybuilders and gym sluts, her alien syphilis fast degrading their bodies until soon she can use their marrowless bones as

straws with which to slurp up her latest Windex-colored drink. *insert Hannibal Lecter noise here*

2. Sing the Ululating Goat Song

Horror is best when it's about tragedy in its truest and most theatrical form: Tragedy is born through character flaws, through bad choices, through grave missteps. When the girl in the horror movie goes to investigate the creepy noise rather than turn and run like hell, that's a micro-moment of tragedy. We *know* that's a bad goddamn decision and yet she does it. It is her downfall—possibly literally, as the slasher tosses her down an elevator shaft where she's impaled on a bunch of fixed spear points or something. Sidenote: The original translation of tragedy is "goat song." So, whenever you're writing horror, just say, "I'M WRITING ANOTHER GOAT SONG, MOTHER." And the person will be like, "I'm not your mother. It's me, Steve." And you just bleat and scream.

3. Horror's Been in Our Hearts for a Long Time

From *Beowulf* to Nathaniel Hawthorne, from Greek myth to Horace Walpole, horror's been around for a long, long time. Everything's all crushed bodies and extracted tongues and doom and devils and demigods. This is our literary legacy: The flower bed of our fiction is seeded with these seeds of horror and watered with gallons of blood and a sprinkling of tears. Horror is part of our narrative make-up.

4. Look to Ghost Stories and Urban Legends

If you want to see the simplest heart of horror, you could do worse than dissecting ghost stories and urban legends, two types of tales we tell even as young deviants and miscreants. They contain many of the elements that make horror what it is: subversion, admonition, and fear of the unknown.

5. We're All Afraid of the Dark

We fear the unknown because we fear the dark. We fear the dark because we're biologically programmed to do so: At some point we gain the awareness that outside the light of our fire lurks ... well, who knows? Sabretoothed tigers. Serial killers. The Octomom. Horror often operates best when it plays off this core notion that the unknown is a far freakier quantity than the known. The more we know, the less frightening it becomes. Lovecraft is like a really advanced version of this. Our sanity is the firelight, and beyond it lurks not sabretoothed tigers but a whole giant, squirming, seething pantheon of madness whose very existence is too much for mortal man's mind to parse.

6. Plain Stakes, Stabbed Hard Through Breastbone

On the other hand, creating horror is easier and more effective when the stakes are so plain that they're on the table for all to see. We must know what can be gained—and, more importantly, what can be lost—for horror to work. Fear is built off of understanding consequences. We can be afraid of the unknown of the dark, but horror works best when we know that the dark is worth fearing.

7. Dread and Revulsion In An Endless Tango

Beneath plot and beneath story is a greasy, grimy subtextual layer of pacing—the tension and recoil of dread and revulsion. *Dread* is a kind of septic fear, a grim certainty that bad things are coming. *Revulsion* occurs when we see how these bad things unfold. We know that the monster is coming, and at some point we must see the wretchedness of the beast laid bare. *Dread, revulsion, dread, revulsion.*

8. Stab the Gut, Spear the Heart, Sever the Head

Horror works on three levels: mind, heart, and gut. Our minds reel at trying to dissect horror, and good horror asks troubling questions. Our hearts feel a surge of emotions—terror, fear, and suspense, all felt deep in the ventricles, like a wedge of rancid fat clogging our aortas. Our guts feel all the leftover, baser emotions—the bowel-churn, the stomach-turn, the saline rush of icy sepsis as if our intestinal contents have turned to some kind of *wretched fecal slushie*. Which, for the record, is the name of my new Satanic ska band.

9. The Squick Factor

My father used to walk up, hands cupped and closed so as to hide something, and then he'd tell me to open my hands, the goal being that he would dump whatever he was hiding into my palm. Could have been anything. Cicada skin. A frog or frog's egg. The still-beating heart of a magnificent elk. The point was always the same: for me to find delight in being grossed out. Horror still plays on this. And why shouldn't it? It's both primal and fun. Sidenote: We should do a new gross-out reality show called *The Squick Factor*. Hollywood, call me. You know my number from the last time we made love under the overpass.

10. That Said, You Do Not Actually Require Buckets of Overflowing Viscera for Horror

The Squick Factor is not actually a prerequisite for good horror. Some of the best and most insidious horror is devoid of any grossness at all. A great ghost story, for instance, is often told without any blood and guts.

11. Characters You Love Making Choices You Hate

Suspense and tension are key components to the horror-making process. When you see a beloved character about to step *toward* the closet where the unseen serial killer is hiding, your sphincter tightens so hard it could break someone's finger. We recoil at mistakes made by loved ones, and this is doubly true when these mistakes put their lives, souls and sanities in danger.

12. Horror and Humor Are Gym Buddies

Horror and humor, hanging out at the gym, snapping each other's asses with wet towels. Horror and humor both work to stimulate that same place in our gutty-works, a place that defies explanation. Sometimes you don't know why you think this thing is funny or that thing is scary. *They just are.* It's why it's hard to *explain* a horror story or a joke: You can't explain it, you can only tell it. And both have a set-up, ask a question, and respond with a punchline or a twist. It's just, they go in separate directions—one aims for amusement, the other for anxiety. But the reason you can find these two working sometimes in tandem is because they're ultimately kissing cousins.

13. Sex and Death Also Play Well Together

There are two more kissing cousins: sex and death. Shakespeare didn't call the orgasm the "little death" for nothing. (I, on the other hand, refer to it as "The Monkey's Pinata.") Both are taboo subjects, both kept to the dark—and, as we know, horror lives in the dark, too. We all fear death, so sex—procreative and seductive—feels like an antidote to that, but then you also have the baggage where OMG SEX KILLS, whether it's via a venereal disease or as part of the unwritten rules contained within a slasher film. In this way, horror, sex, and death are the Ouroboros, the snake biting its own tail.

14. Car Crashes and Two Girls With One Cup

If you want to understand horror, you have to understand the impulse that drives us to click on a video that everybody tells us we don't want to see, or the urge to slow down at car crashes and gawk at blood on the highway. That urge is part of what informs our need to write *and* read horror fiction. It's a baser impulse, but an important one. We deny it, but if you ask me, it's universal.

15. The Real Horror Story Is What's Happening to the Horror Genre

Horror's once again a difficult genre. It had a heyday in the 80s and 90s, as evidenced by the fact that it had its very own shelf at most bookstores. That's no longer the case at Barnes & Noble, and Borders broke its leg in the woods and was eaten by hungry possums. I've heard that some self-published authors have pulled away from marketing their books as horror because they sell better when labeled as other genres.

16. Ripe for Resurgence?

That said, I wonder if it's not time for horror to rise again, a gore-caked phoenix screaming like a crazed hell-beast. The times we live in often dictate the type of entertainment we seek—and we're starting to slide once more into a very dark and scary corner of American life. Horror may serve as a reflection of that—equal parts escapist and exploratory—maybe it's time again to let monsters be monsters, giving a fictional face to the fiends we see all around us. Then again, maybe shit's just too screwed up. Who can say? It's worth a shot, though. I submit that it's a good time to try writing horror.

17. Horror Writers Tend to Be Very Nice

I don't know what it is, but goddamn if horror writers aren't some of the nicest writers on the planet. I think it's because their fiction is like constantly lancing a boil: The poison is purged, and all that's left is smiles.

18. Horror Needs Hope

Good is known by its proximity to evil. You don't know what a great burger tastes like until you've eaten a shitty one. You can't know great sex from awful sex until you'd experienced both (pro tip: Great sex is the one where you don't cry and eat a whole container of cake frosting after). And so it is that for horror to be horrific, it must also have hope. Unceasing and unflinching horror ceases to actually be horrific until we have its opposite present: that doesn't mean that hope needs to prevail. Horror always asks which will win the day: the eyes of hope or the jaws of hell?

19. Lessons Learned
Horror stories can serve as modern-day fables. They work to convey messages and lessons, rules about truth and consequence. If you're looking to say something, *really say something*, you've worse ways of doing so than by going down the horror fiction route. A great example of this is the underrated *Drag Me To Hell*, by Sam Raimi; a grim parable about our present economic recession.

20. The Stick of a Short, Sharp Needle
Sometimes, horror needs to be really goddamn screwed up. It just can't do what it needs to do unless it's going to cut out one of your kidneys, bend you over a nightstand, and shove the kidney back up inside your nether-burrow. Horror all but demands you don't pull your punches, but that kind of unceasing assault on one's own senses and sanity cannot be easily sustained for a novel-length or film-length project (looking at you, *Human Centipede*). Hence, short fiction and short films do well to deliver the sharp shock that horror may require.

21. We Need New Monsters
The old monsters—vampires, zombies, ghosts, werewolves—have their place. They mean something. But they may also be monsters for another time. Never be afraid to find new monsters. In this way, horror is a pit without a bottom—you will always discover new creatures writhing in the depths, reflecting the time in which they are born. Just go to a Juggalo convocation or a Tea Party gathering. You'll see.

22. Never Tell the Audience They Should Be Scared
Show, Don't Tell is a critical rule in all of storytelling, so critical that you should probably have it tattooed on your forehead backward so that ev-

ery time you look in the mirror, there it is. But in horror it's doubly important not to convey the fear that the audience is ideally supposed to feel. You can't tell someone to be scared. You just have to shove the reader outside the firelight and hope that what you've hidden there in the shadows does the trick. You can lead a horse to horror, but you can't make him piss his horsey diapers when something leaps out of the depths to bite his face and plant eggs in his nose holes.

23. Break Your Flashlight

If you write horror, you're trying to shine a light in dark corners. The key word there is "trying"—the flashlight needs to be broken. A light too bright will burn the fear away—the beam must waver, the batteries half-dead, the bulb on the verge of popping like a glass blister. It's like, what the light finds is so unpleasant, you can't look at it for too long. Look too long it'll burn out your sanity sensors. Horror isn't always concerned with the *why* or the *how*—but it is most certainly concerned with the *what*.

24. Horror Still Needs All the Things That Make Stories Great

You can't just jam some scary shit into a book and be like, "Boom, done, game over." Slow down, Slick. Come back to the story. You still need all the things that make a story great. Horror—really, any genre—ain't squat unless you can commit to the page a story filled with great characters, compelling ideas, strong writing, and a sensible plot. Don't just dump a bucket of blood on our heads and expect us to slurp it up. We wade *through* the blood to get to great storytelling.

25. Horror Is Personal

Horror needs to work on you, the author. You need to be troubled, a little unsettled, by your own material. Write about what scares you. Doesn't matter what it is or how absurd—hell, some people think that being terrified of clowns is ridiculous, until you realize *how many people find clowns spooky as shit.* Dig deep into your own dark places. Tear off the manhole cover and stare down into the unanswered abyss. Speak to your own experiences, your own fears and frights. Shake up your anxieties and let them tumble onto the page. Because horror works best when horror is honest. The audience will feel that. The truth you bring to the genre will resonate, an eerie and unsettling echo that turns the mind upon itself.

25 WAYS TO DEFEAT WRITER'S BLOCK

1. Write Through It

You are confronted by a tangle of jungle vines and Amazonian thicket. The only way forward is forward. You have a machete. What do you do? You chop, goddammit. Take the blade. Start hacking. Won't be fun. Won't be fast. But it's the only way to gain ground. Your first way through writer's block is just to write. Clench your jaw, tighten your sphincter, and write. The key is to write badly if you must. Write without regard for quality or care. Flail about with your word machete until the tangle is clear.

2. Write Through It, Part II: All Work and No Play

This is the same as the first but bears special mention: Sometimes it's not even about writing words in your stor; sometimes it's about just *writing*. Writer's block is often about jarring loose stubborn bullshit. It feels like you're trying to shave the back of a meth-cranked raccoon, but that's an act of finesse. Write crazy. Write big. Write insane. *All work and no play makes writermonkey a twitchy serial murderer.* Write one word over and over. One sentence. One paragraph. Don't worry about what you're writing. Turn on the spigot. Let the madness flow.

3. The Blood Must Flow

Science lesson: Blood carries nutrients to your brain. One of those nutrients is *imagozen*, the vitamin that governs our imagination. I may just be making that up. But there's some truth there: We do need good blood-flow to the brain to think clearly. Been sitting on your ass a while? All the blood and sweet, sweet *imagozen* is pooling in your ass parts. Get up. Move around. Take a walk. Exercise. Do some push-ups. Hell, *have sex.* You gotta love a guy who will tell you to solve writer's block by "banging it out." Right? No, seriously, you *have* to love me. Take off your pants. Mine are already on the floor. LOVE ME.

4. Prepare Yourself for the High-Octane Energy Drink Enema!

I am not actually recommending an energy drink enema, just so we're clear. I will not be held liable for the embarrassing X-rays that make it onto the Internet. What I am saying is that caffeine can be your buddy. It can give your brain a much-needed jolt, as if from those electrified paddles. CLEAR. Bzzt. Start with tea. Tea has a mellower edge than coffee. If that doesn't work, try coffee. Mmm. Coffee. Speaking of—*slurrrp*

5. Booze Booze Booze Booze Booze *vomits*

Caffeine creates tension. But maybe what you need is recoil. Could be that you're just too ratcheted up to write. No problem. *Switch your chem-*

ical dance partner. From caffeine to liquor. I'm not saying you should make a habit of writing drunk—in fact, I'm suggesting you write *merely tipsy.* Whatever amount of alcohol lubricates your social gears may also lubricate your writing gears. Just this once. Just to ooze past this block. To get your mind chatting up the birds at the word bar. (Please note that alcohol is a drug and you should not partake if you or your family has a history of alcoholism or heart conditions or a tendency to get really drunk and throw up in potted plants at parties. Drink and write responsibly. And more seriously, never ever get in a car if you've had something to drink.)

6. Chatty Cathy, Don't Clip Those Strings

Talk to yourself. Seriously. Use your mouth. Vocalize words. Have a conversation *with yourself.* Talk about the story. Talk about what's clogging the pipes. Yammer away like a crazy person. (For bonus points, do so at a public bus terminal.) If you're so inclined, record the conversation. Label the file, "MY MANIFESTO." E-mail it to all the newspapers.

7. Reach Out and Touch Somebody

Perhaps a masturbatory chat with yourself isn't quite enough. Fine. Find another human being (or if you're reading this after the year 2028, find a sentient appliance bot, like the Dishflenser 500 or the Toast-Aborter v2.0), and have this chat with them. Talk out your problem. Get their input. Human interaction can go a long way toward jarring loose whatever grubby suppository is stuck inside your narrative butthole.

8. Converse With Your Imaginary Friend

This one will make you certifiable, so don't perform it in front of any sensitive family members. But take one of your characters, and talk to them. Out loud or on the page. Do a little role-playing. (And any writer who hasn't engaged in a little role-playing—either the kind with dice or the kind with a librarian's outfit and an orangutan mask—is missing out on learning how to let your fiction find its path.)

9. Fiddle With the Feng Shui

Get up off your ass. Pack up your writing. Go elsewhere. Across the room. To the kitchen table. To a Starbucks. To a Jersey rest stop. Hell, wander outside, and do some writing there. Sometimes just the change of scenery is enough to free the word demons from their restrictive cages.

10. Tinker With the Guts

You ever get lost while traveling? "We're supposed to be at the aquarium. And yet here we are, atop an ancient hill, trapped inside a giant wicker effigy, surrounded by torch-wielding cultists. I think we took a wrong turn somewhere, honey. Sorry, kids." Sometimes you have to backtrack. Find out where things went awry. So too with your fiction. Read back. Find where you screwed up. Your reluctance to continue writing may be born of the unconscious discomfort that something in your tale is wrong, like a picture hanging askew on the wall. Go back. Straighten the picture.

11. You Need a Motherfizzucking Map

It can be hard to see the forest for the trees when writing a big project. You feel like you're wandering in the swamp, walking in weeds as high as your ears. Do you have a map? Probably not. Listen, some writers are pantsers. They love to operate off the narrative grid. You may not be one of them. Go back. Write an outline. Beat out the story the way you'd beat a confession out of a perp. Know where you've been and discover where you're going and then go back and write. Sometimes writer's block is just you missing the big picture.

12. Throw the Map in a Bag and Burn It

Alternately, maybe you need to "pants" it a little. Maybe you're too married to an outline that just isn't tickling your pink parts anymore. Fine. Throw caution to the wind. It's time to do something dramatic. Christa Faust has a killer tattoo that cuts to the heart of it: "When in doubt, have a man come through the door with a gun in his hand." That's a specific example, but you can blow up the story however you choose. Fire! Death! Betrayal! Cataclysm! Deception! Adultery! Whatever it is, take the map you've written, burn it, and inhale the sweet story vapors.

13. Put Lipstick on That Monkey

Sometimes, a cosmetic change goes a long way. Me? I'm a font whore. I like to find the right font that fits well with my story. Yes, this is ludicrous. Yes, this is a waste of time. Yes, I do it anyway. And once I take thirty minutes to find the right font, the story's style locks for me. Try it. Or maybe you mess with margins. Or line spacing. Or you choose to write longhand. Your call.

14. A-Scripting-We-Will-Go

Depart from your narrative, and turn your fiction into a script. Just for now. Just for the part that's blocking you. Of course, if you're already writing a script, then do the reverse—switch it up, and move into the more languid and longer form afforded by prose. Again, this "switching of gears" can uncage the story bears. By the way, "uncage the story bear" is the metaphor I choose when I proclaim I am about to make love. I walk into the room, I scratch my beard, unmoor my pants, and I announce that in a booming voice. I just wanted to let you in on that part of my life. Thank me later.

15. Dear Missus Frittershire

Familiar with the epistolary? Any story that takes the form of a series of documents is considered epistolary. The novel might manifest as a collection of letters, e-mails, newspaper clippings, diary entries, tweets, the ravings of an impudent spam-bot, etc. Try this out. I don't mean for the whole story. But for today, try writing through your writer's block by embracing this form. "Today, my character will write a blog entry." "I will use the art of the *takeout Chinese menu* to tell this story." Shit, you never know.

16. Wander Down an Alley

Er, not literally. I will not be held responsible if you are captured and eaten by Oscar the Grouch. (You gotta watch that guy. *Terrible hungers.*) Let's say you're writing a novel. Let's say you're banging your head on that novel the way a bumblebee bats his head against the window glass. I want you to take the protagonist, or some aspect of the storyworld, and *deviate*. Write some flash fiction, maybe a short story, some ancillary, tacked-on, doesn't-connect-directly-to-the-novel story. Indirect, yes. Direct, no. Take today, and write only that. It may open doors for the larger project at hand.

17. Kill the Shiny

As modern souls we are besieged by distractions. Text messages and tweets and spam-bots and porn and TV on demand and cyber-LSD and digital cupcakes *and only the gods know what else.* Escape the gravity of your own distractions. Turn it off. Power it down. Use a program like Mac Freedom or Write Or Die. Close the door on all the piffling, waffling, middling bullshit, and make sure it's just you and the word count.

18. Hear a Buzzer, Start to Drool

Tell yourself, "If I write 1,000 words, I get [fill-in-the-blank]." Doesn't matter what it is. Ice cream? Another cup of coffee? An hour of television? A jet boat made of pony bones? Like I said, whatever. But establishing a reward gives you motivation to do the one thing that really defeats writer's block: writing through the anguish and coming out the other side. Covered in blood. And smiling.

19. The Penmonkey Diet

Carbs are great if you're going to be, y'know, *using* that energy for something like, say, moving your laggardly slugabed body around. But writers live a sedentary existence, at least while working, and so it behooves you not to hoover a bowl of Corn Pops into your gut. Do that, and the carbs will only drag you down, make you mentally foggy. Stick with protein while writing. By the way, bacon is protein. Just saying.

20. Hop Around Like a Coked-Up Jackrabbit

Nobody said you had to write your work in order. I like to write in sequence for the most part just because it keeps me on point but if I'm at a section I'm just not "feeling" that day, I'll skip around and write something else. "I want to write a fight scene between two stompy robots," I'll say. Hell, you're the god of the story. You may experience it in whatever order you so choose.

21. Get Visual

I like to take photos. Or screw around with Photoshop. You think I haven't been vain enough to do up fake book covers for my as-yet-unpublished books? *Oh, I have.* Point is, sometimes writer's block is just about flexing those creative muscles on the right side of your brain. Hell, fingerpainting poop on your Plexiglass enclosure like I do. Seriously. Look, I drew a monkey! *The flies are his eyes.*

22. Down the Rabbit Hole of Research

Research can be a trigger to get you moving again. No matter what you're writing about, you will always find more to know, and in this case research qualifies as a "good" distraction as long as you keep a relative focus. If you play it right, research can be the key that unlocks whatever mental door got slammed shut.

23. Recognize Why You Don't Want to Write This Part

Sometimes you get stuck on a part and are too stubborn to do anything about it, so you just stand there and stare it down, growling and stomping your feet. Here's a secret: Maybe that part you're stuck on is a part you just don't want to write. And if you don't want to write it, what are the chances that someone might not want to read it? You know what you do? Skip it. Kill it. Move past it. Find another way through.

24. Screw Off for a Day, Willya?

You get one day. *One.* Free pass. No writing today. Just flit away, little butterfly. Flit, flit, flit. Clear your head. Have some fun. Tomorrow the work returns. The block, undone. Or it damn well better be.

25. Deny the Existence of Writer's Block

If you're being skewered by a unicorn, tell the unicorn he doesn't exist. If you do that, he'll disappear in a puff of Trix cereal. That's true. That's *fact.* Same thing goes for writer's block. If it's an incubus clinging to your back, you just tell that mythological being that you don't believe in him. If you do that, you steal his power. Suck his breath away. Make him turn into so much vapor. You have to harden your heart and your head against it and believe that the one way through is that old saw everyone repeats but always forgets: *Writers write.* That's the one tried and true way through writer's block. Because a writer who writes isn't blocked, is he? (Sidenote: It's worth noting that sometimes the thing you think is writer's block is actually depression. Depression is neither helped nor fixed by attending to it as if it's writing block—no amount of "writing through it" will solve depression. Depression requires its own solutions that you should discuss with family, friends, and any medical personnel you trust with such a decision.)

25 WAYS TO PLOT, PLAN, AND PREP YOUR STORY

1. The Basic, Vanilla, Tried-And-True Outline

The basic and essential outline: Numbers, Roman numerals, letters. Items in order. Separated out by section if need be (say, Act I, Act II, Act III). Easy peazy, Lyme diseasey.

2. The Reverse Outline

Start at the end, instead. Write it down. "Sir Pimdrip Chicory of Bath slays the dragon-badger but not before the dragon-badger bites the head off Chicory's one true love, Lady Miss Wermathette Kildare of the Manchester Kildares." Rewind the clock. Reverse the gears. Find out how you built to that.

3. Tentpole Moments

A story in your head may require certain keystone events to be part of the plot. "Betty-Sue must get sucked into the time portal outside Schenectady because that's why her ex-boyfriend Booboo begins to build a time machine in earnest which will accidentally unravel space and time." You might have five, maybe ten of these. Write them down. These are the elements that, were they not included, would make the plot collapse (like a tent without its poles). The narrative space *between* the tentpoles is uncharted territory.

4. Beginning, Middle, End

Write three paragraphs, each detailing the rough three acts found in every story: the inciting incident and outcome of the beginning (Act I), the escalation and conflict in the middle (Act II), the climactic culmination of events and the ease-down denouement (Act III). You can, if you want, choose the elemental changes-in-state you might find at the end of each act, too—the pivot points on which the story shifts. This document probably isn't more than a page's worth of wordsmithy. Simple and elegant.

5. A Series of Sequences

The saying goes that an average screenplay usually offers up eight or nine sequences (a sequence being a series of scenes that add together to form common narrative purpose, like, say, the Attack On The Death Star sequence from *Star Wars* or the Kevin James Makes Love To All The Animals In Order To Make The Audience Feel Shame sequence from *Paul Blart, Zoo Abortion*). So chart the sequences that will go into your screenplay. If you're writing prose, I don't know how many sequences a novel should have—more than a film, probably (or alternately, each sequence is granted a greater conglomeration of scenes).

6. Chapter by Chapter

For novel writers, you can chart your story by its chapters. A standard outline is more about dictating plot and story without marrying one-self to narrative structure. This, however, puts the ring on that finger and locks it down tight. A chapter-by-chapter outline is visualizing the reader's way through the novel.

7. Beat Sheet

This one's for you real granular-types, the ones who want to count each grain of sand on your story's beach. Chart each beat of the story in every scene. This is you writing tout he entire story's out, but you're writing it without much dialogue or narrative flair. It's you laying out all the pieces. The order-of-operations made plain.

8. Mind Maps

Happy blocks and bubbles connected to winding, bendy spokes connected to a central topical hub. You can use a mind map to chart ... well, anything your mind so desires. It is, after all, a map of said mind. Sequence of events? Character arcs? Exploration of theme? Story-world ideas? Family trees? The crazy hats worn by your villains? Catchphrases? Your inchoate rage and shame made manifest? Your call.

9. Zero Draft

AKA, "The Vomit Draft." Puke up the story. Just yarf it up—*bleaaaarrghsputter.* A big ol' Technicolor yawn. You aren't aiming for structure. Aren't aiming for art or even craft. This is just you getting everything onto the page so that it's out there and can now be cleaned up. You've puked up the story, now it's time to form it into little idols and totems—the heretic statuaries of your story.

10. In the Document, as You Go

AKA, "The Bring Your Flashlight" technique. You outline only as you go. Write a scene or chapter. Roughly sketch the next. Then write it. Onward and upward until you've got a proper story.

11. Write a Script

For those of you writing scripts, this sounds absurd. "He wants me to outline my script by writing a script? Has this guy been licking colorful toads?" Sorry, screenwriters—this one ain't for you. Novelists, however, will find writing a script useful for the plotting. Scripts are lean and mean: description, dialogue, description, dialogue. It'll get you through the story fast—then you translate into prose.

12. Dialogue Pass

Let the characters talk and nothing else. Put those squirrely bastards in a room, lock the door, and let the story unfold. It won't stay that way, of course. You'll need to add meat to the bones. But it's a good way to establish the characters, find their voices, and discover their stories. Remember that dialogue reads fast and tends to write fast, too. Dialogue is like Astroglide—it lubricates the tale.

13. Character Arcs

Characters often have arcs. They start at A, go to B, and end at C (with added steps if you're feeling particularly saucy). Commander Jim Nipplesplitter, Jr. starts at "gruff and loyal soldier boy in the war against the Ant People" (A) and heads to "is crippled and betrayed by his country, left to die in the distant hills of the Ant Planet" (B) and ends up at "falls in love with a young Ant Squaw and he must fight to protect his ant-man larvae" (C). A character arc can track plotty bits, emotional shifts, outfit changes, whatever.

14. Synopsis First

You might think to write your query letter, treatment, or synopsis last. Bzzt. Wrong move, donkeyface. Write it up front. It's not etched in stone, but it'll give you a good idea of how to stay on target with this story.

15. Index Cards

Index cards are a kick-ass organization tool. You can use them to do anything—list characters, track scenes, list chapters, identify emotional shifts, make little Origami throwing stars that will give your neighbors wicked-ass papercuts. Lay them on a table, or pin 'em to a corkboard. Might I recommend John August's "10 Hints for Index Cards?" Go Google that NOW. Also look for the Index Card app for iOS.

16. Whiteboard

A whiteboard represents a great thinking space. Notes, mind maps, character sketches, drawings of weird alien penises. Get some different colored pens, and chart your story in whatever way feels most appropriate.

17. The Crazy Person's Notebook

Once in a while, a story of mine demands a hyper-psycho notebook experience. My handwriting is messier than a garbage disposal choked with hair, but even so, sometimes I just like to put pen to paper and scribble. And I sometimes print stuff out, chop it up, and tape it into the notebook. Weird, right?

18. Collage

You're like, "What's next? A shoebox diorama of the Lincoln assassination?" That's a different blog post. Seriously, on my YA-cornpunk novel Popcorn, I took a whole corkboard and covered it in images and quotes that were relevant to the work. Then I'd just wander over there from time to time, stare at it, and get my head around the story I was telling and the feel of the world the story portrayed. Surprisingly helpful.

19. Spreadsheets
Stare too long into the grid of a spreadsheet and you will feel your soul entangled there—a dolphin caught in a tuna net. Even still, you may find a spreadsheet very helpful. Track plots and beats to your heart's delight. J.K. Rowling has an amazing hand-written spreadsheet detailing various Harry Potter plots and characters. (I will leave it to your capable Google Magic to find it.)

20. Story Bible
Everything and anything goes into the story bible: worldbuilding, character descriptions, the "rules" of the story, plot, theme, and mood. An IKEA furniture manual. (Goddamn Allen wrenches.) The *Bioshock* story bible was reputedly a 400+ page beast, which means that yes, your story bible may be bigger than your actual novel. The key is not to let this—or any planning technique—become an exercise in procrastination. You plan. Then you do. That's the only way this works.

21. The Power of Templates
Film and TV scripts already follow a fairly rigorous template, but you can go further afield. Look to Blake Snyder's *Save The Cat* beats. Or Joseph Campbell's hero's journey. Go weirder with the Proppian morphology of fairy tales. You may think it unimaginative but the power of art and story lives easily within such borders as it does outside of them.

22. Stream-of-Consciousness Story Babble
Slap on a diving bell, and jump deep into the waters of the stream of consciousness. Order, you see, is sometimes born first from chaos, wriggling free from a uterus made up of fractal swirls and Kamikaze squirrels. Open yourself to All The Frequencies: Get into your word processor,

or find a blank notebook page and just scribble wantonly without regard to sense or quality. You may find your story lives in the noise and madness and that on that snowy screen you will find structure. Like a Magic Eye painting that reveals the image of a dolphin riding a motorbike and shooting Japanese whalers with twin chattering Uzis.

23. Visual Storyboards

Sometimes the words only come when given the boost of a visual hook. Sketch it out yourself. Get an artist friend. Find images from the Internet. Ingest some kind of dew-slick jungle mushroom and paint your story on the wall in an array of bodily fluids. Sometimes you really need to *visualize* the story.

24. The Test Drive

Take your characters, storyworld, and ideas, and run them through a totally separate story. Let's call it apocryphal or "noncanonical." It's not a story you intend to keep. Not a story you want to publish. You're just taking your story elements through their paces. Run them through a test drive. "This is where Detective Shirtless McGoggins solves the murder of the goblin seamstress." Sure, your Detective lives in the real world, a world not populated by goblins. Screw it, it's just an exercise. A test run to find his voice and yours.

25. Pants the Shit Out of It

All this plotting and scheming just isn't working for you? Go ahead, and pants the hell out of it. (Me? I don't wear pants. Pants are the first tool of your oppressors.) Sometimes trying to wrestle your story into even the biggest box is just an exercise in frustration, so do what works for you and avoid what doesn't. Once again, however, I'll exhort you to at least learn the skill of outlining—because eventually, someone's going to ask for a demonstration of your ability.

PART TWO
THE CRAFT

25 THINGS YOU SHOULD KNOW ABOUT CHARACTER

1. The Character as Fulcrum: All Things Rest Upon Him
Without character, you have nothing. Great plot? Robust storyworld? Potent themes? Elegant font? Matters little if your character is a dud. The punch might be delicious but not if someone threw up in it. The character is why we come to the table. The character is our way through all those other things. We engage with stories because we relate to them: They are mirrors. Characters are the mirror-side version of "us" staring back. Twisted, warped, uncertain—but still us through and through.

2. The Cure for All That Ails the Audience
A great character can be the line between narrative life and story death. She's a powerful Band-Aid, a strong swaddling of gauze to staunch the

bleeding. Think of the character like duct tape: She can piece the whole thing back together. I will forgive your sins of a so-so plot, of muddy themes, of a *meh-ehhh-enh* storyworld if you're letting me live for a while with a great character. But don't think character will close truly grievous injuries. A gaping chest wound—meaning, poor writing, asinine plot, or perhaps a duller-than-two-dead-goats storyworld—will only swallow your great character into its gory depths.

3. And Yet the Character Must Be Connected

Don't believe that all those other aspects are separate from the character. The character is—or should be—bound inextricably to those other elements. The character is your vehicle through the plot. The character carries the story. Theme, mood, description: Focus them through the prism of character, not vice versa. The character is the DNA in every goddamn cell of your story.

4. You Are the Dealer; the Character Is the Drug

The audience will do anything to spend time with a great character. We're junkies for it. We'll gnaw our own arms off to read just *one more page* with a killer character. It's why sequels and series are so popular— we want to see where the character's going. If you give us a great character, it becomes out only desire to lick him like he's a hallucinogenic toad and take a crazy trip-ass ride wherever he has to go.

5. Tell Us What She Wants

It is critical to know what a character wants from the start. She may not know what she wants, but the audience must have that information. Maybe she wants her enemies destroyed, freedom from oppression, her child returned to her, true love, the perfect falafel, a pet monkey, the ultimate wedding, or a secret subterranean moonbase. She can want a number of things, and it's of the utmost importance that we know what it is. How else will we know how far she's come? How else can we see the stakes on the table? How else will you frustrate the piss out of the audience by standing in her way?

6. Not Likability but Rather Livability

It doesn't matter if we "like" your character, or in the parlance of junior high, whether we even "*like*-like" your character. It only matters that we want to live with him. We must see something that makes us want to keep on keeping on, following him into the jaws of Hell and out through the Devil's lava-encrusted keister. For the record, the "Lava Keister" sounds like either a rollercoaster or a Starbucks drink.

7. The Give-a-Shit Factor

Ask this up front as you're crafting the story: *Why will the audience care about this character?* You have unlimited answers to this. Look to the narratives all around us to find reasons to care. We love underdog stories. We love tales of redemption. We love bad boys, good girls, bad girls, and good boys. We want to see characters punished, exalted, triumphant, rewarded, destroyed, stymied, puzzled, and wounded. We gawk at car crashes. We swoon at love. Find a hook. Hang your character upon it.

8. Rub Up Against Remarkability

You must prove this thesis: "This character is worth the audience's time." The character must deserve her own story—or, at least, her own part within it. You prove this thesis by making the character in some way remarkable. This is why you see a lot of stories about doctors, detectives, lawyers, cowboys, bounty hunters, wizards, space rangers, and superheroes ... but you don't see quite so many about copier repairmen, pharmaceutical assistants, piano tuners, or ophthalmologists. The former group is remarkable, in part, by their roles. The latter group can be just as remarkable, however, provided you discover their noteworthiness and put it on the page or the screen. What makes one remarkable can be a secret past, a current attitude, or a future triumph. It can be internal or external. Infinite options. Choose one.

9. Act Upon the World Rather Than Have the World Act Upon Him

Don't let the character be a dingleberry stuck to the ass of a toad as he floats downriver on a bumpy log. We tire of characters who do nothing except react to whatever the world flings at their heads. That's not to say that characters shouldn't be forced to deal with unexpected challenges and left-field conflicts—but that doesn't prevent a character from being proactive, either. Passivity fails to be interesting for long. This is why crime fiction has power: The very nature of a crime is about doing. You don't passively rob a bank, kill your lover, or run a street gang. Simply put: *Characters do shit.*

10. Bad Decisions Are a Good Decision

Nobody ever said an active character had to be a smart character. A character can and perhaps should be *badly* proactive, making all the wrong moves and affecting the world with his piss-poor decisions. At some point a character needs to take control, even if it means taking control in the worst possible way. In fact ...

11. This Is Why Jesus Invented Suspense

Tension is created when characters you love make bad decisions. They lie, cheat, steal, break laws, or shatter taboos. They go into the haunted house. They don't run from the serial killer. They betray a friend. Sleep with an enemy. Eat a forbidden fruit. Jack off in a mad scientist's gizmotron, thus accidentally creating an army of evil baby Hitlers. Tension is when the character sets free his chickens and we know full well that those chickens will come home to roost. But the chickens will come home changed. They will have knives. Prison tats. And evil wizard powers. Don't let tension wriggle free, soft and pliable, from external events. Let the character create the circumstances of suspense.

12. How You Succeed Is by Not Having Them Succeed

You as storyteller are a malevolent presence blocking the character's bliss. Imagine that the character is an ant over here and over *there* is a nugget of food, a dollop of honey, and all the ant wants is to trot his little ant-y ass over to the food so that he may dine upon it. Think of the infinite ways you can stop him from getting to that food. Flick him into the grass. Block his path with twigs, rocks, a line of dish soap, a squeeze of lighter fluid set aflame. Be the wolf to his little piggy, and huff and puff and blow his house down. Pick him up, put him in the cup holder in your car, and drive him a hundred miles in the opposite direction while taunting him with insults. The audience will hate you. But they'll hunger for more. *Will the ant get to the food? Won't he? Will he find his friends again? Can he overcome?* Primal, simple, declarative problem. You are the villain. The character is the hero. The audience thirsts for this most fundamental conflict of storyteller versus character.

13. The Code

Just as a storyworld is beholden to certain laws, norms, and ways, so too is a character: Every character has an internal compass, an invisible set of morals and beliefs that comprise their "code." The audience senses this. They know when a character betrays his own code and violates the program—it's like a glitch in the Matrix, a disturbance in the dream you've crafted. That's not to say characters can't change. They can and do. But a heroic fireman doesn't one day save a cat from a tree and the next day decide to cook and eat a baby. Changes in a character must come out of the story, not out of thin air.

14. A, B, C, 1, 2, 3

The law of threes. Find three beats for your character—be they physical, social, emotional—with each beat graphing a change in the character over the course of a story. *Selfish boy* to *exiled teen* to *heroic man.*

From *maiden* to *mother* to *crone*. Private, Lieutenant, General. Knows everything, everything in question, knows nothing. Birth, life, death. Beginning, middle, end.

15. Boom Goes the Dynamite
Blake Snyder calls this the "Save The Cat" moment, but it needn't be that shiny and happy. The point is that every character needs a kick-ass moment, a reason why we all think, "Hell yeah, that's why I'm behind this dude." What moment will you give your character? Why will we pump our fists and hoot for him?

16. Beware the Everyman, Fear the Chosen One
I'm boring. So are you. We don't all make compelling protagonists despite what we feel in our own heads, and so the Everyman threatens to instead become the Eye-Wateringly-Dull-Man, flat as a coat of cheap paint. The Chosen One—arguably the opposite of the Everyman—has, appropriately, the opposite problem: he's too interesting, a preening peacock of special preciousness. Beware either. Both can work, but know the danger. Find complexity. Seek remarkability.

17. Nobody Sees Themselves as a Supporting Character
Your supporting characters shouldn't act like supporting characters. They have full lives in which they are totally invested and where they are the protagonists. They're not puppets for fiction. They don't know they're not the heroes.

18. The Main MC, DJ Protag
That said, they don't call your "main character" the MC for nothing. Your protagonist at the center of the story should still be the most compelling rockstar in the room.

19. You Are Not Your Character, Except for When You Are

Your character is not a proxy for you. If you see Mary Sue in the mirror, put your foot through the glass and use that reflection instead. But that old chestnut—"write what you know"—applies. You take the things that have happened to you and you bring them to the character. Look for those things in your memory that affected you: fought a bear, won a surfing competition, lost a fist-fight with Dad, eradicated an insectile alien species. Pull out the feelings. Inject them into the face, neck, guts, brain, and heart of the character.

20. Screwed Up

Everybody's a little screwed up inside. Some folks more than that. No character is a saint. Find the darkness inside. Draw their imperfections to the surface like a bead of blood. You don't have to give a rat's ass about Joseph Campbell, but he was right when he said we love people for their imperfections. Same holds true for characters. We love them for their problems.

21. A Tornado Beneath a Cool Breeze

A good character is both simple and complex: Simplicity on the surface eradicates any barrier to entry, and complexity beneath rewards the reader and gives the character both depth and something to do. Complexity on the surface rings hollow and threatens to be confusing, so ease the audience into the character the way you'd get into a clawfoot tub full of steaming hot water—one toe at a time, baby.

22. On the Subject of Archetypes

You can begin with an archetype—or even a stereotype—because people find comfort there. It creates a sense of intimacy even when none exists. But the archetype should be like the leg braces worn by Forrest Gump as a kid—when that kid takes off running, he blasts through the braces and leaves them behind. So too with the "type."

This will help the character stand on his own until it's time to shatter 'em when running.

23. Dialogue Over Description, Action Over Rumination

Don't bludgeon us over the head with description. A line or three about the character is good enough, and it doesn't need to be purely about their physical looks. It can be about movement and body language. It can be about what people think, about what goes on in her head. But throw out a couple-few lines and get out. Dialogue is where a character is revealed. And action. What a character says and does is the sum of her being. It doesn't need to be more than that: a character says shit, then does shit, then says shit about the shit she just did. In there lurks infinite possibilities—a confluence of atoms that reveals who she is.

24. Take the Test Drive

Write the character before you write the character. Take her on adventures that don't count. Who cares about canon? Here I say, "To Hell with the audience." This isn't for them. This is for you. Joyride the character around some flash fiction, a short script, a blog post, a page of dialogue, a poem, whatever.

25. Get All up in Them Guts

Know your character. Every square inch. Empathize, don't sympathize. Understand the character, but don't stand with the character. Get in their skin. The closer you get, the better off you are when a story goes sideways. Any rewriting or additional work comes easy when you know which way the character's gonna jump. Know them like you know yourself; when the character does something, you know it comes justified, with purpose, with meaning, with intimate knowledge that the thing she did is the thing she was always supposed to do.

25 THINGS YOU SHOULD KNOW ABOUT DESCRIPTION

1. Description Is a Misleading Term

If I were to say to you, "Describe for me this lamp," you would begin listing off its traits in earnest. "Base made of ironwood, 60-watt lightbulb, fraying electric cord, lampshade made of human skin," and on and on. But that is not what you do in fiction. I don't want you to describe every detail. I don't seek an accounting of all the brass tacks. The first lesson is: Don't describe everything. Knowing how to write description is often knowing what *not* to describe.

2. Bowling a Spare

Less isn't exactly *more*, here—less is less—but that's the side on which you should err. Better to make the reader hunger for more detail than be bludgeoned about the head and neck with it. A reader who wants to know more keeps reading. A reader who knows too much will put that book or script down and have a nap as if he just ate a whole plate of carnival food. (Sidenote: I'd shank a dude in the kidneys for a bite of funnel cake. Do you have some? Please give me some.)

3. The Reader Came Here to Work
The reader doesn't realize this, but he wants to get his hands dirty. I'm paraphrasing the brilliant Fate RPG game designer Rob Donoghue here, but the apocryphal story goes like this: When Betty Crocker first starting selling mixes, they were super-easy to make. Packet of powder, add water, and bake. But they didn't sell—in part because they were too easy. It felt like a cheat. So Crocker chose to leave out the egg—meaning, a housewife had to *add* an egg, an extra step. And bam! They sold like a sonofabitch. The lesson is that your audience wants to work. When they work, they feel invested. Hand them a pickaxe, a pith helmet. Don't give them all parts of the description—let them fill in details with their imagination. Let them add the egg.

4. Your Bloated Ego Makes for Swollen Description
To put it differently, the author likes to be in control. And you are. But you have to cede some intellectual and imaginary control to the audience. You don't need strict autocracy over description. You only need agency over those details that are critical for the story to be what you want the story to be. Leave everything else to the reader to invent inside their crazy head caves.

5. Zelazny's Rule of Three
This reportedly goes back to Roger Zelazny, who said you should stop at three details in description. People aren't going to remember much more than that, anyway. It's a good rule, although I don't think you need to be quite this mathematical about it. Rather, like with most writing

advice, the tenet and the *practice* of that tenet are a bit divergent. After all, does he mean three details about one character? All characters? The room? A lamp? The heating vent? If I'm allowed three details *per item in the room*, then suddenly I'm writing 1,436 details. I think it just means, "Keep the details to a minimum, asshole."

6. Describe What Matters

Describe only what matters to the story. If the reader must know something, then ensure she knows it. I don't give a damn about your lamp. Or what leaf rot is on the oak tree outside. Or what the tag on the dog's collar looks like. If you choose to describe these things, it should be because I need to know them: A character is going to brain another with the lamp; the leaf rot is part of a larger plot point about some sort of botanical *doom fungus*; the tag on the dog's collar is shaped like a lucky four-leaf clover because his owner is William "Irish Billy" McArdle, an ex-IRA bomber turned merc thug, and the clover is his signature.

7. Speedbumps and Slammed Doors

Over description slows down the pace of reading, and if it's truly too egregious, the reader will slam the door and walk away. (In Internet parlance? tl;dr = "too long, didn't read.") This is true when writing scripts, too—description separates out action and dialogue, and those two things keep a script's story moving. Heavy description can kill a script like a hammer to the skull.

8. And Yet, Fat Is an Essential Flavor

That's not to say a reader won't find those extra details compelling. Fat can be flavorful. Simply describing the antagonist's Dodge Charger as "cherry red" seems like a nonessential detail. But always look for the ways that description can do doubleduty. The fact that the muscle car is *cherry red* suggests deeper meaning. We know that red cars are likely to be pulled over. We intuit that red is a color of anger, blood, and fire.

The character's choice of color can tell us something about that character. Thus, the detail seems fatty, and it is—but it's also an *essential* fat. Like what you get from olive oil, avocados, or the unctuous barnacles scraped from the thighs of Oprah Winfrey.

9. That Goes for the Goddamn Weather, Too

To hell with weather. Too many writers go straight to describing the weather. I think it comes from that old saw, "It was a dark and stormy night," except everyone seems to forget that it comes from a laughably bad book. Describe the weather only if it matters. If a storm has physical effects on the plot, describe it. A miserably cold day might cause a car accident (ice) or lost visibility (blizzard). If the weather matters, tell us. Pro tip: It usually doesn't matter.

10. Well, Somebody's a Moody Little Monkey

You can use description to create or enhance mood, sure. That is, I think, why some writers try to describe the weather—"Oh! It's thundering, and I'm creating a mood of *impending doom*." Really? You can't do any better? It's thunder or nothing? Here's the thing: You can describe something in a way that is both meaningful to the story and conveys mood. Were you interested in stirring up a pervasive mood of *rot and decay*, you could describe the rust on the character's gun or some skin disorder he's suffering. Those things can affect the plot (the gun eventually jams, the skin disorder worsens). Description there serves both mood *and* story.

11. Time to Take a Test

Walk into a room. Preferably one with which you're not intimately familiar. Look around for thirty seconds. Time that shit. Don't wing it. Then walk out. Wait five minutes. Make some toast. Pour a drink. Pet the dog. Twerk wantonly against your dining room wall. After five minutes, write down those details you believe are essential to capturing the "roomness" of that room. Write down as many details as you'd like. By the end, cut it down to three. Then cut it down to one. Just to see. How'd you do? You failed. F+. I'm kidding. I could never fail you. Not as long as you keep sending me checks.

12. Don't Bury the Lede

Stories often rely on critical details that come out through description. A facial tic. A bomb under the table. A mysterious artifact known as the "Astronaut's Anal Beads." But some writers bury critical details in a mushy glop of description. Don't bury the things the audience needs to know. Highlight them. Make them stand out. I don't want to get to page 156 and say, "Whoa, whoa, whoa, the antagonist only has one hand? Shouldn't I have known that?" Then it turns out that yes, you told me back on page 32, but you told me in the middle of a generally descriptive paragraph. Blah blah blah, red hair, nice shoes, toe bunions, one hand, big belt buckle, blah blah blah.

13. Here's the Truth:
I Might Just Skip That Descriptive Shit You Wrote

My eyes catch onto dialogue like a hangnail on a fuzzy sweater. My eyes slide over big patches of description like a hippo going down a log flume greased with bacon fat. Description is like sex with someone unpleasant: Get in, get the job done, and get out. We call that a "combat landing."

14. Break Description Apart With Your Word-Hammer

No, "word-hammer" is not a euphemism for your penis. My penis, yes. Your penis, no. What I'm saying is, shatter descriptive passages like toffee—break it into pieces. Incorporate it into dialogue and action. Description doesn't need to exist as if time stands still so the protagonist can "take it all in." He can be running, talking, scheming, hiding—the details he notices are the details *he has to notice*, and thus, are the details the reader must notice, too.

15. Pricking the Reader's Oculus With This Grim and Gleaming Lancet

Purple prose is the act of gussying up your words so that they sound more poetic. (Of course, that misunderstands poetry as some flowery, haughty thing.) If you dress up your language in such frills and frippery, you stand in the way of your own story. You do nothing but sound haughty, ludicrous, or some combination of the two. And yes, I said "frippery." If that's too purple for you, then pretend I said, "If you dress your language up in a bedazzled prom gown and give it a gaudy spray-tan..." Put differently: Use the words that live inside your head. And if the words that live inside your head are those of an sentimental Victorian troubadour, then please close your head in a door jamb until you kill all that overwrought prose in a heroic act of brain damage.

16. "The Thing Is Blue, The Dog Is Making Sounds"

If you need to take the time to describe something, then aim for specifics. You can't just tell me it was a dog. I don't know what to do with that. Big dog? Little dog? Mutt? Pit bull? Rat terrier? Big-balled bulldog? Just telling me *what the thing is* goes a long way toward helping me place that object, character, or situation into the context of the story you're telling. Was she a leggy blonde? Was he a dumpy child? Description doesn't need to be long or drawn out to matter. It just needs to be specific.

17. Metaphor Is the Tendon Connecting Muscle to Bone

See what I did there? I used *metaphor* to describe metaphor. That's how a writer does things. That's some hard-ass penmonkey trickery, son. What? What? You gonna step? You gonna front all up in my face-grill? Ahem. Sorry. Where was I? Right. Metaphor takes a *mundane part of the story* and connects it to the *larger experience of the audience*. It says, "This little thing is like this bigger thing, this *other* thing." Metaphor is less about fact and more about feel.

18. Metaphors Are Always Wrong

They're not wrong to use. But like I said, metaphors aren't about fact. They provide inaccurate information, but offer instead keen artistic and figurative data. When I say, "On our sales team, Bob's the last sled dog in the line—he's always got a butthole view of the world," nobody really expects that Bob is a dog, or that during a sales conference he's staring down the poop chute of a snow-covered Malamute. Metaphors have power *because* they're wildly inaccurate, because they take two very unlike things and bring them together in the reader's mind.

19. And Yet Metaphors Must Find Essential Truth

A metaphor has to make some goddamn sense. "Man, working night-shift is a real can of earwax, isn't it?" What? What does that mean? That doesn't mean anything. Maybe you have some keen understanding of night work and ... cans ... of earwax (can you buy earwax in cans?), but the reader doesn't grok your lingo. That's why a metaphor bridges a part of the story with the *reader* experience, not with your experience as an author. Everybody needs to get the metaphor. The Thing That Is Like Another Thing must share an essential truth. That's the connective tissue.

20. Everything Cannot Be Metaphor

Metaphors allow description to transcend a mere accounting, but even so, sometimes I just want to know if the girl has long legs or if the gun is loaded. Not everything needs to be a metaphor.

21. Clichés Are a Brick Wall You Make the Reader Crash Into

Clichés work because we all understand them, but they're also a little sad because, really? Can't you do better? "He ran like the wind?" Yeah, well, I kicked your nuts like a soccer ball. You're a writer. It's your job to avoid clichés. It's your job to *do better* than the bare minimum.

22. Show Me What the Donkey Smells Like

You don't need to rely on visuals. Many writers do. So you shouldn't. You have four other senses and so do your characters, so use them. Actually, there's a sixth sense, too: common sense. Common sense says you shouldn't overdo the "other senses" thing, and furthermore you should only do so when it's appropriate. You might see or smell a donkey, but you don't taste it. Or you might touch it. Mmm. Yeah. Yeah, baby. Touch that donkey. Go on. Do it. What? Ohh, uhh … nothing.

23. The Hardest Description
Is When You Invent Stuff Out of Thin Air

Creating a new monster out of nothing? Inventing some wretched clockwork gewgaw whose flywheel mechanism could destroy the world? Unfolding a whole new fantasy realm or planetary scape? This is when it becomes tempting to hunker down and *describe the unholy shit* out of stuff. Resist this temptation. I know. You're thinking, "But how will the audience know what I'm talking about? This creature, the Dreaded Horvasham Gorblim, has never before existed. The audience won't know that his horns are studded with thorns, or that his nipples look like crispy pepperoni. I have to build this monster for them. On the page. Inside their heads." No, seriously, resist the urge. By not going much further than "thorny horns and crispy pepperoni nipples," you've already created an image in your head of the beast. So too have you pictured the wretched clockwork flywheel gewgaw. Like I said, the audience is willing to work. They will carry your water. Even through made-up lands.

24. Novelists, Read Screenplays (and Screenwriters, Read Novels)

Novelists could learn a thing or two from the brevity of description found in screenplays. Therein you will find short, collapsed descriptive nuggets that still manage to paint the picture and get the story moving. Furthermore, screenwriters could learn a thing or two from novelists. Remember, screenwriters: Your script needs to be *readable* before it needs to be *filmable*. It lives in the reader's head before it ever makes it to screen. Description must feel alive.

25. As With All Things: Everything in Moderation

That's an old Greek idea, right? "Everything in moderation?" Of course, those guys were all huffing Zeus juice and banging satyrs. Point is, description is a powerful tool in your narrative kit because, as it turns out, readers like you to help set the stage inside the theater of their minds. You can underdo it. You can overdo it. You need to walk the line, look at the shape of your page. Sentences or small paragraphs punctuated by stretches of dialogue and/or action is certainly a good shape for which to strive. Find the middle path and you shall appease the reader.

25 THINGS YOU SHOULD KNOW ABOUT WRITING A GODDAMN SENTENCE

1. A Sentence Has One Job Above All Others

That job is to convey information. Its job is not to be clever. Its job is not to sound nice. Its primary task is to present information. That's not to say it can't, or shouldn't, sound nice. Or be clever. But those are *value adds*. A sentence has another, more important job, and that is as an *information delivery system*.

2. It Is a Fundamental Building Block

Sentences comprise all that you write. They chain together to form ideas. Learning how to write a sentence properly, with clarity, and in a way that engages the reader or listener is the cornerstone of good writing. Sentences are made up of words and clauses (a clause being a *subject* and a *verb*).

3. This Noun Is Going to Verb You in the Naughtyhole

The simplest sentence is a nearly naked clause of subject and verb: Becky ran; The dog barks; The robot will dance. Never be afraid to use a simple construction. It's short. Sharp. Punchy. Equal parts "flick to the ear" and "grenade going off under your chair." Throw a direct object in there (and maybe an indirect object, to boot), and now we're cooking with a deadly biotoxin. I mean, "gas." Just gas. Definitely not making bathtub biotoxin over here. You didn't see anything.

4. Some Clauses Still Live at Home With Their Parents ...

... while others go and strike out on their own. This means that some clauses are independent, and others are dependent. The former stand on their own. I'm not going to get into a whole compositional lesson here, but sentence construction relies on you knowing that dependent clauses cannot form their own sentences because they are immature assholes. They are subordinate, and like the remora fish must cling to the shark-like independent clause to survive. Independent clauses can come together to form sentences, if you care to do that. "Hiram likes cheese, but he thinks milk is for dickheads." Two independent clauses, connected by that little word *but*. (*and* works, too.) If I were to instead write, "Hiram likes cheese more than he likes milk," then you can see that *more than he likes milk* is the dependent clause because it cannot stand by its lonesome.

5. On the Subject of Sentence Fragments

Sentence fragments are generally a no-no. And yet, I use them. They work when they help to establish flow in the ear of the reader, and they fail when they break that flow. Nine times out of ten, they break the flow. But roughly 10 percent of the time, they allow your prose to pop. Use, but use sparingly.

6. Simplicity Is Not the Enemy of a Strong Sentence

In fact, simplicity is the good neighbor of a strong sentence. He mows his neighbor's lawn. Picks up the mail. Doesn't tell the other neighbors about the weird bleating coming from the basement. A simple sentence can be thought of as "dumbed down," but that's not true, not true at all. Elegance and profundity may lurk within simplicity. Consider these two words: *John died.* That's heavy. Two words like lead fists in your gut. *John died.* Oh, shit.

7. Simplicity Begets Mystery

John died. Two words. Not a lot of information. But that's okay. Because the reader wants that information. It creates in his mind an open variable in the story equation you're building. John died, yes, but how, why, when, and where? (Probably of bathtub biotoxin. In my basement. Ten minutes ago. Because he was an asshole who couldn't keep his mouth shut about the goddamn biotoxin.)

8. Go Read a Kid's Book

Children's books are written for, duh, children. The sentence construction in those books is about as simple as it can get, and admittedly, some of the stories are simple, too. But some of those stories can be quite complex, with a bubbling sub-layer of biotoxin ... er, I mean, profundity beneath the surface of those basic, straightforward sentences. If you want to get back to the heart of learning how to write a goddamn sentence, you could do worse than nabbing a couple of kiddie books and studying their elegance.

9. Clarity Defeats Confusion

Whenever I do development or editing work, the most troubling things I see are sentences I must mark with the dreaded three-word abbreviation of AWK. Which, admittedly, sounds like the cry of a petulant seabird, but no, it stands for *AWKward*. As in, this sentence sticks out like a hammerstruck boner. Something about it is positively Lovecraftian: It unsettles the mind; it curdles the marrow. Its angles do not add up. What I'm really saying with that tag is, "This sentence doesn't make nearly enough sense." And frequently that confusion stems from a poorly-constructed and often overcomplicated sentence. You must strive for clarity. As mentioned, a sentence must convey information, and information is not properly conveyed if I don't know what the hell you're talking about.

10. How a Sentence Gets Lost

Long sentences reduce comprehension in readers. The longer and more convoluted the sentence, the greater chance you will lose the reader's attention and understanding.

11. The Forrest Gump of Sentences

A run-on sentence is technically a sentence that takes a bunch of independent clauses and smooshes them together like melting gummi bears without the pleasure of punctuation or conjunction. In practice, just know that a run-on sentence is one that goes on and on and on. Feels rambly. Loses cohesion. Run-on sentences are loose butthole. Concise sentences are tight butthole.

12. I Want to Buy the Semicolon a Private Sex Island

I love those winking little cheeky bastards like you wouldn't believe. You can't use them too often, but when you do, you use them to link two independent clauses without a word like *but* or *and*. Mmm. Semicolons. Come to me, semicolon. Wink at me. Touch my man parts. Don't tell my wife. Wink. ;)

13. Destroy, Rebuild
The way to fix a screwed-up sentence is the same way we'll end up fixing civilization: You have to destroy it and rebuild it. Break it down into its constituent parts, and just rewrite that slippery sonofabitch. The real secret here? Most times, you'll end up breaking the sentence in twain as if you were Solomon. One boggy, busted-ass sentence is almost always made better when it becomes two leaner, meaner sentences. Bisect those bitches.

14. Sentences Rarely Exist in Isolation
Novels, scripts, blog posts, ransom notes—whatever the body of writing, you will find more than one sentence living together. So, writing a good sentence isn't just about nailing one sentence but about nailing the sentence before it and after it. They live in colonies, these goddamn things, like termites, or ants, or polyamorous space marines. It's like what they say about roaches: If you find one, you know there's bound to be a whole lot more behind the walls.

15. The Dancing Diagram
Where the Sentence Shakes Its Word Booty
Each individual sentence has a rhythm, and you can diagram it—Shakespeare was quite concerned with this, what with all that *iambic pentameter*. You can see it too in children's verse. Or even in unmetered poetry—read free verse aloud and you'll find the rhythm, the way each word and idea flows into the next. And that's the key, right there—"into the next." Each sentence establishes a rhythm with the one before it and the one after it. They flow into each other like water—calm water here, rapids here, waterfall there, and back again to still waters. We think of sentences as being written down and thus related to the eyes, not the

ears—but good writing sounds good when spoken. Great writing is as much about the ear as it is about the eye.

16. The Doctor Sentence Q. Sentenceworth Variety Hour

Each sentence must be different from the last. Variety creates a chain of interest. If I gaze upon wallpaper with an endless pattern, my eyes glaze over and I wet myself. But look upon a wall with variety—a photo, a painting, a swatch of torn wallpaper—and your eye will continue moving from one thing to the next. Sentences work like this. Vary your usage. Short sentence moves into a long sentence. Sentence openings never repeated twice in a row. Simplicity yields to complexity. Each sentence, different in sound and content from the last.

17. Each Sentence Is a Gateway Drug

Like I said earlier, a good sentence begets mystery. It makes you want to get to the next sentence. No one sentence should try to say it all. Think of each sentence like a tiny iteration of a cliffhanger. Each is an opportunity to convince the reader to keep on reading.

18. Is "Is?" or Isn't "Is?"

Some folks say that cutting any and all instances of the verb *to be* from your work will make that work stronger. They're probably not wrong because *is* ends up fairly limp dicked as far as verbs go. As with all things, practice moderation. Don't go psycho on every iteration of the verb. If you see a sentence that uses some form of *to be* and you think, *Dang, this sentence could be stronger*, then rip out that verb and dose it up with the corticosteroid of a tougher, more assertive verb.

19. Passive Constructions Were Killed by Me, in the Study, With a Lead Pipe

See what I did there? Yeah. You see it. Avoid passive constructions. They *wussify* your sentences. What makes a sentence passive? When the actor in a sentence is not the subject of that sentence. "Bob strangles Betty." Bob is the actor and the subject. But if you rewrote that to be, "Betty was strangled by Bob," you've made the subject of the sentence separate from the actor. You can spot passive language generally with the verb *to be* bound up with the past participle (*was strangled by*).

20. I Murders the Nasty Adverbses!
An adjective modifies a noun; an adverb modifies a verb. Adjectives seem okay, yet adverbs get a bad rap. What's the deal? Adverbs alone are not poison. They do not by themselves sink a sentence. In fact, what people often identify as adverbs is a small subset of the whole pie. For instance, that word I just used—*often*—is an adverb. It modifies *identify* as an element of frequency. If I say, "John lives here," then know that *here* is an adverb (modifying *lives*—he lives where? Here.) How do you know if an adverb belongs? Read the sentence aloud. "Gary giggled delightedly" has two problems—first, *giggling* already indicates delight, and second, *delightedly* sounds clunky when you speak that sentence aloud. You notice it when you speak it. Again, we read with our ears as well as our eyes.

21. Beware the Sentence With a Big Ass
What I mean is, you don't want a sentence with a lot of junk in the trunk. Junk language, like junk food, is both easy and delicious. Writing a good sentence is often about what to omit as much as it is about what goes into the mix. Beware: clichés, redundancies, pleonasms, needlessly complicated clauses, bullshit intensifiers (*really, actually, truly, severely, totally*), euphemisms, and passive constructions.

22. Sometimes We Like a Little Junk Food
Adding in rare junk language *can*, if done right, add a conversational feel to your writing. You don't want to eat a chocolate bar every meal, but an occasional dose of junk food (or junk language) won't kill you.

23. My Greatest Foe: The Expletive Construction

You might think I'd love the expletive construction, what with me being such a fan of, well, *expletives*. But this isn't that. No shit-ass sonofagoddamnbastard here, I'm afraid. Nay, the expletive construction is when you begin a sentence with "there is." (Found quite frequently in movie trailers, or in the opening lines of novels.) This construction is often both lazy and passive. Don't use it. Your sentence is better than that. Here's why: you can always rewrite a "there is" sentence in a better, more confident manner. "There is a fly in my soup" sounds much better when written as, "A fly flew into my soup," or, "I see a fly in my soup," or, "Why the hell is there a fly in my soup? Get me your manager. I want to watch him eat the fly in front of all the other restaurant patrons, because if he doesn't, I'm going to deliver an epic testicular kicking to all parties present." Or something like that.

24. You Have 15,000 Chances to Screw It Up

But, you also have as many chances to make it sing. What I'm saying is, the average novel has 15,000 sentences. Each one can't be poetry. Find your own tricks to write a kick-ass sentence from the get-go—a sentence that sings, a sentence that bites. A sentence that conveys information clearly and without confusion and with a cadence beating in its heart.

25. You Don't Need to Be a Compositional Grammar Nerd to Write a Cracking Good Sentence

A sentence is home to endless possible complexities. The entire power of language composition lives inside a sentence. You should know how to write. Know where punctuation goes, know what works and what doesn't. But you'll eventually hit a limit of when it becomes useful and when it just becomes obsessive. Do you need to know about the nominative case? Do you need to know what a "predeterminer" is? What about a subordinating conjunction? Or a bearitive grotanical modifier? I might've made that last one up. The point is, knowing those things isn't bad. It's just not always that helpful. You're not trying to get your doctorate, here. You're free to get a little crazy. But not "hobo genius mathematically solving the world's troubles with sidewalk chalk and cat poop" crazy.

25 THINGS YOU SHOULD KNOW ABOUT PLOT

1. What the Hell Is "Plot," Anyway?
A plot is the sequence of narrative events as witnessed by the audience.

2. The Wrong Question
Some folks will ask, incorrectly, "What's the plot?" Were you to answer them strictly, you would begin to recite for them a litany of events, each separated by a deep breath and the words, *And then ... .* They probably don't want that. What they mean to ask is, "What's the story?" or, "What's this about?" Otherwise you're just telling them what happened, start to finish. In other words: Snore.

3. A Good Plot Is Like a Skeleton: Critical, Yet Unseen

A plot functions like a skeleton in that it's both structural and supportive. Furthermore, it isn't entirely linear. A plot has many moving parts (sub-plots and pivot points) that act as limbs and joints. The best plots are plots we don't see, or rather, that the audience never has to think about. As soon as we think about it, it's like a needle manifests out of thin air and pops the balloon or lances that blister. Remember, we don't walk around with our skeletons on the outside of our bodies, which is good because, *ew*. What are we, ants? So don't show off your plot. Let the plot remain hidden.

4. Shit's Gotta Make Sense, Son

The biggest plot crime of them all is a plot that doesn't make a lick of goddamn sense. That's a one-way ticket to plot jail. Do not pass GO. Do not collect $200. Do not drop the soap. The elegance of a great plot is that, when the events are all strung together, there exists a natural order as if this was the only way they could fit together. It's like dominoes tumbling. Your plot is not a chimera—random parts mashed together because you didn't think it through. Test the plot. Pull the pieces apart and ask, "Is there a better way?" Nonsense plots betray the potency of story.

5. The Quintessential Plot

The simplest thing to remember about plot is this: Things get worse until they get better. A straight-up escalation of conflict. It goes from "Uh oh, that's bad," to, "Uh oh, it's getting worse," to "Oh, holy shit, it can't get any worse," to, "I think I maybe fixed it, or at least stopped it from being so totally and completely borked." When in doubt, just know that your next step as a storyteller is to bring the pain, amp the misery, and escalate the conflict. That's what Chandler meant by the advice, "Have a man with a gun walk through the door." You can take that literally, sure, but what it means is that the bad news just got worse.

6. In Life We Avoid Conflict, but in Fiction We Seek It

Fiction is driven by characters in conflict, or, put differently, the flame of *fiction* grows brighter through *friction*. A match tip lights only when struck; so too is the mechanism by which a gun fires a bullet. Impact. Tension. Fear. Danger. Need to know what impels your plot forward? Look to the theme of Man Versus [fill-in-the-blank]. Man versus his fellow man. Woman versus nature. Man versus himself. Woman versus an angry badger high on bath salts. Find the essential conflict and look for events that are emblematic of that.

7. Want Versus Fear

Of course, the essence of the essential conflict—the one below all that Wo/Man versus stuff—is a character's *wants* versus a character's *fears*. Plot grows from this fecund garden. The character wants life, revenge, children, a pony—and that which he fears must stand in his way. John McClane must battle terrorists to return to his wife. Indiana Jones must put up with snakes and irritating sidekicks to uncover the artifact. I must put up with the onerous task of walking downstairs to make myself a gin and tonic. Everything that stands in a character's way—the speedbumps, roadblocks, knife-wielding monkeys, ninja clones, tornadoes, and sentient Krispy Kreme donuts sent from the future to destroy man via morbid obesity—are events in the greater narrative sequence: They are pieces of the plot.

8. Grow the Plot, but Don't Build It

A plot grows within the story you're telling. A story is all the important parts swirling together: world, character, theme, mood, and of course, plot. An artificial plot is something you have to wrestle into place, a structure you have to bend and mutilate and duct tape to get it to work. It is external. It is artifice. You want a plot that is internal and organic.

9. The Tension and Recoil of Choice and Consequence

An organic plot grows like this: Characters make decisions—sometimes bad decisions, other times decisions whose risks outweigh the rewards, and other times still decisions that are just plain uncertain in their outcome—and then characters must deal with the consequences of those decisions. A character gives up a baby. Or buys a gun. Or enters the dark forest to slay the dread beast, Lady Gaga. Anytime a character makes a choice, the narrative branches. Events unfold because she chose a path. That's it. That's plot. Choice and consequence tighten together, ratcheting tension, creating suspense. Choice begets event.

10. Plot Is Promise

Plot offers the promise of Chekov and his gun, of Hitchcock and his bomb under the table. An event *here* leads to a choice *there* which spawns another event over there. Foreshadowing isn't just a literary technique used sparingly; it lurks in the shadow of every plot turn. Plot promises payoff. A good plot often betrays this promise and does something different than the audience expects. That's not a bad thing. You don't owe the audience anything but your best story. But a plot can also make hay by doing exactly what you expect: If you show them the gun, they will want to see it fire.

11. Let Characters Do the Heavy Lifting

Characters will tell you your plot. Even better, let them run and they'll goddamn give it to you on a platter. Certainly plot can happen from an external locus of control, but you're not charting the extinction of the dinosaurs or the life cycle of the slow loris. Plot is Soylent Green: *It's made of people.* Characters say things and do things, and that creates plot. It really can be that simple. Authentic plot comes from internal emotions, not external mechanics.

12. Chart the Shortest Point Between Beginning and End

One way to avoid the nonsensical, untenable plot is to cut through all the knots. If we are to assume that a plot is motivated by the characters' choices and actions—and we must assume that, because who else acts as prime mover? —then we can also assume that characters will take the most direct path through the story that they can. That's not to say it'll be the smartest path, but it will be forthright as the character sees it. No character creates for himself a convoluted path. Complex, perhaps. But convoluted? Never. Characters want what they want and that means they will cut as clear a path to that goal as they can. A convoluted, needlessly complex plot is the result of an overly clever storyteller—or an overly confused one.

13. On the Subject of "Plot Holes"

Plot holes—where logic and good sense and comprehensible sequence fall into a sinking story pit—happen for a handful of reasons. One, you weren't paying attention. Two, your plot is too convoluted and its untenable nature cannot sustain itself. Three, you don't know what the hell is happening, and maybe also, you're drunk. Four, the plot is artificial, not organic, and isn't coming out naturally from what the characters need and want to do. Five, you offended the Plot Gods by not sacrificing a goat. You can't just fix a plot hole by spackling it over. It's like a busted pipe in a wall. You need to do some demo. Get in there. Rip out more than what's broken. Fill in more than what's missing.

13. If the Characters Have to Plan, So Do You

Many writers don't like to outline. Here's how you know if you should, though: If your characters are required to plan and plot something—a heist, an attack on a moon bunker, a corporate takeover—then you're a fool if you think these imaginary people have to plan but you don't. This is doubly true of genre material. A murder mystery, for example, lives and dies by a compelling, sensible plot. So plan the plot, for Chrissakes. This isn't improvisational dance. Take some goddamn notes.

14. Set Up Your Tentpoles

A big tent is propped up by tentpoles. So too is your plot. An easy way to plan without getting crazy is to find those events in your plot that are critical, that must happen for the whole story to come together. "Mary Meets Gordon. Belial Betrays Satan. Sir Bieber slays the Dread Gaga." Chart these half-dozen events. Know that you must get to them somehow.

15. The Herky Jerky Plot Shuffle Pivot Point Boogie

You've seen Freytag's Triangle. (If not, go employ Google.) It's fine. But it doesn't tell the whole story. This is the *future*. We have CGI. We have 3-D. Gaze upon the plot from the top down. It isn't a linear stomp up a steep mountain. It's a zig-zagging quad ride through dunes and jungles, over rivers and across gulleys. You're a hawk over the quad rider's shoulder—watch it jerk left, pull right, jump a log, squash a frog. More obstacles. Greater danger. Faster and faster. Every turn is a pivot point. A point when the narrative shifts, when the audience goes right and the story feints left.

16. Plot Is the Beat That Sets the Story's Rhythm

Plot comprises beats. Each action, a new beat, a new bullet point in the sequence of events. These establish rhythm. Stories are paced according to the emotions and moods they are presently attempting to evoke. Plot is the drummer. Plot keeps the sizzling beat. Like Enrique "Kiki" Garcia of Miami Sound Machine.

17. Every Night Needs a Slow Dance

I know I said that plot, at its core, is how everything gets worse and worse and worse until it gets better. Overall, that's true. But you need to pull back from that. Release the tension. Soften the recoil. Not constantly but periodically. Learn to embrace the false victories, the fun and games, the momentary lapses of danger. If only to mess with the heads of the audience. Which, after all, is your totally awesome job.

18. The Name of My New Band Is "Beat Sheet Manifesto"

You can move well beyond the tentpoles. You can free-fall from the 30,000-foot view, smash into the earth, and get a macrolevel microview of all the ants and the pillbugs and the sprouts from seeds. What I mean is, you can track every single beat—every tiny action—that pops up in your plot. You don't need to do this before you write, but you can and should do it after. You'll see where stuff doesn't make sense. You'll see where plot holes occur.

19. Beats Become Scenes Become Sequences Become Acts

Plot is narrative, and narrative has units of measurement: Momentary beats become scenes of a single place, scenes glom together to form whole sequences of action and event, and sequences elbow one another in the giant elevator known as an "act," where the story manifests a single direction before zig-zagging to another (at which point, another act shifts). Think first in acts. Then sequences. Then scenes. And finally, beats. Again, take that 30,000-foot view, but then jump out of the plane and watch the ground rush up to meet you.

20. Your Sexy Mistress, the Subplot

In real life, don't cheat on your spouse or lover. Not cool, man. *Not cool.* As a writer, you don't cheat on your manuscript, either: While working on one script or novel, don't go porking another one behind the shed. But inside the narrative? The laws change. You *need* to cheat on your primary plot. Have dalliances with subplots—this is a side story, or the "B-story." Lighter impact. Smaller significance. Highlights supporting characters. But the subplot always has the DNA of the larger plot and supports or runs parallel to the themes present. Better still is when the subplot affects, influences, or dovetails with the larger plot.

21. Beneath Subplot, a Nougaty Layer of Microplot

Every little component of your story threatens—in a good way, like how storms threaten to give way to sun, or how your date threatens to dress up as your favorite Farscape puppet and sex you down to galaxy-town—to spin off into its own plot. Your tale is unwittingly composed of tiny microplots—filaments woven together. A character needs to buy a gun but can't pass the legal check. His dog runs away. He hasn't paid his power bill. Small inciting incidents. Itty-bitty conflicts. They don't overwhelm the story, but they exist just the same, enriching the whole. A big plot is in some ways just a lot of little plots lashed together and moving in a singular direction. Like a herd of stampeding marmots.

22. Exposition Is Sand in the Story's Panties

Look at plot construction advice and you'll see a portion set aside for "exposition." Consider exposition a dirty word. It is a synonym for "info dump," and an info dump is when you relentlessly shovel your narrative waste into the reader's open maw. Take the section reserved for exposition and fold it gently into the rest of the work as if you were baking a light and fluffy cake. Let information come out through action. Even better, withhold exposition as long as you can. Tantric storytelling, ladies and germs. Deny the audience's climax expectation until you can do so no longer.

23. On the Subject of the "Plot Twist"

A plot twist runs the danger of being the kid who's too cool for school—ultimately shallow, without substance, and a total tool. They can feel gimmicky. Let your story be magic, not a magic trick. Plot twists only work when they are organic, not artificial. Meaning, when it happens, the audience isn't left flummoxed. The audience is instead left feeling like the twist was the only way the story could've gone.

24. The Ending Is the Answer to a Very Long Equation

Plot is math, but instead of numbers and variables it's characters, events, themes, and yes, variables. The ending is one such variable. An ending should feel like it's the only answer one can get when he adds up all parts of the plot. This actually isn't true: You can try on any number of endings, and you likely have a whole host that can work. But there's *one* ending that works for *you*, and when it works for you, it works for them. And by "them" I don't mean the men in the flower delivery van who are watching your every move. I mean "them" as in the audience. P.S., don't forget to wear your tinfoil hat because the *flowers are listening*.

25. Plot Is Only a Means to an End

Speaking of ends, plot is just a tool. A means to an end. Think of it as a *character-* and *conflict-delivery system*. Plot is conveyance. It still needs to work, still needs to hang together, and make sense, but plot is rarely the reason someone cares about a story. They care about characters. Note, though, that the opposite is true: Plot may not make them love a story, but it can damn sure make them hate it.

25 THINGS YOU SHOULD KNOW ABOUT NARRATIVE STRUCTURE

1. Every Story Has Structure

Whether you put it there or not, no story goes from start to finish without structure. Structure is either something you design as a storyteller or something that just happens. Sometimes the structure is the right one. Sometimes it's the wrong one. If you have a good gut for a story, then you will intuit a strong structure as you go. If your instincts aren't that sharp, it helps to design the story's structure before moving forward.

2. Think of It as Story Architecture

Structure serves story; story does not serve structure. A cathedral is built toward certain considerations: the beauty of God, the presence of God's story, the need for acoustics, the accommodation of seating, the sacrificial altar, the Daft Punk DJ booth, and so on. You design a structure to highlight the type of story you're telling. Using a nonlinear structure in a mystery story means you maximize the uncertainty and use the rejiggered narrative to create suspense. Structure has purpose. Structure is where art and craft collide.

3. The Two Essential Pieces

Most stories have at their core two critical components: The Screw Up and Trying To Fix The Screw Up. Something goes wrong, or something changes—a divorce, the Apocalypse, a lost child, someone puts ALF back on the air—and then one or several characters strive to right that wrong. (In effect, reversing or correcting—or sometimes exploring—the narrative *change of state*.) Maybe they succeed. Maybe they fail. Maybe they achieve a Pyrrhic victory where they succeed but not without significant cost. What this really reveals are the most critical components to structural storytelling: A *conflict* is as essential as the *character agency* to correct that conflict. Without those, your structure is naught but a straight line. A straight line is the most boring construction a story can take. Aim for any shape but straight.

4. Said Differently, From Order to Chaos

Storytelling is the push and pull of order and chaos, the horny tumble and tangle of limbs as each struggles to overcome the other. Signal moves up and down, transitioning from a clear frequency to an inky squiggle of chaotic uncertainty which in turn reveals the structure. And that structure highlights the *up and down* and *push and pull*. The flat lines of order give way to the ascent (or more properly, descent) into chaos.

5. Narrative Measurement

I have explained this before, but screw it, you're duct-taped to that chair nice and tight and I know you can't squirm away HA HA HA: Narrative, like all things, can be measured. You don't have to measure it, same as you don't have to measure that fish you caught or the fishing rod that caught it (insert your own keenly-veiled sexual metaphor here!). If you do measure, know that beats make scenes, scenes make sequences, sequences make acts, and between each act is a turn of sorts, a shifting of the story's hips, cocking this way or that. Ignore these story measurements if you like, but if you're building a house, you might want to know what a brick looks like.

6. Sliced in Thrice Nicely With My Knife
You could argue that all stories fall into three acts—and, in filmmaking, if they don't fall that way they're damn well pushed. Act One is the *Set Up* (first 25 percent), Act Two is the *Confrontation* (next 50 percent), Act Three is the *Resolution* (final 25 percent). It's an imperfect description and damn sure not the only description, and in the grand scheme of things you could, if you chose, distill it down to beginning, middle, and end.

7. Microcosmos
Whatever structure you give to a story is also a structure you can give to an individual act. In this way, each act is like a story within a story, with its own ups and downs and conflicts and resolutions. As an act closes, the tale told there either evolves or transforms entirely to manifest new aspects of the tale. For an example, look to the stages of our lives: child to teen to adult to doddering, Depends-wearing gadabout (or at least that's how I hope my own final arc plays out). While we remain the same person through such life changes, our story grows and shifts and becomes something else. Thus is the way a story's acts flow into one another.

8. Complexity Breeds Complexity
The more complicated your story, the more acts that story is likely to feature—like how when you get gremlins wet, they just make more goddamn gremlins. A bigger, stranger, crazier story is likely to demand a

bigger, crazier, stranger structure. The reason a film tends to only have three acts is because a film is around a hundred minutes long, and because audiences crave the comfort of simplicity for a number of reasons good and bad. Shakespeare, for instance, rocked a five-act structure.

9. Omne Trium Perfectum

That's Latin for, "I'm sorry, there are two girls in my bathroom." *checks notes* No, wait, that can't be right. Oh! Oh. Here it is. Loosely translated, "Every set of three is complete." Even if you ignore all other structural components, this is a good one to keep an eye on—the Rule of Threes suggests that all aspects of your story should have at least three beats. Anything that has any value or importance should be touched on three times and, further, evolve a little bit each time. Every character arc, ever act, every scene, every setting, every motif or theme, needs you the storyteller to call it back *at least* three times.

10. The Power of the Pivot

The story must from time to time *pivot*—as the saying goes, the tiger must change his panties. *checks notes* Damn it, who wrote these? *Stripes.* Stripes. The tiger must change his stripes. This is true of characters, too. Or the world and its rules. *Change* is a critical element to storytelling, but you cannot change aspects wildly and completely. It must be gradual and believable, moving only a single phase shift over, the way water becomes ice—it's an expected and believable shift. It's why I prefer to think of this and call it a *pivot*. That word intimates a turn of the body, not a dizzying backflip. Pivot points will mark those narrative moments when your structure turns and things change. When one act becomes another, for instance, that is when the story pivots for the audience. This could mean an evolution of conflict, a revelation of new information, a major character life change. Any major shift in the story will do.

11. Escalations and Reversals

Again, if you don't care much about formal structure, just tune your intestinal frequency to these two ideas: First, the story must escalate, or in all-caps speak, SHIT GOTTA GET DOUBLE-BIG SCREWED UP YO; second, the story must feature occasional reversals where One State (order, victory, hope) becomes the Opposite State (chaos, loss, despair), or in all-caps speak, YO BRO THE STORY SWITCHED IT AND FLIPPED IT AND BOGGLED MY SHIT, SON. Dang, if I could write a novel in all caps, I would.

12. Why the Ejaculatory Arc Works

Freytag's Pyramid (or triangle) shows the rise and fall of narrative. We'll talk a wee bit more about Freytag and his arcing glob of narrative progeny (it was Douglas Rushkoff who I first heard use the term "male ejaculatory arc" to describe the standard structural shape of modern narrative) in just a moment, but the reason this general shape works is because it reveals escalation—things grow worse or more complicated or more intense as the tale moves forward.

13. The Arc as Microstructure

Having a hard time thinking about plotlines or subplots or act structures? Think instead of how a story comprises a number of smaller and larger arcs—an arc just being a component of your story that begins and ends (or, even better, rises and falls). Characters, themes, events, settings—these can have arcs. Some fill a whole story; some are just little belt loops popping up here and there. Some arcs begin where others end. Many overlap, rubbing elbows or shoulders or other filthier parts. Television is a great place to study arcs (and if I may suggest a show: *Justified* on FX). Comic books, too.

14. For Every Story, a Structure

Every story demands a different structure. No universal structure exists. It's why that mopey old saw about there being only seven plots or some bullshit is, well, bullshit. If you distill them down to their barest (and in many ways most meaningless) essence, sure, that's true. But the art is in the arrangement. The structure you build around the plot to support the story is where the elegance lies.

15. Back to That Freytag Dude

One structure you can look at is Freytag's Pyramid. Or Triangle. Or Pubic Thatch. Whatever you care to call it. Gustav Freytag said, *Mein Gott, all diesen plottenheimer schmeckt der same to meinein mouthenpartsen.* Translated, every story features five key structural beats mirroring five acts: Exposition (introduce characters and world) --> Rising Action (conflict creates tension) --> Climax (confrontation leads to a major change) --> Falling Action (conflict resolves) --> Denouement (dangly bits are all tied up or trimmed away). It is, like all structural explorations, equal parts "useful" and "a garbage scow set aflame." Not every plot fits. Furthermore, modern storytelling (which usually trims five acts to three) pushes that climax further toward the end, which means the falling action and denouement get squished, as if between two Sumo wrestlers.

16. From Five to Seven

Behold, a rough seven-act structure: Intro (duh) --> Problem or Attack (duh) --> Initial Struggle (character first tussles with source of conflict) --> Complications (conflict worsens, deepens, changes) --> Failed Attempts (oops, that didn't work) --> Major Crisis (holy goathumping shitbomb, everything's gone pear shaped) --> Climax and Resolution (duh). Not a bad look at the way many modern stories play out.

17. Ain't Nothin' but an Aristotle Thang

Two words: *anagnorisis* and *peripeteia*. Both from Aristotle's theory of tragedy (and two words that if you can make in Scrabble, you automatically win a balloon ride). Anagnorisis is a discovery made by a character. Peripeteia is a dramatic change (either positive or negative) within the story. Each feeds into the other in the same way I spoke of order and chaos earlier—a character's discovery may lead to a change in fortune, or a change in fortune may lead to a new discovery. These two things tumble around and around like a pair of hedgehogs battling one another in a washing machine until finally they reach *catastrophe*, which in Aristotelian terms is what closes the story—either the character wins or is defeated by the conflict or by himself (and in true tragic form, the character often defeats himself).

18. The Monomyth:
Storytelling Epiphany or Sublime Bullshit—You Decide!

Ever since *Star Wars* hit, a lot has been made of Joseph Campbell's *hero's journey*—AKA "The Monomyth." It is neither The Best Thing Since [Insert favorite Sexual Position Here] or The Worst Thing To Happen To Modern Fiction. It's just a thing—one more structural consideration you can choose to use or toss in the medical waste bin at your local health clinic. While it's got a lot of extra fiddly bits, the Monomyth can be distilled as: Departure (hero leaves normalcy and comfort on an adventure spurred by some call to action) --> Initiation (hero meets trials and tribulations both personal and impersonal) --> Return (hero comes back to the world changed and brings with him boons for his buddies). It's got 17 total steps (or 8, if you want the distilled version). Want to examine its application? The hell with George Lucas. Seek James Joyce.

19. The Morphology of the Folktale

I do not have the space or the time in this list to explore all thirty-one of Vladimir Propp's structural steps, which are meant to explicate the narrative nature of folktales (Russian folk-tales in particular). I mean, dang, I got shit to do. Like eat a sandwich. Or stare at the floor. It's a very specific rendering of narrative structure, but it could be enlightening in some fashion. I'll trust your Google-Fu to get started.

20. Did You See Last Night's Episode?

And no, by "episode" I do not mean, "that time when Chuck went apeshit at Arby's and started slathering his nude goblin body in Horsey Sauce." Different kind of episode. No, here I mean episode-as-narrative-structure. Television and comic books tend to be episodic, with any serialized elements packaged away as story arcs (noted earlier). Episodic storytelling tends to chop up each tale in to neatly-packaged plot pieces, with each piece theoretically resolving by its end and then together forming a larger story. Generally, television works on acts separated out by commercial breaks. Episodic narrative may make your story feel more manageable—*but*, at the same time, placing an episodic structure inside a nonepisodic format (say, a novel or a film) is likely to feel artificial and/or inauthentic.

21. My Porn Director Name Will Be "Therefore Butts"

There must exist a chain of cause and effect, of action and opposite reaction, of *consequence*. Dominoes do not fall separate from one another. They fall against one another. Embroider *that* profound shit on a throw pillow. Each scene does not lead ineluctably toward one another so much as the complications of each scene result in the one following—*therefore*, a thing happens. *But*, the opposite occurs. *Because of*, indicating consequence. But never merely: *and then*.

22. From Aperitif to Digestif

Shut up, I like food metaphors. So, here's one—consider how the structure of a seven-course meal works in terms of storytelling. You start with an aperitif (guests become acquainted over a drink) and progress through a series of dishes meant to both embody the meal and challenge the palate, with certain contextual shifts in taste (sorbet and/or cheese) to punctuate larger events. Dessert rolls along as kind of a climactic moment, and then coffee and the digestif appear to give one final strong dose of taste-punching goodness in order to help the eater digest the meal he just consumed. You could chart it on a graph, and it might look similar to narrative structure. Then again, maybe I'm just hungry.

23. You Can't Structuralize Me, Man

Nonlinear storytelling would seem to have a nontraditional structure, and that's true, to a point. But what you'll ultimately find is that, while the plot events may bounce around like a meth-cranked dormouse, the structure that occurs is still one that you can identify, (which tells us that plot and narrative structure are there to complement one another but are not actually the same thing).

24. Tend to Your Organic Story Garden, You Silly Hippie

Writing without structure is a challenge equivalent to writing with structure—if you do it right, you get something that feels organic and unexpected. If you do it poorly, you'll end up with the storytelling equivalent of the Winchester House: doors that never open, stairways that end in walls, rooms that serve little purpose. If one method's not working? Duh, try the other. Which leads me to ...

25. The Final Word

If the application of structure helps you tell a better tale, use it. If you find it artificial and it only hampers your efforts, *kick it in the mouth and chuck it down an open manhole cover.* This stuff isn't here to oppress you—it's a tool for when you need it and invisible when you don't. Some stories will call for the strong spine of structure. Some stories need to be altogether hazier, stranger, less pin-downable. Just know that if you're having some trouble grasping how the plot moves from one piece to another, it might be time to take a gander at borrowing from the many structural storytelling examples that exist. Either that or you need to eat a baggie of magic mushrooms or something. Your call.

25 THINGS YOU SHOULD KNOW ABOUT PROTAGONISTS

1. Prime Mover

The protagonist is the prime mover of the story. He shapes the tale and is in turn reshaped himself. If you can remove the character from the story and the story still happens in the same way, then what you've written is not a protagonist so much as "some shmoe who wanders through events like an old person lost at the mall." Activity over passivity. The character should *act upon* the world, not merely *react to* the world. Put differently: The character is driving the car; the car is not driving the character.

2. Yo, Yo, Yo, It's MC Protag in the House, Motherfizzuckers

Generally, the "main character" and "protagonist" are the same—that isn't an automatic, however. A main character can be the narrator telling the story of a protagonist (think *A Prayer for Owen Meany*). But, unless you're a particularly talented writer, that's probably going to suck a bucket of bubbly hippo spit.

3. Wuzza Wooza Hero Buzza Booza Quest?

Yes, sure, fine, your protagonist is a "hero" going on a "quest." Strike this language from your vocabulary, at least at the outset. It's not that these terms are wildly inappropriate—given certain modes of genre-writing, they are the hats the protagonist will wear. But for now, let's pretend that a protagonist is more complicated and nuanced and *sophisticated* than the overly simplistic "hero going on a quest" allows. Even characters existing in a fantasy realm or fighting, I dunno, *space bees in space,* should all be written as real people with real goals and real problems. Real people are not purely heroic. Real people do not go on quests. Let the audience call the protag a questing hero. You should endeavor to dig deeper.

4. Replace the *K* With a *V*

The old saying is that the protagonist should be *likable*. That we should want to go out and grab a beer with him and paint our nails and giggle as we rub our genitals together. Put that out of your head. Forget *likable*. Likable is not a meaningful quality. The audience *says* that, but they don't *mean* it—otherwise, they wouldn't be interested in the likes of Tony Soprano. Or Don Draper. Or Lisbeth Salander. (It's harder to pull off an unlikable female protagonist, but that's because we're a screwed-up society who embraces flawed men but not flawed women.) Instead of likable, aim for *livable*. Meaning, we need to find this character compelling enough to *live* with them for the duration of the tale. I don't want to get a beer with Lisbeth Salander any more than I want to get a beer with a Bengal tiger. But I'm happy to watch them do their thing.

5. The Worst Crime You Can Commit ...

... is to create a boring protagonist. I'd rather loathe the protagonist than be bored by him. If your character has all the personality of chewed-up cardboard, I'm out, I'm done, I'm hitting the eject button. And don't try any of those excuses—"But the world is exciting! The plot is zing! Bang! Boom!" No, no, no. You take those excuses and cram them in your pee-pee hole on the end of a rusty ramrod. The protagonist is why we stick around. This is the problem with the Everyman protagonist, by the way—recognize instead that we're not all John Q. Who-Gives-A-Shit and that the Everyman is a false notion and embrace what makes each person interesting as opposed to what makes us all one slack-jawed superorganism.

6. Combat Landing

I need to know who your protagonist is right out of the gate. Don't jerk me around. It's like a combat landing—drop hard and fast out of the atmosphere. From the first five pages of your book or five minutes of your script, I need to know why I care about your protagonist. Dally not, word herder.

7. The Ability to Act Upon the World

I want to read about a character who can do something. I don't want to read about some dude who has no marketable skills—"I'm really good at watching *Wheel of Fortune* drunk" is not a compelling reason for me to stick around. I don't care if he's a ninja, a lawyer, a detective, a doctor, a boat captain, or Captain Doctor Detective Stormshadow, Esquire—I want to know he is *in some way* capable. (Be advised, however: Capable is not the same as *perfect*.)

8. Standard Questions May Apply

The four cardinal questions: Who is she? What does she want? What conflicts and/or fears are standing in her way? And what is at stake (stakes as in *what will be won or lost*) if she fails?

9. The Three Beats of Doctor Protagonist

At the bare minimum, track the protagonist's character arc by plotting three beats—these beats indicate change (positive or negative) in that character. Werner goes from *self-destructive --> loses everything --> turns life around*. Roy-Anne goes from cloistered *farm girl --> dragged along on crazy adventure --> world-wise but cynical*. Bobo the Hobo has an arc of *homeless otter whisperer --> half-robot hobo machine --> destroys world in staticky burst of cybernetic rage*. Okay, maybe not that last one. The point is, track the way the character changes for the better and/or the worse across the swath of the story.

10. Change Is More Interesting Than Stasis

Storytelling is the narrative accounting of how one thing becomes another. It is a fictional accounting of a *change of state*. The protagonist is the arbiter of this change, and without change, we have a narrative structure that's basically just a straight line with a period at the end of it. In your story, either the world changes the protagonist or the protagonist changes the world. But something must change.

11. The Two Faces of Change

A protagonist either changes gradually over time as he encounters new events and other characters *or* he changes dramatically in response to a dramatic situation. The degree of change must match the degree of the events that urge that change. For example, you can't have a protagonist whose girlfriend breaks up with him and next thing you know he's throwing babies into the shark tank at the local aquarium. "NOBODY LOVES ME, NOW I HATE BABIES RAAAAR." You must seek out believability by way of consistency—and, when consistency breaks, empathy. A protagonist who suffers trauma changes drastically because we expect and allow that change. We must accept it. To some degree we even expect it.

12. Are You an Innie or an Outie?

The protagonist tends to have an inner story and an outer story. The internal tracks the protagonist's emotional, mental, and spiritual state, whereas the external story tracks the character's actions and movements and corporeal health. The external story is obvious because, duh, it's external. The internal story is hidden on purpose—exposing it to the light makes it feel twee, cloying, artificial. This is how we are as humans: Our physical lives are plainly seen, but our inner existence is guarded, concealed, hush-hush. The two stories also don't need to go the same way: A character who karate-kicks all the villains to death reaches a positive outcome in his external story, but his internal story may be one of guilt and strife over the violence caused by his karate-wielding death-hands.

13. The Necessity of That One Ass-Kicking Moment

We want to see the protagonist do something awesome. Sure, it can be some rad-ass karate bullshit, but it can just as easily be him telling off his villainous mother, or graduating high school when the odds were stacked against him, or saving a baby penguin from the slashing knife of a serial killer. A small version of that moment can come early in the story, but toward the final act of the story we need to see this again—crank the volume knob to Maximum Awesome.

14. The D&D Alignment Chart Is Not the Worst Thing in the World

This is *overly* simplistic, but bear with me—the D&D alignment chart can help get you started in terms of determining the shape of your protagonist's actions. Does the character lean more lawful or more chaotic? Is she neutral, or does she take sides on either side of the moral spectrum? WILL SHE DO BATTLE WITH THE CATOBLEPAS, OR THE DREAD MIND FLAYERS? Okay, maybe not so much with the *Monster Manual* stuff, but I think you get the idea.

15. Know Which Way the Character Will Jump

Some authors will go deep into a protagonist's history and chart every breakfast she had since she was but a snot-glazed toddler. Do that if you'd like, but in my experience it's best to dig deeper into the choices the character might make. In other words: Know what way the protag'll jump in any given situation. Who she was should work backward from who she is—at least, for you, the writer. Knowing how she'll behave and what choices she'll make will inform the history necessary for the protag to have gotten to this point. By the way, "protag" is short-hand for "protagonist." All the kids are using it. Just yesterday a twelve-year-old was like, "Hey, what up, Protag!" Or maybe I have it wrong. Maybe he was like, "Hey, what up, you old, bearded asshole!" I'm sure *protagonist* is what he meant.

16. Painting With Shadow: The Power of the Antagonist

The antagonist opposes the protagonist not just once but throughout. In this way the antagonist helps define the protagonist in the same way you invoke a shape by coloring in everything but that shape. Note that the antagonist needn't be another character—it traditionally is, yes, but any persistent conflict can be truly antagonistic. A looming house foreclosure, a cancer diagnosis, a tornado made of biting squirrels.

17. Suit up for the Protagonist Tango (AKA: "The Protangoist")

Yes, Virginia, you *can* have multiple protagonists. Multiple "main" characters just assumes that you have several characters pushing and pulling on the story. Any ensemble piece or story with strong multiple-POV characters could be said to have several protagonists. They should get equal time and have equal effect on the world lest they be demoted to the cast of supporting characters, AKA "People who might get eaten by alligators or dispatched by Klingons somewhere in the story."

18. Time to Practice Your Most Insidious Laugh

I like Moo-hoo-*ha-HA-HA-HAHAHAHA*—start slow and quiet, and then go loud and fast. Which is also how I masturbate, just in case you were wondering. And you were. Anyway. My point here is, you have to hurt your protagonist. You have to be willing to cut them to the marrow physically, emotionally, spiritually—you know the protag well enough to know what and where his most vulnerable pressure points are. This works because you've drawn a connection between the audience and the protagonist. The audience cares—or, at least, wants to remain compelled by the character's journey. By messing with the protagonist, you're messing with the audience. Which makes you sort of a dick, so way to go. No wonder nobody liked you in high school. Jeez.

19. Fake Out, Sucker

You can have a "false protagonist." You set up one character as a protagonist, the audience buys into it, and then you switch it. Often by killing that false protagonist and revealing the real one. (I'm looking at you, George R. R. Martin.) It's kind of a dick move, but we've already established that you're a dick. The key is to be an *effective* dick. Or something.

20. Theme and Character: Car Crash or Pubic Braid? You Decide!

The protagonist interacts with theme in one of two ways: *intersection* or *interweaving*. At an intersection, the protagonist crashes head on into the theme in a perpendicular twenty-car pile up. The protagonist is at odds with the theme and rails against it, eventually overcoming it, overturning it, or succumbing to it and proving it. *Or*, the protagonist and theme are interwoven together, wherein each reflects the other.

21. The Definition of "Mary Sue"

You will find multiple definitions of a "Mary Sue." What you need to know is that your protagonist should not be a pap, waffling, twee stand-in for your most perfect ideals. An unconflicted, untroubled, unrealistic icon of flawless goody-two-shoedness is a shitballs protagonist no matter what you call her. So don't do that. (Note: The male version of this is known as "Gary Stu.")

22. We Love Characters for Their Imperfections

We want characters who have flaws. Flaws are interesting. We like to watch flaws. Maybe we see them as representative of our own damaged goods? Maybe we just like to watch awful stuff, like when a conversion van full of bees drives into a Kodiak bear stuffed with explosives and sticky honey. Further, flaws offer a practical component: They make for a source of excellent conflict and, in fact, represent a nearly-perfect, internal self-generating conflict because the flaw forces the protagonist to act as his own antagonist. HOLY POOPFIRE DID I BLOW YOUR MIND? Ahem. Sorry. Had a little too much coffee. Anyway. Some protagonists are subject to a "fatal flaw," which is a tragic-in-the-truest-sense weakness that forever threatens to undo all the good that the protagonist has done. My fatal flaw is writing POOPFIRE in all caps. And drinking too much coffee. Mmm. Coffee.

23. Discover the Sadness

That sounds like a new Sarah McLachlan song, doesn't it? Anyway, sadness lingers at the nucleus of every story. It may not be dominant or prominent, but it's there—and I think you can find the same thing inside the protagonist. Every protagonist should be wounded in some way; the wound may be a small but potent one or it may be the all-consuming spiritual equivalent of a sucking chest wound, but it should be present. In this wound grows sadness, and by digging for this griefstruck little pearl and unearthing it you will expose a critical part of the protagonist's makeup.

24. Find Yourself Inside the Protagonist

I don't mean that literally, of course (as sexy as it may sound). I mean that, to discover what lies at the heart of your protagonist you should endeavor to find some shared human experience, some *critical emotional core sample* that is a match betwixt the both of you. It can be anything, of course—"We're both orphans! We both have anger issues! We both enjoy wrestling chimpanzees while goofy on decongestants!"—but it helps to channel a bit of yourself into the main character. If only so you create that sense of empathy needed to grok the protagonist's motives, fears, and goals.

25. The Superglue of Shared Story

And therein lies the secret. When we respond to a protagonist, it's because we see a bit of Our Story in Her Story. That's the glue that affixes us to the character, that makes us want to cling to him or her like a cuddly little marmoset. The protagonist can be wildly different from us as long we can see in him some aspect of shared human experience, some piece of driftwood bobbing in the great, big, chaotic ocean that is that protagonist's persona. (This is, I'd argue, why we respond to Luke Skywalker but not to Anakin—it's easier to see ourselves in Luke than his whiny, child-slaying father.) Don't keep the protagonist at arm's length by giving her traits and experiences understood by only a small subset of the audience. That's not to say the protag cannot be a serial killer, alien, or star fighter pilot; it just means that some part of that character's makeup must reach across the abyss between *story* and *audience*. We need that bridge built so that we may cross it.

25 THINGS YOU SHOULD KNOW ABOUT SETTING

1. What Is Setting?

Setting anchors your story in a place and a time. A short story or film may hover over a single setting; a longer-form film or novel may bounce across dozens of settings. You often have a larger setting ("The town of Shartlesburg!") and many microsettings within ("Pappy's Hardware! The Egg-Timer Diner! The Shartlesburg Geriatric Sex Dungeon!").

2. What Does Setting Do for You?

It props everything else up. It's like the desk on which you write—it has function (it holds up all your writing tools, your liquor bottles, your Ukrainian pornography), it has detail (the wood is nicked from where you got into that knife fight with that Bhutan assassin), it has an overall feel (the desk dominates the room, making everything else feel big—or perhaps the opposite is true, where the desk is crammed into the corner like you're some third-rate citizen). Setting props up plot, character, theme, and atmosphere. And it gives the audience that critical sense of place and time so it doesn't feel like she's floating around in a big ol' sensory-deprivation tank of recycled amniotic fluid. Which does not, despite its appearance, smell like bubblegum.

3. Establish That Shit Early, Then Reveal Gradually
You don't want to keep the reader in the dark as to the setting because it's disorienting and disconcerting. Even if the character on the page doesn't know, you the author sure do, and it's up to you to provide those hints ("She hears a church bell ringing and smells the heady stink of hobo musk"). You don't need to spend two paragraphs outlining setting right from the get-go, though—we just need that filmic establishing shot to say, "Ohh, okay, we're in a convenience store next door to an insane asylum. Boom, got it." Then, as you write, *over time* you reveal more details about setting as they become important to the story. Revealing setting should be a sexy striptease act. A little flash of skin that gradually uncovers the midriff, then the thighs, then the curve of the OH MY GOD SHE HAS A TENTACLE IT'S GOT MY MMGPPHABRABglurk

4. Setting as Character
It may help to think of setting as just another character. It looks and acts a certain way. It may change over the course of the story. Other characters interact with it and have feelings about it that may not be entirely rational. Think about how, on those awful (and totally fake!) house-hunting shows on HGTV, someone's always looking for a house "with character." That means they want a house that is uniquely their own, that has, in a sense, a personality. (And probably a poltergeist, let's be honest. Houses with "character" always have poltergeists.) That's a

fact. I saw it on the BBC and British people cannot lie. It's in their regal charter or something.

5. Paint in as Few Strokes as Possible

Play a game—go somewhere and describe it in as few details as possible. Keep whittling it down. See how you do. This is key for setting description (and, in fact, all description). Description must not overwhelm.

6. Exercise: Three Details and No More

Find any place at any time and use three details to describe it. You get to paint your image with three strokes and no more.

7. What Details? The Ones the Audience Needs to See

The details you choose are the ones that *add* to the overall story. Maybe they're tied to the plot. Maybe they enhance the mood. Maybe they signal some aspect of the theme. Maybe they offer a dash of humor at a time when the story really needs it. Each detail has text and subtext—the text is what it is ("a toilet"). The subtext is what it adds to the deeper story ("the toilet's clogged and broken like everything else in this building, spilling water over the bowl rim"—saying this adds to the overall atmosphere and theme offered by the setting).

8. Abnormalities Are Your Friend

Another tip for finding out which details matter most: they're the ones that break the status quo. It's like this: I know what a Starbucks looks like. Or a pine forest. Or a men's restroom. You don't need to tell me that the restroom has a sink, a floor, a lightbulb, and a toilet. You need to tell me there's a mouse crawling around in the sink. That the fluorescent light above is flickering and buzzing like a bug zapper. You need to show me the weird guy sitting in stall three playing with himself while reading an issue of *Field and Stream* magazine. Show me the details that defy my expectations. Those are the details that matter.

9. The Reader Will Do Work for You

No, I don't mean the reader will come to your house and grout your kitchen. Or maybe she will? I should look into that. Anyway. What I'm saying is, the reader will fill in many of the details that you do not. In a variant of what I just said above, it's your job to give the reader the details that she cannot supply for herself.

10. Description Should Be Active and Action Based

Describe the setting as a character moves and operates through it—which means that it features action and takes into account that character's point of view. You don't introduce the Shartlesburg Geriatric Dungeon by giving a paragraph of setting description before the character even steps into the room. As the character sees it, the reader sees it. As the character picks up that riding crop that smells like Vicks Vaporub and horehound lozenges, *the reader* picks up the same. We take in a setting one bite at a time. Not in a giant gulp.

11. Why the POV Matters

The character is our vehicle through any story. We like to think that the vehicle is our narration as the author, but the truth is, it's not. The audience duct tapes its experiences (and hopes and dreams and fears and a whole host of other things) to the character, and that's how we make it to the end of any story. So setting as seen through a character's eyes—or, a setting affected *by* the character, as well—matters more than any inert rendering you might offer.

12. Really? The Five Senses?

I hate that advice. "Writing good setting is about detailing all five senses." Umm, I don't know about you, but my experiences in this world are rarely about how a place tastes and how it feels when I touch it. When my gunman character throws open the convenience store door with his shotgun held high in order to rob the joint, the last thing I'm going to do is have him taste the air like a snake, or have him run his hands along the smooth countertop as he waits for the poor sap to throw all the money in the bag. Go with the senses that matter—in particular, the three senses whose input we do not so easily control: sight, sound, and smell.

13. Keep Your Shit Consistent

Er, no, I don't mean your actual feces. That's between you and your bathroom gods. What I mean is that setting details are the easiest to lose in the muddled mass of words that comprise your story. Before you know it, you forget that it's raining or the road is icy or the walls are covered in blood, and two scenes later you've completely lost the thread—and, by proxy, the reader—because of these inconsistent details. A good way to track details on your editing is to highlight critical details in the manuscript and move forward to make sure they match.

14. Setting as Reflective of Theme

If your theme is "Man will always be outdone by Mother Nature," then your setting must reflect that—a harsh and untamed forest whose thicket is impenetrable and whose every barb and briar cuts the flesh of those who pass? Yes. A Minnesota shopping mall holding a pageant for little girls dressed like strippers? No. That setting props up a different theme which is, "Pageant moms should be airdropped onto a distant tropical island, and then we should use that island for nuclear tests."

15. Setting as Source of Conflict

Setting is fertile ground for providing conflict. A car chase on icy roads? Rock on. An old house that reminds the character of the house in which she grew up—a house in which she suffered great abuse? Done. A geriatric sex dungeon home to a parliament of octogenarian S&M vampires? Ew. But yeah, I guess.

16. Grok That Vibe

Setting can be used to enhance the atmosphere of the tale at hand. If you want an oppressive atmosphere, for instance, details like *fog* and *heavy air* and *claustrophobic passages* lend themselves toward that sense of being trapped. Setting is in fact probably the best "seedbed" you have in terms of planting the roots for mood in your work.

17. Go to Real Places, Look at Them, and Take Notes

Anywhere you go, note the details of the place. Like with fiction, note most of all those details out of place—from this not only will you get good descriptions for your work, but you might even nab a story idea or two out of it. Bonus: Hey, you get to travel!

18. Cheat: Google Maps

Okay, listen, here's the deal. The Internet is not a replacement for reality—I can't write about a place I've never been with total authenticity, and the Internet doesn't fill that gap perfectly any more than reading a recipe for pad thai substitutes for the eating of pad thai. But shit, sometimes you gotta fake it. When I wrote *Double Dead*, I set some of the story in Texas—and I have never been to Texas. So, I used Google Maps. Not just the map portion but that thing where you zoom to Street View and you can see the roads and street signs and, I dunno, people taking dumps on the side of the road. It's enough to give you a sense of what you're looking at, and you can still cheat some convincing details this way. In other news: I love the Internet so much I want to have sex with it. That's healthy, right?

19. Authenticity Over Reality

Authenticity is perceived reality above actual reality. In terms of fiction writing, the fact of actual reality is meaningless. The feeling of fact is paramount. It just has to feel correct. So, in terms of setting, you want to make sure that the details feel true—even if it's a cheat and the audience wouldn't know the truth of the thing if it crawled up their asses and laid eggs.

20. The Reality of the Unreal

Fiction in general concerns itself with countless places that don't exist. Atlantis or the Endor Moon or that geriatric sex dungeon I keep blathering on about—these are all imaginary places. But they can still feel real, and this cuts to the heart of that old chestnut, *Write What You Know.* You take details from places you've been, and apply them to the invented setting. I know what horse saddles smell like (oiled leather) and I know what old people sometimes smell like (peppermint candies, Vicks Vaporub, rosehips, Depends), so I can tell you what the geriatric sex dungeon smells like.

21. Complex Complications Are Complicated Complexly

The logistics of certain settings are tricky. You're trying to move characters through some weird, three-dimensional, gravity-free space arena, and you don't know how to describe it. Or they're moving across the Prom dance floor. Or working their way through a tangled hedge maze in pursuit of goblin thieves. Whatever. The more complex the setting, the harder it is—or, seems to be—to describe. Here's three tricks. First, ask how you'd describe it verbally. Talk your way through it. Second, figure out what you can cut out. A lot of what you want to describe does not need to be described. Third, use stage blocking technique—blocking being how a theater director determines how the actors are going to move onstage. Literally block it out. Draw it, or use your G.I. Joes (you still have them hanging around, *don't lie*) to set the scene.

22. Destroy Stereotypes of Setting

Stereotypes offer a kind of shorthand in fiction—you write, "truck-stop bathroom" or "bordello bedroom," and you don't have to go much further in order to paint the picture. I get it. I already know what those things look like in my head. But, just the same, doing that too often results in a series of under-described, hand-waved, over-generic settings. Break the stereotype. Just as you would with people, so too should you go beyond the expected in reaching for unique settings. An English professor's office doesn't need to look like some stuffy library—maybe the guy's office is covered in movie posters. Or maybe it's just a nasty-ass mess with papers and Chinese food cartons everywhere. Maybe he's got a dead hobo stuffed in a too-small wastebasket! *Those randy English professors.* Always murdering train hobos!

23. Imagine the People There

A setting is shaped by people. Okay, fine, that's not true in terms of, say, a distant mountain pass or a long tract of desert—though there you might suggest that it's the lack of people that have shaped such places. Regardless, most of the world has been touched by humanity's greasy, grubby hands, and so it behooves you to imagine how—and then, of course, it behooves you to reflect that in your imagining. Or, in Disney-speak, "Imagineering."

24. "Every Tool Is a Weapon If You Hold It Right"

Well said, Ani DiFranco. Anyway. A setting should not be devoid of objects and items. Just look at your writer's desk and all the objects upon it—some of them are obvious, sure (coffee cup, iPhone charger, pens, notebooks, whatever), but as I noted earlier, choose those items that are less than obvious, that highlight the character of the writer you are. The eczema cream, the handgun, the creepy binoculars so you can watch your neighbors do the rumpy-pumpy. Furthermore, if you're like me, you occasionally glance around the room and think about what items would make good weapons. You know, in case of zombies.

25. Setting Is Not the Red-Headed Stepchild of Your Story

Setting is essential. It props up all the parts of your story. It is the stage where the characters act. It is a place reflective of character motivations, fears, and goals. Setting reveals theme, complicates plot, and creates and enhances atmosphere. Setting is not a sidelined byproduct. Don't treat it like an afterthought—just as you want the floor beneath your feet and the walls and rooftops around you to be strong, you want the floors and walls and ceilings of your *fiction* to be strong, too. Setting is more than just the box your story comes in—no, it's the house in which your story lives.

25 THINGS YOU SHOULD KNOW ABOUT SUSPENSE AND TENSION IN STORYTELLING

1. True of Every Story

We assume suspense and tension are reserved for those stories that showcase such emotions. "This is a suspense-thriller about the mad ursinologist who runs around town leaving behind enraged bears, and the beautiful scientist lady who seeks to undo his sinister plans." Bzzt. Wrongo. Every story must offer suspense and tension. Will Harry get together with Sally? Will the Millennium Falcon escape the gauntlet of TIE fighters? Will Ross and Rachel finally consummate their love and give birth to the Satanic hell-child that the prophets foretold? Suspense and tension drive our narrative need to consume stories.

2. Predicated on Giving a Shit

A small disclaimer: Suspense and tension only work if the story offers something for the audience to care about. If the audience neither likes nor cares to discover the truth about *La Bufadora*, the Assassin Baby of Madrid, then any suspense or tension you build around this infantile killer will flop against the forest floor like a deer with its insides vacuumed out of its corn chute. VOOMP. Just a gutted pelt. Never ignore the Give-A-Shit factor. And stop messing around with deer and their poor deer buttholes. Weirdo.

3. Ratchet and Release

Constant tension can be trouble for a story: a story where pain and fear and conflict are piled endlessly atop one another may wear down the audience. Creating suspense works by contrast: You must relax and release the tension before ratcheting it back up again. Pressure builds, and then you vent the steam. Then it builds again, and again you vent. This is pacing, the constant tightness and recoil of conflict into resolution and back into conflict. Think of Jenga: You remove a piece, and, *if the tower remains standing*, everybody breathes a sigh of relief. Tension, release, tension, release. Give the story time to breathe.

4. Harder, Harder, Haaaaarderrr, Ngggghh

In winding tension tighter, escalation is everything. How could it not be? Tension is about hands closing around one's neck, so the grip must grow tighter for the fear to be there. A rollercoaster doesn't waste the big loopty-loop on the first hill. Rather, you see it in the distance. You know it's coming. Each hill, bigger and meaner and faster than the last. The final hill is the culmination, the climax, a roller coaster loop where you crash through plate-glass windows and have jars filled with bees pitched at your head. Mounting danger. Rising fear. The hits keep coming. The Jenga tower teeters ...

5. The Bear Under the Table

It's the Hitchcockian "bomb under the table" example—you create shock by having a bomb randomly go off, but you create suspense and tension by *revealing* the bomb and letting the audience see what's coming. The first day of a new school year creates tension not because it's random (SURPRISE MOTHERF***ER! IT'S 4TH GRADE!) but because you know *all summer long* that shit is coming. Also, for the record, I think we should revise the "bomb under the table" example to a "bear under the table" example. Bombs are so overdone. But two characters sitting there with a Kodiak bear slumbering secretly at their feet? Oh, snap! Sweet tension, I seek your ursine embrace!

6. Danger as a Known Quantity: The Power of Dramatic Irony

This, by the way, is dramatic irony. Dramatic irony is best friend and old frat buddy to *Herr Doktor Suspenseundtension*. Dramatic irony is when the audience knows something that the characters do not. Suspense is created whether or not the characters are aware of the problem, but if the audience is the only one in on the secret, that may go a long way toward heightening tension.

7. The Question Mark-Shaped Hole in All of Our Dark Hearts

That's not to say every quantity must be known: The most refined tension grows out of a balance between known and unknown elements. Yes, the boy realizes that the first day of 4th grade is coming, but inherent to that are a number of unanswered questions: Did his bully and elementary nemesis Brutus "Smeggy" Smegbottom get held back? What will his new teacher be like? Who will he sit next to? Will Peggy Spoonblossom finally accept his Valentine's Day card? The first day of school is a known quantity, but what will happen on that day is not.

8. Always Tell Han Solo the Odds

Han Solo says, "Never tell me the odds." But we need to know the odds. (Which is why C-3P0 starts to tell him—so we as the audience understand the magnitude of the situation.) This is another component of the transparency sometimes needed to create tension: We *must* know when the stakes are high and the odds of success are totally astronomically screwed.

9. Save the Date!

Let's say you're a total dickhead parent to the aforementioned soon-to-be fourth grader. If you wanted to *foment* tension in that child, all summer long you'd occasionally remind him: "Hey, summer's fading fast, kiddo. School's on its way!" Every once in a while you'd lay on him a little something extra: "Hey, I heard Brutus Smegbottom got a new pair of brass knuckles." Or, "I think I saw Peggy Spoonblossom down at the mall eating a froyo with her new boyfriend." You'd needle him. *Remind* him of his tension. That's what the storyteller does because the storyteller is a total asshole. The storyteller must occasionally—not constantly, but just enough to keep it *hovering*, to keep it *orbiting*—remind the audience that something wicked this way comes.

10. The Character You Love Does Something You Hate

An easy way to create tension: when a character the audience loves does something the audience hates. It's the whole, "Oh, I'm going to go *investigate* the creepy noise rather than flee from it, load my shotgun, and call all the cops." John McClane jumps off the building's edge! Harry ruins his relationship with Sally! They mysteriously elect JarJar Binks to the Galactic Senate! It's a moment when the audience winces. One's butthole *tightens* up so hard it could pulverize a ruby. You say, "Oooh. That was a bad call. This is not going to end well." That septic feeling in one's gut—the anticipation of worse things to come—is the splendor of effective suspense.

11. Or, the Character You Hate Does Something You Hate

Of course, it's also effective to have a character the audience hates do something bad, too—that, then, is the power of a killer antagonist, nemesis, and villain. That sense of OH GRR GOD SO MAD RIGHT NOW is a powerful one. Tug on that puppet string whenever you need to for maximum storyteller cruelty.

12. Physical Tension Is the Shallowest of Tension

A threat against one's life and limb is totally workable—a character in physical danger is a good way to create fast tension. But sometimes you want to go deeper. You want to stab your sharpened toothbrush shiv into the heart and the brain. Emotional tension is the most palpable and troubling to the reader (and that's a good thing): Fear of damaged love, and intimate betrayals and irreversible emotional wounds creates a more vibrant and spectacular tension in the audience. It's cruel, yes. But as noted, it is not the storyteller's job to be kind. The storyteller should not be a safe haven. She is not to be trusted.

13. The Pain Sandwich

For maximum evil, ensure that the tension is multilayered. The protagonist's wife being in danger represents both physical (she might die) and emotional (he might lose her) tension. Apply with the mayonnaise of escalation and the bread-and-butter pickles of dramatic irony for one dastardly sandwich.

14. Personal Suspense Above Global Suspense

Sure. The world's gonna end. That's tough. Mos def. I feel it in here. *thumps heart with fist* Except, really, I don't care. I never do. The global threat is never ever (and once more for good measure: *ever*) as interesting as the personal threat. Yes, all the world is going to die but if that happens *so too shall the protagonist's daughter die.* Boom. Personal. Connection. Meaning. Suspense and tension are best when the personal is in addition to (and ultimately above) the global or the cosmic.

15. The Tongues of Tension, the Speech of Suspense

How you write matters in terms of creating suspense and tension. If you're trying for tension that is fast, frenetic, and born of collapsed moments and microscopic beats, then you wouldn't use big ponderous paragraphs to tell that tale. Just the same, you wouldn't hope to convey that slow creeping sour-gut dread with short, sharp, truncated sentences. As with all things, language matters. The architecture of your language means something—are you building a Gothic cathedral, a one-room studio apartment, or the Winchester Mansion?

16. Drug Dealers and Cliffhangers

The storyteller is a drug dealer meting out pain and pleasure in equal measure—a hard slap to the face and then a free taste of balm and salve to soothe the sting. Once they're hooked, you keep them hooked with cliffhangers. Not all the time, no, but whenever they might start to pull away, you surge within the audience that sense of suspense by leaving them dangling from the edge of the cliff. "My favorite character is in danger! Who just walked into the room? Is that a *Kodiak bear* under the table?" Mm-hmm. It is. Hooked again!

17. Flaws and Foibles and Frailties and Other Awesome *F*-Words

Character flaws. Use them as excellent tension creators. Knowing that a character has a drug habit or a propensity to break hearts lets us know that *at any point* they might fall off the wagon and lash out with the whip of their most intimate frailties, sending ruination far and wide. But we must know that the flaw is on the table, or at least have it hinted at—this does not work in a vacuum. You know what else doesn't work in a vacuum? A vacuum. True story!

18. The Itchy Panties

Comfort is the enemy of tension. You want characters and readers alike to remain in a state of agitation and discomfort. Even during times where the tension is relaxing rather than ratcheting up you still want to create a sense of dread and foreboding using language, circumstance, and situation to deepen discomfort.

19. Failure Most Certainly Is an Option

The audience needs to know that things can go wrong. If they become trained by you as a storyteller that you'll save everything and everyone at the last minute, the storyteller will no longer suspect you of being an untrustworthy malefactor. You are not the reader's buddy. Failure must be on the table. You must be willing to let things go all pear shaped once in a while. Tension without fear is a defanged and declawed tiger dressed as a banana. Harmless and deserving mockery over fear.

20. Speak of Ke$ha and Ke$ha Shall Appear

Never be afraid to use a ticking clock to instill tension and suspense. A character's only got one week to save the little girl? One day to pay the ransom? One hour to defuse the bomb? Works in any type of story— "The girl of my dreams is about to board a plane in thirty minutes! Can I make it to the airport in time to profess my love and tell her that I got her cat pregnant! Uhh? What? Nothing! I didn't say anything about a cat being pregnant! Hey, did you hear that new Ke$ha song?"

21. Deny Your Audience the Satisfaction as Long as You Can

Storytelling is Tantric. You withhold the audience's orgasm as long as you can. The audience wants to know that everything's going to work out, that it's going to be all right. They want answers. Comfort. Solace. Don't give it to them. Not until late (if ever). The longer you can hold out on 'em, the deeper the tension digs into the meat and marrow.

22. Look to Your Life for Suspense

Seriously, that example of the first day or school? Or a new job? Or that feeling you get when you speed past a cop car? Or when your mother goes sniffing around your closet and almost finds the leather-clad gimp you keep in there? That's suspense. Harness those feelings from your own life. Find out what makes them tick. Replicate in your fiction. And seriously, gimps are so 1990s. Get a monkey butler like the rest of us.

23. The Fear Maker's Promise

Suspense and tension are about fear. Plain and simple. Not just fear in the characters, but fear—actual honest-to-Jeebus fear—in the audience. Find a way to invoke fear and dread, and you've won.

24. Suspense Keeps Them Reading

Be content to know that effective implementation of suspense and tension will keep them coming back and turning pages.

25. Suspense Keeps You Writing

The thing is, it's also what keeps you going. Creating powerful suspense takes you along on a journey, too—the writer is not immune to his own magic, or shouldn't be, at least. If you feel like you're not engaged or that your own sense of suspense and dread just isn't in play, then you might need to look at what the problem is. Just as readers need a reason to keep reading, writers need a reason to keep on writing. And you, as writer, are the Proto-Reader, the first line of defense. If the tension is as limp as a dead man's no-no stick, you'll feel it. And that means it's time to find a dose of high-test narrative Viagra to stiffen everything up.

25 THINGS YOU SHOULD KNOW ABOUT THEME

1. Every Story Is an Argument

Every story's trying to say something. It's trying to beam an idea, a message, into the minds of the readers. In this way, every story is an argument. It's the writer making a case. It's the writer saying, "All of life is suffering." Or, "Man will be undone by his prideful reach." Or "Love blows." Or, "If you dance with the Devil Wombat, you get cornholed by the Devil Wombat." This argument is the story's *theme*.

2. The Elements of Story Support That Argument

If the theme, then, is the writer's thesis statement, then all elements of the story—character, plot, word choice, scene development, inclusion of the Devil Wombat—go toward proving that thesis.

3. Unearthed or Engineered

The theme needn't be something the writer is explicitly aware of—it may be an unconscious argument, a message that has crept into the work like a virus capable of overwriting narrative DNA, like a freaky dwarven stalker hiding in your panty drawers and getting his greasy Norseman stink all over your undergarments. A writer can engineer the theme, building it into the work. Or a writer can unearth it, discovering its tendrils after the work is written.

4. Theme: A Lens That Levels the Laser

Knowing your theme can give your story focus. If you know the theme before you write, it helps you make your argument. If you discover the theme before a *re*write, it helps you go back through and filter the story, discovering which elements speak to your argument and which elements are either vestigial (your story's stubby, grubby tail) or which elements go against your core argument ("so far, nobody is getting cornholed by the Devil Wombat").

5. Do I Really Need This Happy Horseshit?

Yes and no. Yes, your story needs a theme. It's what elevates your story to something beyond forgettable entertainment. You can be assured, for instance, that 90 percent of movies starring Dolph Lundgren have no theme present. A story with a theme is a story with a point. No, you don't always need to identify the theme. Sometimes a story will leap out of your head with a theme cradled to its bosom (along with the shattered remains of your skull), regardless of whether or not you intended it. Of course, identifying the theme *at some point* in your storytelling will ensure that it exists and that your story isn't just a hollow scarecrow bereft of his stuffing. Awww. Sad scarecrow. Crying corn syrup tears.

6. Slippery Business

I make it sound easy. Like you can just state a theme or find it tucked away in your story like a mint on a pillow. It isn't. Theme is slippery, uncertain. It's like a lubed-up sex gimp: Every time you think you get your hands around him, the greasy, latex-enveloped sonofabitch is out of the cage and free from your grip and running into traffic where he's trying desperately to unzipper his mouth and scream for help. Be advised that theme is tricky. Chameleonic. Which isn't a word. But it should be.

7. For Instance: You Can Get It Wrong

You might think going in, "What I'm trying to say with this story is that man's inhumanity to man is what keeps civilization going." But then you get done with the story and you're like, "Oh, shit. I wasn't saying that at all, was I? I was saying that man's inhumanity to cake is what keeps civilization going." And then you're like, "Hell yeah, cake." And you eat some cake.

8. Mmm, Speaking of Cake

In cake, every piece is a microcosm of the whole. A slice contains frosting, cake, and filling. Okay, that's not entirely true—sometimes you get a piece of cake where you get something that the other pieces don't get, like a fondant rose, but really, let's be honest, fondant tastes like cardboard. Nasty stuff. So, let's disregard that and go back to the original notion: *All pieces of cake contain the essence of that cake.* So it is with your story: All pieces of the story contain the essence of that story, and the essence of that story is the theme. The theme is cake, frosting, filling. In every slice you cut. Man, now I really want cake.

9. Grand Unification Theory

Another way to look at theme: it unifies story and bridges disparate elements. In this way theme is like The Force. Or like fiber. Or like bondage at an orgy. It ties the whole thing together. Different characters, tangled plotlines, and curious notions, all come together with the magic sticky superglue of theme.

10. Put Down That Baseball Bat, Pick Up That Phial of Poison
Theme can do a story harm. It isn't a bludgeoning device. A story is more than just a conveyance for your message: the message is just *one component* of your story. Overwrought themes become belligerent within the text, like a guy yelling in your ear, smacking you between the shoulder blades with his Bible. Theme is a drop of poison, subtle and unseen but carried in the bloodstream to the heart and brain just the same. Repeat after me, penmonkeys: *Your story is not a sermon.*

11. No Good If Nobody Knows It
A theme so subtle it's imperceptible does your story no good. It'd be like having a character that just never shows up. Or a two-headed ferret in your pants that you never put on YouTube. What's the point?

12. Triangulating Theme
Ask three questions to zero in on your theme: "What is this story about?" "Why do I want to tell this story?" "Why will anyone care?" Three answers. Three beams of light. Illuminating dark spaces. Revealing theme.

13. As Much an Obsession as a Decision
The auteur theory suggests that, throughout an author's body of work, one can find consistent themes—and, studying a number of authors, you'll find this to be true. (Look no further than James Joyce in this respect, where he courts themes exploring the everyday heroism of the common man competing against the paralysis of the same.) In this way theme is sometimes an obsession, the author compelled to explore certain aspects and arguments without ever really meaning to—theme then

needn't be decided upon, nor must it be constrained to a single narrative. Theme is bigger, bolder, madder than all that. Sometimes theme is who we really are as writers.

14. Theme Is Not Motif
I'll sometimes read that theme can be expressed as a single word. *Love. Death. Plastics.* Let me offer my own one word to respond to that: bullshit. Those are motifs. Elements and symbols that show up again and again in the story. Motif is not synonymous with theme. "Death" is not a theme. "Man can learn from death" is a theme. "Life is stupid because we all die" is a theme. "Sex and death are uncomfortable neighbors" is a theme. *Death* is just a word. An inconclusive and unassertive word. Theme says something, goddamnit.

15. Mmm, Speaking Of Cake, I Mean, Motif
That said, motif can be a carrier for theme. Theme is the disease and motif is the little outbreak monkey spreading it. If your theme's making a statement about death, then symbols of death would not be unexpected. Or maybe you'd use symbols of time or decay. I mean, it has to make sense, of course. A theme about what man can learn from death is not well embodied by, say, a series of microwave ovens.

16. Theme Is Also Not a Logline
A logline is plot based. It depicts a sequence of events in brief, almost vignetted, form. Plot embodies breadth. Theme embodies depth. Theme is about story, and story is the weirder, hairier brother of "plot."

17. Piranhasaur Versus Mechatarantula
In English class, I was often told that theme could best be described as X versus Y. Man versus Nature. Man versus Man. Man versus Woman. Fat Guy versus Hammock. Of course, English class was frequently stupid. Once more I'm forced to call *bullshit*. Theme isn't just you, the writer,

identifying a struggle. That's not enough. Theme picks a goddamn side. Theme asserts predictive outcome. It says, "In this struggle, nature always gets the best of man." It predicts, "That hammock is going to *ruin that fat guy's day*, for realsies." Theme does more than merely showcase conflict. Theme puts its money on the table.

18. Take That Question Mark and Shove It

So too it is that theme is never a question. "How far will man go for love?" is a question, not a theme. Theme isn't a big blank spot. Theme is the answer, right or wrong, good or bad.

19. It Is the Question, However, That Drives Us

Plot can carry theme by asking the question—like the aforementioned, "How far will man go for love?"—but then it's theme's job to stick the landing and, by the end of the story, answer the question posed. Theme comes back around and demonstrates, "*This* is how far man will go for love." It shows if man will go into the whale's mouth and out the whale's keister, if man has limitations, or if man's love can be defeated by other elements (greed, lust, fear, microwave ovens, wombats).

20. Of Turtleheads and Passing Comets

Theme might end up like Halley's Comet—once or twice in a story, it emerges from hiding and shows itself. The blood test reveals it, and The Thing springs forth from flesh. In this way, it's okay if the theme is plainly stated (often by a character) once or twice in the story. Forrest Gump tells us that life is like a box of chocolates, you never know what you're gonna get. (And the film is like a box of chocolates, too—all the shitty ones filled with suntan lotion and zit cream.) You could argue that the opening line in *Reservoir Dogs* gives away the whole point of the movie: It is, after all, a metaphor for big dicks.

21. Do Your Due Diligence

Read books. Watch movies. Play games. Find the theme in each. This isn't like math. You may not find one pure answer to the equation. But it's a valuable exercise just the same. It'll teach you that theme works.

22. Your Audience Might Not Give a Damn (but That's Okay)

Theme may not be something the audience sees or even cares about. Furthermore, the audience may find stuff in your work you never intended. Like that old joke goes, the reader sees the blue curtains as some expression of grief, futility, and the author's repressed bestiality, but, in reality, the author just meant, "The curtains are blue." It's all good. This is the squirmy, slippery nature of story. That's the many-headed hydra of art.

23. Not Just for Literary Noses Held High in the Air

Just the same, theme isn't a jungle gym found on a playground meant only for literary snobs. Theme speaks to common experience and thus is for the common reader and the common writer. Theme isn't better than you, and you're not better than theme. Like in *Close Encounters of the Third Kind*, this is you mounding your mashed potatoes into an unexpected shape. "*This means something.*" Hell yeah, it does. That's a beautiful thing.

24. A Weapon in Your Word-Warrior Arsenal

How important is theme at the end of the day? It's one more weapon in your cabinet, one more tool in your box. It is neither the most nor the least important device in there—you determine its value. My only advice is, it helps to get floor time with every weapon just so you know how best to slay every opponent. Play with theme. Learn its power. I mean, why the hell not?

25. Bloody Fingerprints

You want theme distilled down? You want it reduced like a tasty sauce? Theme is you saying something with your fiction. Why wouldn't you want to say something? Big or small, simple or complex, as profound as you care to make it, fiction has the power to do more than just be a recitation of plot events. Your work becomes your own—fingerprinted in blood—when you capitalize on the power of storytelling to *speak your heart and soul*. Take a stand. Let theme be a bold pronouncement of confidence, a message encoded in the DNA of an already-great story.

25 THINGS YOU SHOULD KNOW ABOUT WRITING A SCENE

1. The Narrative Brick in the Wall

A story can be measured—just not in inches, liters, or seconds. A story is measured in beats, scenes, sequences, acts, arcs, and so forth. A scene is just one building block, and it is perhaps our most important one because each brick is critical to holding up the entire building. Every scene must be like that brick: When it's there, it keeps the whole story together; when it's gone, the whole thing falls apart around the audience's ears.

2. Sweet Brevity

Try to describe every scene with a single sentence. Can you do it? "Betty confronts Doctor Barracuda about their secret love child, Barry," is fine. But if you find yourself droning on and on ("… and Betty expresses her displeasure at mid-century modern furniture and transforms into a giant praying mantis and then …") you've probably got too much going on. Break it up. Multiple scenes are okay. Bonus points: The "one-sentence description" is also useful in terms of outlining.

3. No Set Length

A scene has no set length. It isn't 1,000 words or two script pages, but err on the side of "Shorter is better." if you leave a scene too long, it's like opening up a gas leak—it won't be long before your audience is snoring like a lawn mower. Nobody loves a scene that overstays its welcome.

4. A Single Setting

Assume that a given scene never leaves a single location: the protagonist's kitchen, the old stable, the deck of the ISS Mimsy Borogroves, a distant moon brothel, whatever. If it leaves that location, it's best to assume it's a new scene.

5. Who's There?

The most critical narrative components in any scene are the characters that populate it. Characters are the agency by which a plot moves forward, so without characters, a scene is really just a yawning vacuum. A scene gains more mileage and momentum when you decide to put several interesting and conflicting characters together in a scene—like Mentos and Diet Coke, you are hoping to provoke a *reaction*.

6. What Do They Want?

Everybody wants something. Love. Revenge. Sex. Cake. A scene is frequently an expression of characters trying (and often failing) to get what they want. Motivations and fears drive characters, so they drive your story's scenes as well.

7. What's the Problem?

The characters want the thing (*love revenge sex cake*, which is also the name of my new memoir), but of course they can't have it, can they? That's storytelling at its core: People want things and they are denied those things. It's a fundamental human struggle, and so it is with stories and the scenes that comprise them: A straight line is boring, so we throw all manner of jagged angles and sharp inclines in the way of our characters. In this scene, discover what the conflict is that roadblocks the character's goals. Does another character stand in her way? Are they at cross-purposes? Does an act of nature complicate the problem? Does the character complicate her own existence?

8. What Are They Doing?

Interesting characters *do* shit. A scene can be framed very simply by asking what it is the characters are literally doing and saying in a given increment of time. "In this scene, they plan the bank robbery." "In that scene, they have sex when we all know it's a really bad idea." "In the final scene, they try to blow up Ice Station Donkey and save the day from the Terrorist Narwhal."

9. Something Has to Happen, Goddamnit

In other words, if nothing is happening in your scene, throw it into a bag and burn it. Action. Event. Change. Agency. A scene must move, writhe, squirm, *seek*. It's okay if a scene has a little oxygen and is about introspection and dialogue, but at the end of the day, if a scene is pure intellectual indolence, it needs to be thrown out of the airlock and allowed to freeze in the cold dark of space.

10. What Is the Purpose of This Scene?

Identify the purpose behind the scene. "I don't know" is not, by the way, an acceptable answer. What does it do for you, for the audience? "It reveals the true killer." Or, "We learn what *really* happened to our protagonist back at the lighthouse." Or, "We finally figure out why the villain wants sexy revenge against the cake he once loved." If you cannot find the purpose of the scene, then the scene must be shanked in the kidneys and left on the prison shower floor.

11. Why Will Anyone Care?
It's a simple (if troubling) test: A scene gets to stay if the audience has reason to care about its inclusion. You, the author, caring? Not enough. *They* have to care. If you can't say at the end of writing it, "They're going to want this scene," then once again, it's time to butcher it for spare parts.

12. A Scene Must Sing for Its Supper
What's clear in the above questions is that every scene's existance must be justified. Every scene takes up space on the page or the screen and must earn that space. The pages of a book or minutes of screen time are precious goddamn real estate with top-dollar costs; if it can't pay up, it's gotta go. Be merciless in the culling of scenes that do not belong. A story is often improved by such cruelty.

13. Moves the Story Forward
A story is a progression of various things: plot, character, theme, and so on. A scene is the driver for such progression. In each scene *action* and *dialogue* combine to carry our characters, our plots, and our themes forward because *action* and *dialogue* help to change things (sometimes subtly, sometimes dramatically) within the fiction. If a scene fails to change anything and is unable to evolve (or devolve) those critical elements in any way, then it is naught but a boat anchor stuck in the narrative mire. Give the scene energy, impetus, event. Give the scene *movement*.

14. Reveals Something We Didn't Already Know

A good scene shows us things of which we were not already aware. Every scene is a learning opportunity for the audience. Secrets exposed! Betrayals illuminated! Motivations laid bare! Sexual fetish for denim bondage wear revealed! Look for at least one thing that the scene tells the audience that they could not have known before (though it's okay if it's something they *suspected*).

15. For Every Answer, a New Question

The audience is haunted by questions. Just as a scene reveals things, it must also obscure things—just as we hunger to see the character driven by goals she cannot yet achieve, we also hunger to answer questions we cannot yet see resolved. Imagine putting a new question mark into each scene—where is it? What will the audience be asking upon leaving the scene? "Did Betty betray Doctor Barracuda? What the hell is the 'Halberd of Infinite Breakfast?' Does this clown suit make me look fat?"

16. Double Duty

A scene needn't merely do one thing; every scene is a dessert napoleon of sweet layered possibility. It can move the story forward. It can teach us something about a character. It can restate or challenge our theme. It can have great dialogue and snappy action. A scene should be encouraged to do as much as it can without being overburdened—again, since creative real estate is at a premium within our stories, a scene that does a lot is better than a scene that does a little when the reaper's scythe comes to slicey-dicey.

17. Text and Subtext

A scene has two layers—one visible, one less so. The visible layer is the action and the dialogue. Things happen. People say stuff. This is text. But a current of unspoken, unseen event runs through every scene, too: This is *subtext*. The scene may express a theme or mood. Unspoken character motivations (fears, desires, hopes, nightmares) may lurk beneath the surface. Subtext is a whisper, not a shout.

18. Small Story Arc
It may be helpful to think of each scene as having a small narrative arc—a microcosm of the overall narrative arc. An event, a rise of action and possibility, a challenge and complication, a moment of climax—the one difference here is that generally speaking, scenes do not offer much in the way of resolution. It is this lack of resolution that, in part, keeps us reading.

19. Begin the Scene as Late as You Can
You don't need to go through the motions of "getting into" a scene—if it's a scene where two people rob a diner, you don't need to show them driving to the diner, getting out of the car, loading their weapons, pulling down their balaclavas, going in the front door, and so on. Jump right in—*boom*, they kick down the doors, guns up, scene begins. Side note: "Balaclava" is not the same thing as the sweet, layered Greek dessert. Do not wear dessert on your head when committing robbery.

20. Once in a While, Drop a Bomb
Sometimes a scene needs something that completely changes the landscape of a story. Every scene can't have a bunker-buster plot moment (OMG BRUCE WILLIS HAS BEEN DARTH VADER THE WHOLE TIME), but sometimes you'll get the sense in a scene that it's time to take a sharp right turn—shatter the guardrail, leap off the highway, and drive off into an entirely unexpected direction. Do not fear this. Allow the scene to execute in a surprising way.

21. Variation Is the Spice of Life
(Actually, I think "Spice Melange" is the spice of life, GODDAMN YOU BARON HARKONNEN. Whatever.) Scenes should not feel reit-

erative or redundant—same settings, same conflicts, same boring old replay of events and conversations. Scenes should evolve from one to the next, each moving forward and changing and offering us new settings, new or modified conflicts, showing us changed characters and unexpected events. Just as on the page we should see each paragraph start with different sentence forms, so too should our scenes feel fresh, different, and compelling.

22. Strung Together Like Christmas Lights

Scenes connect. They are not islands separate from one another. They are bound by bridges, roads, walkways. They flow one into the next in a natural progression; they're not individual little short stories. Scenes connect via consequence (one scene results from another) or complication (one scene acts against the events of one before it). Note that the most perilous scenes are the ones that are purely bridging—meaning, you need to get characters from Point A to Point B so the audience isn't confused how they got there. Recognize now that the danger is how bridging scenes can be well, *utter snooze-a-paloozas*, and your best bet is to make these transitional scenes loaded with *some other component* (see "Double Duty") to make them interesting.

23. Chekhov's Pebble

Put differently, consider the notion of Chekhov's Gun: if you show a pistol in the first act, the thing better go off by the third act. Every scene is like this: You're introducing elements that must manifest in the scenes that come after (and in many cases, before). Think of each scene as the ripples that result from a thrown pebble; all the ripples will touch circles and affect one another.

24. +/-

A simple way to measure change in a scene is to give the scene values of + or -, meaning, what has changed for the positive and what has changed for the negative in a given exchange? "+: Doctor Barracuda had sex with a cake; -: The cake was a bomb, and now Doctor Barracuda will never love a cake ever again." Not every scene will have one or more of each; it's just a good way to understand change and to gauge how the story-line moves progresses by varying degrees.

25. The Reprieve of Being Interesting

Want to know a secret? None of this stuff matters. It's helpful, of course. But here's the trick: Your only *true crime* in a given scene is being boring. If your scene is interesting, the audience will forgive you for its inclusion. Interesting scenes ... well, for fear of sending a memo from the Department of Redundancy Department, interest the audience. And that's what the audience wants at the end of the day: to be captive to their own interest. To be compelled by what you're writing. If what you write in a scene breaks the above "rules" but still draws the interest of the audience, screw it. Keep it. Being interesting is the best reprieve from execution.

25 THINGS YOU SHOULD KNOW ABOUT DIALOGUE

1. Dialogue Is Easy Like Sunday Morning

Our eyes flow over dialogue like butter on the hood of a hot car. This is true when reading fiction. This is true when reading scripts. What does this tell you? It tells you to use a lot of dialogue.

2. Easy Isn't the Same as Uncomplicated

We like to read dialogue because it's easy, not because it's stupid. Dialogue has a fast flow. We respond to it as humans because, duh, humans make talky-talky. Easy does not translate to uncomplicated or unchallenging. Dialogue isn't, "I like hot dogs," "I think hot dogs are stupid," "I think you're stupid," "I think your Mom's stupid," and "I think your Mom's *vagina* is stupid." Dialogue is a carrier for all aspects of the narrative experience. Put differently, it's the spoonful of sugar that makes the medicine go down.

3. Sweet Minimalism

Let's get this out of the way: don't hang a bunch of gaudy ornaments upon your dialogue. In fiction, use the dialogue tags *said* and *asked* 90 percent of the time. In edge cases you might use *hissed*, *called*, *stammered*, etc. These are strong spices; use minimally. Also, adverbs nuzzled up against dialogue tags are an affront to all things and make Baby Jesus pee out the side of his diaper, and when he does that, people die. In scripts, you don't have this problem but you can still clog the pipes with crap if you overuse stage directions. Oh, heavy dialect and slang? Just more ornamentation that'll break your dialogue's back.

4. Uh, You Do Know the Rules, Right?

Learn the structure of dialogue. If a screenplay, know the format. Capitalized name, centered above parenthetical stage direction and the line of dialogue. VO, OC, OS, cont'd:

SCOOTER (VO)

(shouting)

I always said that life was like a box of marmots. You never know which one's gonna nibble off your privates.

In fiction, know when to use a comma, when to use a period, know where the punctuation goes in relation to quotation marks, and know that a physical gesture (*nodded*, f'rex) is not a dialogue tag.

"To hell with that monkey," John said.

"But," Betty said, "I love that dumb chimp."

John nodded. "I know, Betty. But he's a bad news bonobo, baby. *A bad news bonobo.*"

5. Use It to Set Pace

If you want a pig to run faster, you grease him up with Astroglide and stick a NASA rocket booster up his ass. If you want your story to read faster, you use dialogue to move it along. Like I said, dialogue reads easy. Dialogue's like a waterslide: A reader gets to it, they zip forth fast, fancy and free. Want to slow things down? Pull away from the dialogue. Speed things up? More dialogue. Throttle and brake—dialogue and description.

6. Shape Determines Speed

Short, sharp dialogue is a prison shiv: moves fast 'cause T-Bone only has three seconds in the lunch line with Johnny the Fish to stitch a shank all up in Johnny's kidneys. Longer dialogue moves more slowly. Want to create tension? Fast, short dialogue. Want to create mystery? Longer, slightly more ponderous dialogue. Want to bog your audience in word treacle? Let one character take a lecturing info-dump all over their heads.

7. Expository Dialogue Is a Pair of Cement Shoes

One of dialogue's functions is to convey information within the story (to other characters) and outside the story (to the audience). An info dump is the clumsiest way to make this happen. Might as well bludgeon your audience with a piece of rebar. You have ways to pull this off without dropping an expository turd in the word bowl. Don't let one character lecture; let it be a conversation. Question. Answer. Limit the information learned; pull puzzle pieces out, and take them away to create mystery. Let characters be reluctant to give any info, much less dump it over someone's head.

8. Showing Through Telling

Dialogue is a better way of conveying information than you, the storyteller, just straight up telling the audience. The curious nature of dialogue, however, is that it would *seem* to violate that most sacred of writing chestnuts—show, don't tell. I don't open my mouth and project goddamn holograms. I tell you shit. And yet, the trick with dialogue is to *show through telling*. You reveal things through dialogue *without* a character saying them. This means it's paramount to avoid ...

9. The Wart on the End of the Nose

"On-the-nose" dialogue is where a character says exactly what he feels and what he wants for the purpose of telling the audience what they need to know. When a villain spoils his own sinister plan, that's on-the-nose. Imagine if, in a romantic love triangle, all the characters in that triangle discussed the love triangle in flat, overly truthful language. Then imagine just how that would kill the tension between characters. Trust me, we'd live in a better, happier society if real-world dialogue was all on the nose. On the other side, we'd experience duller, shittier fiction. Characters—and, frankly, real people—reveal things without saying them.

10. The Words Beneath the Words

Text versus subtext. On-the-nose dialogue versus dialogue that is deliciously sub rosa. Meaning exists beneath what's said. The best real world example of this is the dreaded phrase spoken by men and women the world around: "I'm fine." Said with jaw tight. Said with averted eyes. Said in sharp, clipped tongue. Never before have two words so clearly meant something entirely different: "I'm fine" is code for, "Yes, something is goddamn wrong, but I don't want to talk about it. Actually, I *do* want to talk about it but I want you to already know what's wrong, and what's wrong is that you had sex with my mother in a New Jersey rest stop and put it on Youtube *ohmygod-I-hate-you-so-bad*."

11. Pay No Attention to the Dead Man Behind the Curtain

Put differently, pretend that dialogue is more about hiding than it is about revealing. The things we the audience want to know most—who killed his wife, why did he rob that bank, did he really have a romantic dalliance with that insane dancing robot—are the things the character doesn't want to discuss. Dialogue is negotiating that revelation, and it's a revelation that should come as easy as pulling the teeth out of a coked-up Doberman. Meaning, not easy at all.

12. Where Tension, Suspense, and Mystery
Have a Big, Crazy Gang Bang

The fact that characters lie, cheat, conceal, mislead, and betray all in dialogue tells you that dialogue is a critical way of building tension and suspense and conveying mystery. Characters are always prime movers.

13. Quid Pro Quo, Clarice

Hannibal Lecter susses out the truth through dialogue. (Oh, and he also eats people.) But he's also performing meta-work for the audience by sussing out character through dialogue. Clarice Starling is painted in part by Lecter's own strokes. A character's blood, sweat, and tears, live inside their dialogue. How they speak and what they say reveals who they are, though only obliquely. After writing a conversation, ask yourself, "What does this say about the characters? Is this true to who they are?"

14. Let the Character Sign Their Own Work

A character dialogue is that character's unique signature. It contains their voice and personality. One speaks in gruff, clipped phrasing. Another goes on at length. This character is ponderous and poetic while that one is meaner than two rattlesnakes bumping uglies in a dirty boot. Don't let a character's voice be defined by dialect, slang, or other trickery. It's not just how they speak. It's what they say more than how they say it.

15. Dialogue Is a Theme Park
Theme is one of those things you as the author don't really speak out loud, but sometimes characters do. They might orbit the theme. They might challenge it. They might speak it outright. Not often, and never out of nowhere. But it's okay once in awhile to let a character be an avatar of theme. It's doubly okay if that character is played by Morgan Freeman. God, that guy's voice. He could say anything—"Beans are a musical fruit"—and I'm like, "There it is! Such gravitas! Such *power*. It's the theme. *It's the theme!*"

16. Dialogue Is Action
We expect that dialogue and action are separate, but they are not. *Speak* is a verb. So is *talk*. Or *discuss, argue, yell, banter, rant, rave*. Verb means action. That means, duh, dialogue is action, not separate from it. Furthermore, dialogue works best when treated this way. Don't stand two characters across from one another and have them talk at each other like it's a ping-pong game. Characters act while speaking. They walk. Kick stones. Clean dishes. Load rifles. Eat messy sandwiches. Pleasure themselves. Build thermonuclear penile implants. This creates a sense of dynamism. Of an authentic world. It adds variety and interest.

17. The Real World Is Not Your Friend
I'm not talking about the MTV reality show, although one supposes there the lesson is the same (so not your friend). What I mean is that if you want to ruin good dialogue, the fastest path to that is by mimicking dialogue you hear in the real world. Dialogue in the real world is dull. It's herky-jerky. Lots of um, mmm, hmm, uhhh, like, y'know. If you listen really hard to how people speak to one another, it's amazing anybody communicates anything at all. A little bit of

this authenticity is fine; overdoing it will muddy the dialogue so as to make it unreadable.

18. For the Record, You're Not David Mamet

Yes, yes, I know. David Mamet writes "realistic" dialogue. Everyone interrupts everyone. They say inexplicable shit. They barely manage to communicate. *Subtextapalooza*. It's great. It works. You're also not David Mamet. I mean, unless you are, in which case, thanks for stopping by. Would you sign my copy of *Glengarry Glen Ross*? All that being said ...

19. Again: Not a Ping-Pong Match

Characters don't stand nose to nose and take turns speaking. People are selfish. So too are characters. Characters want to talk. They want to be heard. They don't wait their turn like polite automatons. They can interrupt each other. Finish one another's sentences. Derail conversations. Pursue agendas. Dialogue is a little bit jazz, a little bit hand-to-hand combat. It's a battle of energy, wits, and dominance.

20. Conversation Is Conflict

Dialogue can represent a pure and potent form of conflict. Two or more characters want something, and they're using words to get it. Before you write conversation, ask: What does each participant want? Set a goal. One character wants money. Another wants affirmation to justify her self-righteousness. A third just needs a hug. Find motive. Purpose. Conscious or not. Let the conversation reflect this battle.

21. Authenticity Trumps Reality

"But it really happened," is never an excuse for something to exist in fiction. Weird shit happens all the time in reality. Ever have something happen where you say, "Gosh, that was really convenient?" If you put that in your story, the audience is going to kick you in the gut and spit in your cereal. Dialogue suffers from similar pitfalls. Just because you hear it in reality doesn't mean it works in the context of story. Story has its own secret laws. You can make dialogue sound real without mimicking reality. One might term this "natural" dialogue; authenticity is about feeling real, not about being real.

22. Sometimes You Just Gotta Babble That Shit Out
Writing dialogue sometimes means you just let two characters babble for awhile. Small talk, big talk, crazy talk. Let 'em circumvent the real topic. Give them voices. Open the floodgates to your subconscious mind. And let the conversation flow. Write big, write messy, and write long. Cut later in comfort.

23. Nothing Wrong With Banter
You might write two characters just sitting down and shooting the shit and think, "I'll cut this down later." But don't be so sure. Sometimes characters just need to chat, babble, mouth off. Who they are can be revealed in two people just screwing around, seeing what comes out of their heads. That can work if it's interesting, if it puts the character on the map in terms of the audience's mental picture, and if it eventually crystalizes into something bigger than how it began. Oh, and did I mention it has to be interesting?

24. The Greatest Crime Against Humanity Is Writing Boring Dialogue
Like I said, dialogue is easy to read. Or it's supposed to be. Anybody who writes dialogue that's dull, that doesn't flow like water and pop like popcorn, needs to be taken out back and shaken like a baby. Find the boring parts. The unnecessary stuff. The junk. Anything that doesn't feel a) necessary and b) interesting. Stick it in a bag and set it on fire. Want to read great dialogue? Sharp, fast, entertaining, witty as hell, with a lot going on? Go watch the TV show *Gilmore Girls*. No, I'm not kidding. Stop making that face.

25. Double-Duty Dialogue

Heh, "duty." Heh, "log." Shut up. If you take one thing away from these twenty-five "gems" of wisdom, it 's this: Let dialogue do the heavy lifting and perform double- or even triple-duty. Dialogue isn't just dialogue. It's a vehicle for character, theme, mood, plot, conflict, mystery, tension, and horror. Dialogue does a lot of work in very short space: It's the goddamn Swiss Army knife of storytelling. Or MacGyver. Or Trojan Horse. Or MacGyver hiding in a Trojan Horse carrying a Swiss Army knife. Didn't I tell you to shut up already? Where's Morgan Freeman when you need him? He'll tell you to shut up, and *you'll listen*.

25 THINGS YOU SHOULD KNOW ABOUT ENDINGS

1. Behold My Clumsy and Confusing Definition

Let's pretend for a moment that the end of any story is a hazy thing—it doesn't begin at any precise point and spans the nebulous territory between "the beginning of the end and the last moment of the story that reaches the reader's mind." The ending is when there's no turning back, when the story can't be stopped, when everything's in motion and moving forward like a racehorse on angel dust.

2. Okay, Fine, You Won't Stop Staring at Me
So Here's Your Goddamn Definition

If you want the *technical* definition, then the ending begins at the start of the final act. In screenwriting, it begins at the end of the *third* act. It encompasses the climax of the piece and then tumbles forth through the falling action and into the denouement. It is triggered by the turning point (where the story offers its final pivot) which leads into the final act, which sets up the last conflict and the resolution of that conflict. There. Are you happy now, *Mom*?

3. Boom Goes the Dynamite

The climax and falling action are the flashier components of the ending—this is the big-ass fireworks finale where everyone goes *oooh* and *ahhh* and stares into the pretty lights and receives commands from their alien masters on when precisely to assassinate the Archduke. Or whatever. Know that the climax is when, metaphorically or literally, everything explodes. The falling action is the gathering and rearrangement of those pieces. The zeppelin blows up—CHOOM! (the climax)—and then as it sinks toward Earth, the hero's mission to save the lovely lass is in question as the antagonist's plan appears to be successful. But the hero has his mad hero skills and turns the tide and saves the girl and slays the antagonist and has a litter of puppies, blah blah blah. Note that some stories conflate climax and falling action into one moment: I'd argue that *Star Wars* does this, tying everything up with the Big Boom of the Death Star going kaflooey. (Yes, "kaflooey" is a technical term.) *Die Hard* doesn't—the big explosion on the roof is your climax, and McClane versus Hans is the falling action (er, quite literally).

4. All the Little Strings Tied Around Fingers

The denouement is not a critical component, and some stories just say, "Screw it," and kick it into the mouth of a hungry alligator to be eaten and forgotten. The denouement (it's French, and pronounced Day-NOO-MAAAAWWHHHH, with that last syllable comprising about forty-two seconds of actual vocal time) offers what you might consider "narrative cleanup." It takes all the niggling details and ties them into little bows. Sometimes a denouement is just a handful of moments—again, in *Die Hard*, it's that short scene as they leave Nakitomi Plaza. In the film *Return Of The King*, it's the last six thousand minutes as the audience bears witness to an endless procession of hobbit-flavored not-quite-happy endings! Mmm. Hobbit happy endings. Tiny hands. But so soft. Worth the money you pay.

5. A Good Ending Answers Questions

A story raises questions both within the story and outside it—"Will Steve woo Betty? Will Orange Julius save Cabana Boy from the jaws of The Cramposaur? Can love survive in the face of war? Is bacon overrated?" A good ending takes these questions and answers them. Most mysteries are solved. Most concerns are addressed.

6. A Great Ending Asks New Questions

An author should never be afraid to let an ending offer new questions heaped upon the answers of the old. Yes, *the old questions*, the ones you introduced, should be addressed—but things needn't be so simple. Exposing the truth might force the reader to ask new questions, and those questions are likely to never be answered (unless there's another story in the sequence). That's okay. Hell, that's not only okay—*that's awesome*. That leaves people thinking about the story. It doesn't just close the door and kick them out of the house—it Manchurian Candidates those bastards (yes, I turned that movie title into a verb, and shut up) and leaves the story top of mind. You want people to come away from your story talking and thinking about it, not letting it fall to the dreary fog of forgetfulness.

7. Time to Confirm or Deny Your Theme

Your story is an argument—a thesis positing a thematic notion, an idea, a conceit. The ending is where you (purposefully or inadvertently) prove or disprove that thesis. It's when you say, "Man *will* embrace nature over nurture." Or, "True love *won't* save the day." Or,

"Yes, indeed, Fruit Roll-Ups *are* secretly the leathered skin of popular cartoon characters such as Smurfs and/or Snorks." Just as an ending answers a question, it also takes one last look at your theme and concludes that argument.

8. Endings Don't Need to Be Pat

I dunno who "Pat" actually is, but my assumption is that he's a nice guy and everything works out for him. When an ending is pat, it's the same way: It's a nice ending, and hey, lookie-loo, everything works out just dandy. You are not required to create nice, neat, tidy little endings—an ending shouldn't look like a Christmas ornament designed by Martha Stewart.

9. Sometimes, a Nice, Neat Happy Ending Is Appropriate

Sometimes, sure, okay, you want a happy ending. Here's the difference, though, between a *happy ending* and a *pat ending*. A "pat" ending ties things up artificially—it uses coincidence and narrative hand waving to bring disparate elements together and make sure everything is all toothy smiles and unicorn hats and rainbow poop. A happy ending ties everything up nicely because that's how it has to be—that's what the story demands and has been building to all this time.

10. Strongbad's Little Buddy

Some endings are a cheat. That's worse than being "pat," by the way—a cheat is an ending that comes out of leftfield and crams a square peg into the circle hole that is the reader's anus. You know when you're cheating an ending because it feels just like cheating on a test: It's a technical success but some kind of spiritual, moral failure. For the record, many twist endings (including the endings to many murder mysteries) are a total cheat. Cheat is generally related to plot above anything else, but you can cheat a character, too.

11. Sometimes It Pays to Get a Little Messy

It's like that sexual phenomenon where people have sex in big piles of sloppy food? Okay, now that I say it out loud, it's nothing like that. Just the same, sometimes an ending needs to be messy, complicated, just a kick to the nuts where it leaves some questions unanswered and expects a lot of work and trust from the audience. This is a hard ending to pull off, by the way—but you generally know when a story deserves a complex ending because the story itself is complex. A simple fairy tale would do poorly with a messy ending, and a messy moral treatise would do poorly with a neat and simple ending. The tenor of your story will help to determine the tone of the ending.

12. Final Destination

A tip: Concoct the ending of your story before you begin writing. Outliners and planners do this already, for the most part, but pantsers may begin without a clear ending in mind. Having an ending—if only that—in mind allows you rove all over the map but still know where the story is going. "The knight kisses the damsel, and together they hold hands and drive the Jeep up into the dragon's butthole and everybody explodes. *Everything must add up to that.*"

13. Ain't Over Till the Fat Penmonkey Sings (and Maybe Drinks Himself Into a Blackout)

All that being said, no ending is written until … well, until it's written. Conceiving of an ending before you write the story does not somehow mystically lock you into it, trapping you in a sigil-ridden prison of your own design. It's just an idea. Once you get there and cross that threshold, you'll see if the ending stays or if a new ending has written itself into existence. In my experience, some piece of the original ending tends to remain even if the rest changes.

14. Dominoes Tumbling Ineluctably Forward

An ending should feel natural. Like it's the only ending you could write. That's nonsense, of course—you have a theoretically infinite number of endings you could write—but *as you write*, all the elements will start to feel like they're moving toward one thing, one place where they all intersect. Once you write it and once the audience reads or sees it, they should all feel like it's the only ending the story deserves—an unswerving and inarguable narrative conclusion.

15. Momentum Is Some Powerful Shiznit

Know that some endings will almost literally write themselves. You cross the Rubicon, and it's like a log flume ride where you're riding not on water but rather a giant chute slick with Astroglide. A lot of the time my daily writing output easily doubles when writing an ending. This doesn't mean the ending's any *good*—but it does indicate that your vision and direction is clear as polished glass.

16. Every Ending Has a Face

And that face is the face of the character. Remember that an ending may technically be about plot but characters are our vehicle through the story—what matters most is that the ending ties up their arc. Nothing leaves me feeling less satisfied than when an ending is pure plot mechanics and leaves character questions or concerns on the table, ensuring that the protagonist's arc is naught but a sad, sputtering, pleasureless ejaculation. Pbbbbt.

17. Welcome to Trenton

It's the journey, not the destination. That's what they say. However, you can take the most beautiful drive in the world, but if it takes you to a downtown Trenton bus terminal as your final destination, then that's one trip I won't be making, thanks. Imagine eating a truly delicious bowl of soup, and then *right at the end* the waiter hocks a phlegmy spit-gob into your mouth. Ruins the meal, yeah? Yeah. A bad ending will be the thing the audience remembers. So don't spit in their mouths at the culmination of the meal.

18. Good Example of Bad Endings: Most Video Games

Seriously, so many video games have total bullshit endings. They always seem so rushed, so hurried, like all the energy went into the Last Boss Battle but not the story of the game you've been invested in for thirty hours. So many video game endings are like watching a balloon deflate and then get caught in the ceiling fan. If you want a lesson in shitty endings, play a bunch of video games to fruition. Learning about bad endings helps you understand how to formulate good ones.

19. You Will Be Mule-Kicked Off Your Soapbox, Moralizer

Don't let the ending be a sermon. It's okay if it makes a point, especially if that point is braided into the subtext. But if it's you getting up on your soapbox and screaming about some moral lesson, then you should be ashamed of yourself. And tasered, frankly.

20. To Genre or Not to Genre

Genre comes replete with expectations. Romance novels generally end with the two principal characters getting together, for example. Slasher films often end with one female survivor and a number of other conceits (oh hey, he's not dead—watch out). It's up to you whether you're going to stick with conventions and tropes or defy them. For my money, defy any and all conventions if they're what's best for your story. Then again, it's not my money that's going to publish you, izzit?

21. The Tightrope Bridge Between "Surprising" and "Expected"

We want to be surprised at the end, yet we also want the ending to operate within some expected parameters. It's a hard line to walk, and you've no easy way to walk it. I liken it to the experience one has at a haunted house. You walk in and you know you're going to be scared and startled, but you don't know how and you don't know when—the surprise operates somehow within expectations. Like I said, tricky but doable.

22. Sobs and Smiles

The best thing you can say about an ending is that it made you happy you read it but sad that it's over. It really is that simple.

23. It's Calling From Inside the House

If you're having trouble figuring out the ending, it usually means that something is wrong earlier in the draft—maybe all the way back to the beginning. This is a common screenwriting "truism" where many will suggest that a problem with the third act indicates problems in the first. This is sometimes true but I imagine it's just as likely that you might have a problem smack dab in the middle or even in the run up to the final act. It's like sciatica pain: I've got pain radiating down to my widdle toesy-woesies because of a nerve getting rubbed the wrong way somewhere in my goddamn hip. The location of the pain is not always the cause of said pain.

24. Go Big, or Go Home

The ending of your story should show no fear. It should aim big and seek to be more than the sum of its parts—that doesn't mean big as in *event, explosion, cataclysm*, but rather, big as in risky, unafraid, willing to pull no punches. It should go beyond just tying up plot ends. An ending says something about the story and the characters. It also says something about you, the author.

25. Must Satisfy You Above All Others

You'll know if the ending works. You'll know because you're happy with it. It's that simple. The ending lights up like Baghdad during the war, and your jaw drops, the curtains close, and you feel part of something much bigger and much weirder than yourself—the mighty power of storytelling, a power embodied by the conclusion of narrative. The ending to any story is a potent moment, a supercharged dose of a story's capability to make you feel something and to leave you reeling, wondering, *feeling*. You're the first line of defense in the story, and if the ending works for you, that's a good sign.

25 THINGS YOU SHOULD KNOW ABOUT EDITING, REVISING, AND REWRITING

1. Forging the Sword

The first draft is basically just you flailing around and throwing up. All subsequent drafts are you taking that barf and molding it into shape. Except, ew, that's gross. Hm. Okay. Let's pretend you're the Greek God Hephaestus, then. You throw up a lump of hot iron, and that's your first draft. The rewrites are when you forge that regurgitated iron into a sword that will slay your enemies. Did Hephaestus puke up metal? He probably did. Greek myths are weird.

2. Break It to Fix It

Pipe breaks. Water damage. Carpet, pad, floor, ceiling on the other side, furniture. You can't fix that with duct tape and good wishes. Can't just repair the pipe. You have to get in there. Tear shit out. Demolish. Obliterate. Replace. Your story is like that. Sometimes you find something that's broken through and through—a cancer. And a cancer needs to be cut out. New flesh grown over excised tissue.

3. It's Cruel to Be Kind

You will do more damage to your work by being merciful. Go in cold. Emotionless. Scissors in one hand, silenced pistol in the other. The manuscript is not human. You are free to torture it wantonly until it yields what you require. You'd be amazed at how satisfying it is when you break a manuscript and force it to kneel.

4. The Aspiration of Reinvention

I'm not saying this needs to be the case, and it sounds horrible now, but just wait: if your final draft looks nothing like your first draft, for some bizarro reason you feel really accomplished. It's the same way that I look at myself now and I'm all like, "Hey, awesome, I'm not a baby anymore." I mean, except for the diaper. What? It's convenient. And surprisingly comfortable.

5. Palate Cleanser

Take time away from the manuscript before you go at it all tooth and claw. You need time. You need to wash that man right out of your hair. Right now, you either love it too much or hate its every fiber. You're viewing it as the writer. You need to view it as a reader, as a distant third-party editor flying in from out of town who damn well don't give a shit. From subjective to objective. Take a month if you can afford it. Or write something else. Even a short story will serve as a dollop of sorbet on your brain-tongue to cleanse the mind palate. Anything to shift perspective from "writer" to "reader."

6. The Bugshit Contingency

You'll know if it's not time to edit. Here's a sign: You go to tackle the edit, and it feels like your head and heart are filled with bees. You don't know where to start. You're thinking of either just walking away forever or planting a narrative suitcase bomb in the middle of the story and blowing it all to H-E-Double-Hockey-Sticks. That means you're not ready. You're too bugshit to go forward. Ease off the throttle, hoss. Come back another time, another way. Cool down.

7. The Proper Mindset

Editing, revising, and rewriting require a certain mindset. That mindset is, "I am excited to destroy the enemy that resists good fiction; I am ready to fix all the shit that I broke; I am eager to shave off barnacles, burn off fat and add layers of laser-proof steel, and get this bastard in fit, fighting shape so that no other story may stand before it." You gotta be hungry to rend the flesh from your own work in the name of good storytelling.

8. Go in With a Plan, or Drown in Darkness

You write your first draft however you want. Outline, no outline, finger-painted on the back of a Waffle House placemat in your own feces, I don't care. But if you go to attack a rewrite without a plan in mind, you might as well be an orangutan humping a watermelon. How do you know what to fix if you haven't identified what's broken? This isn't time for intuition. Have notes. Put a plan in place. Surgical strike.

9. Don't Rewrite in a Vacuum

You write the first draft in isolation. Just you, your keyboard, a story, and a whole lot of wild-eyed gumption. All other drafts are part of a team initiative. SWAT, kicking in windows, identifying perps. Beta readers, editors, agents, wives, friends, itinerant strangers, hostages, whatever. Get someone to read your nonsense. Get notes. Attend to those notes. Third parties will see things you do not.

10. Embrace the Intervention of Notes

When you get notes, it's tough. It's like coming home and being surrounded by friends and family who want you to sit down and listen as they talk about getting you unfettered from your addiction to obscure 80s hair-bands and foul Lithuanian pornography. But listen to those notes. They may be hard, but they're both instructive and constructive. They are a dear favor, so do not waste them.

11. But Also, Check Your Gut

When someone says "Follow your gut," it's because your intestinal tract is home to an infinite multitude of hyperintelligent bacterial flora. It knows what's up; you merely need to tune in to its gurgling frequency. If you get notes or need to make decisions and they don't feel exactly right, check the gut. Here's the thing, though. Notes, even when you don't agree, usually point out something about your manuscript. It may highlight a flaw or a gap. But it can also be instructive in the sense that each note is a test, and if you come up more resolute about some part of your manuscript, that's okay, too. Two opinions enter one opinion leaves. Welcome to Chunderdome.

12. When in Doubt, Hire an Editor

Editors do not exist to hurt you. They exist to hurt your manuscript. In the best way possible. They are the arbiters of the toughest, smartest love. A good editor shall set you—and the work—free.

13, Multitasking Is for Assholes

It is the mark of the modern man if he can do multiple things at once. He can do a PowerPoint presentation and mix a martini and train a cat to quilt the Confederate flag all at the same time. Your story will not benefit from this. Furthermore, it's not a "one shot and I'm done" approach. This isn't the Death Star, and you're not Luke in the X-Wing. You have to approach a rewrite in layers and passes. Fix one thing at a time. Make a dialogue pass. A description pass. A plot run. You don't just fix it with one pull of the trigger, nor can you do ten things at once.

14. Not Always About What's on the Page

Story lives beyond margins. It's in context and theme and mood—incalculable and uncertain data. But these vapors, these ghosts, must line up with the rest, and the rest must line up with them.

15. Content, Context, Then Copy

Behold the layer cake of editing. Start with content: character, plot, description, dialogue. Move to context: those vapors and ghosts I just told you about. The final nail in the revision coffin is copy: spelling, grammar, all those fiddly bits, the skin tags and hangnails and ingrown hairs. Do these last so you don't have to keep sweeping up after yourself.

16. Evolution Begins as Devolution

Two steps forward, one step backward where you fall down the steps and void your bowels in front of company. Here is a common, though not universal, issue: You write a draft, identify changes, and choose a direction to jump—and the next draft embodies that direction. And it's the wrong direction. The second draft is worse than the first draft. That's fine. It's a good thing. Definition through negative space. Now you can understand your choices more clearly. Now you know what not to do and can defend that.

17. Two Words: Track Revisions

You know how when there's a murder they need to recreate the timeline? 10:30 AM, murderer stopped off for a pudding cup, 10:45 AM, victim took a shit in the ball pit at Chuck E. Cheese, etc.? Right. Track the timeline of your revisions. Keep a record of them all. First, if your word processor allows you to track changes and revisions, do that. If your program doesn't (Word and Final Draft both do), then get one that does. Second, any time you make a revision change, mark the revision and save a new file. I don't care if you have 152 files by the end of it. You'll be happy if you need to go back.

18. Spreadsheets, Yay!

Spreadsheets seem anathema to writing, because writing is "creative." Well, rewriting is clinical and strategic. A spreadsheet can help you track story beats, theme, mood, characters, plot points, quirks and foibles, conflicts, and so on. Any narrative component can be tracked by spreadsheet. Here's one way: Track narrative data per page or word count. "Oh, this character drops off the map for these ten pages of my script." "This plot needs a middle bit here around the 45,000-word mark." "Not nearly enough laser guns and elf porn at the turn of the third act."

19. A Reiteration Of Opinion Regarding "Creativity"

If you looked at that note about spreadsheets and thought something-something blah blah blah about how it will destroy your creativity and ruin the magic of the story, then form hand into fist and punch self in ear. If you need every day of writing to be a nougat-filled boat ride through Pez-brick tunnels of creativity, you're screwed. Rewriting is hard. Creative comes from "create," and often, revision is about destruction. In other words, harden the hell up, Strawberry Shortcake, 'cause the boat ride's about to get bumpy.

20. Put the Fun in Fundamentals

You can't revise if you don't know how to write. Same if you don't know the tenets of a good story. How would you fix basic goddamn problems if you can't find them in the first place?

21. A Trail of Dead Darlings

Don't misread that old chestnut, "Kill your darlings." Too many writers read this as, "Excise those parts of the work that I love." That would be like, "Find the most attractive feature on your body, and cut it off with garden shears." You should leave the parts you love intact ... provided they work. Killing your darlings is about that word: *darling*. Elements that are precious, preening peacocks, that exist only to draw attention to themselves? Those are the components that deserve an ice axe to the back of the brainstem.

22. Look for These Things and Beat Them to Death, Then Replace

In no particular order: Awkward and unclear language. Malapropisms. Punctuation abuse. A lack of variety in sentences. A lack of variety in the page's structure. Plot holes. Inconsistency (John wears a porkpie hat on page 70, but a ferret coiled around his head on page 75). Passive language. Wishy-washy writing. Purple prose. An excess of adverbs. Bad or broken formatting. Clichés. Wobbly tense and/or POV. Redundant language. Run-on sentences. Sentence fragments. Junk language. Cold sores. Mouse turds. Light switches that don't turn anything on. Porno mustaches. Dancing elves.

23. Clarity Above Cleverness, or, "How Poetry Lives in Simplicity"

Poetry gets a bad rap. Everyone always assumes it's the source of purple, overwrought language, like it's some kind of virus that infects good clean American language and turns it into something a poncey eleventh-grade poet might sing. Poetry lurks in simple language. Great story does, too. You don't need big words or tangled phrasings or clever stunting to convey beautiful and profound ideas. In subsequent drafts, seek clarity. Be forthright in your language. Clarity and confidence should rule your writing, and the revision process is the time to demonstrate this. Write with strength. Write to be understood. That doesn't mean "no metaphors." It just means, "metaphors whose beauty exists in their simplicity."

24. Don't Make Me Say It Again: Read. Your Shit. Aloud.

I don't care if the dog is looking at you like you're crazy. If you're on the subway, hey, people think you're a mental patient. Oh well. Seriously though, I hate to repeat myself, but I am nothing if not a parrot squawking my own beliefs back at you again and again: Take your work—script, fiction, nonfiction, whatever—and read it aloud. *Read it aloud.* READ IT ALOUD. When you read your work aloud, you'll be amazed at the things you catch, the things that sound off, that don't make sense, that are awkward or wishy washy or inconsistent. Read it aloud, read it aloud, read it aloud, read that bastard *aloud*.

25. Get Clean

Ultimate lesson: Clinging to a first draft and resisting revision is a symptom of addiction—you may be huffing the smell coming off your own stink. The only way you can get clean is when you want to get clean, and the same goes with revisions: You're only going to manage strong and proper revisions when you're eager and willing to do so. Revising and rewriting is the purest, most fanfrackingtastic way of taking a mediocre manifestation of an otherwise good idea and making the execution match what exists inside your head. Your willingness to revise well and revise deep is the thing that will deliver your draft from the creamy loins of the story angels.

PART THREE
PUBLISHING & EARNING YOUR AUDIENCE

25 THINGS YOU SHOULD KNOW ABOUT GETTING PUBLISHED

1. Publishing, Like Barbecue, Takes Time

Publishing should never happen quickly. If it does, get worried. You know how in stories a character experiences a false victory and is all like, "That was too easy?" Yeah. This is like that. Publishing anything takes effort, and effort requires time. Drafts and editors and beta readers and agents and submissions and such. Even self-publishing needs a heavy foot on the brake. Take time with it. Make sure it's right before you barf a bunch of nonsense into the laps of readers. Let your work—and its emergence into the world—come low and slow until it tastes so good you can't feel your legs.

2. The Dog You Choose to Be

This probably sounds dismissive, until maybe you realize I like dogs. Either way, "legacy" publishing is about being a kept dog. A pet, of sorts. You're cared for and fed, and as long as you perform as expected, nobody's taking your ass to the pound. The self-published dog is on his own—free to roam alone or form packs, free to hunt up his own food, free to pee where he wants to pee. This sounds like an easy decision, but keep in mind that many kept dogs are quite happy and many free dogs go feral or are killed.

3. The First Way: Trod the Old Paths

Like it or not, they call it "legacy" or "traditional" publishing for a reason—this is the system that's been in place since Jesus came down from space and taught the Egyptians how to make iPhones. Or something. The point is, this remains the primary path. It has many advantages. Your mother will buy it. It'll be in bookstores (all seven of them). You'll get to have a hard copy. Someone will pay you an advance. You're also likelier (although not guaranteed) to end up with a more professional, polished product. But this path has disadvantages, too. You lose control over the product. You also lose control over the timeframe—legacy publishing moves with all the get up and go of a glacial epoch. Your percentage per book is likely worse, too.

4. The Second Way: Hack Your Own Path Through the Jungle

Self-publishing is, well, duh, when you publish something yourself. Did I really need to spell that out? Some call it "indie," but others hate that because "indie" indicates a publishing company not owned by a Big Wordmongering Biblioconglomerate (aka "The Uber-Pubs" or "The Big Six"). I think of it as micropublishing. It's you, the story, and an outlet. It's both easier and harder than you think. It's easier because in the time it takes to move your bowels, you could upload something, *anything*, to Amazon and put it in the Kindle Marketplace queue. It's harder because here you are thinking you're a writer when you're also a publisher with all the burdens of *being* a publisher. But if you're willing to dance for your dinner, you can start out earning faster than with traditional publishing. Maybe more money. Probably less respect. For now.

5. I Hear You Go Both Ways

Which path to choose? That's between you and your heretic gods, but if you subscribe to my gospel, you'll do both. *One for you, one for you.* Self-publish one thing. Reserve another thing for the legacy route. Some material just won't sell well to publishers, and that's what you put out there yourself. Some stuff is primed for the bigger market, and that's the meaty gobbet that goes to the bigger dogs. The great thing here is, that the legacy publishers are no longer bulletproof and the micropublishers are no longer a nest of tangled pubic hairs wadded up in the bathroom drain. Both are legitimate paths. So walk both to gain the advantages of each. This is the path of the "hybrid" author.

6. Distrust Zealots

Some will tell you legacy publishing is for chumps. Others will tell you self-publishing is for the talentless and eternal guests of the slush pile. Wrong on both counts. Never judge another for their choice of publication route. Writers are part of an ecosystem, and diversity is a feature, not a bug. If you see a zealot, brand them with a hot iron and kick them down the cellar steps. Where the dragon will eat them and then lay dragon eggs in their corpsely orifices.

7. Crap Still Floats

Self-publishing means a flood of new material in the marketplace. Crap floats. I watched a self-published, certifiable piece of shit with six reviews—all one-star ratings—sit on the top ten at Amazon Horror for a good week. Self-pubbers don't like to admit this to be true. But legacy publishers don't like to admit that it's true for them, too—

let us remind them that they published a book by Snooki. Which is like letting a baby chimp teach a class or allowing some kind of sewer-dwelling goblin-folk to babysit your children. Whatever the case, crap floats everywhere. Self-publishing. Legacy publishing. Television. Film. (How big a box office draw is the *Transformers* franchise? Yeah.) Just because its buoyant doesn't mean it's good. Your job is to be both good *and* buoyant.

8. Proxies and Avatars

Publishing is a team effort. You need editors. You want an agent. You can do it without an agent, sure. You can also sell your house without a real-estate agent, drive your car without a seatbelt, and make sweet love to a bucking centaur without wearing a helmet. An agent can help even the self-published author—after all, certain rights remain open for most self-pubbers. Print, foreign, film. Also, your right to party. Nobody can take that away from you.

9. Gatekeepers Do the Reading Body Good

Don't hate the gatekeepers. Even in the legacy-publishing world, they usually represent a modicum of standards. Readers want quality, not undercooked narcissistic offal. In any situation you can put your own gatekeepers in place: Someone who will challenge the work and make sure it's worth publishing—and if it's not worth publishing, either fix it or say screw it.

10. If You Get Screwed, It's by Your Own Ignorant Hand

Here, see this jar? It's got bees in it. But I've labeled it, "FREE MONEY." You're right if you don't see any money in there. It's seriously just a jar of bees. But if you stick your hand in there anyway thinking you're going to get some unclaimed cash, you're going to get stung. Because you're a dummy. In publishing, if you get screwed over, it's your own fault. Get an agent. Manager. Lawyer. Somebody to read contracts.

11. Don't Fear the Query

Sung to the tune of "Don't Fear The Reaper." (More cowbell?) Writing a query can be a misery. Practice writing them. Learn how to sum up your work in a single sentence, a single paragraph, and three paragraphs. You want to know not just what happens, but be able to explain what it's *about*. Agents and publishers want to know why it's awesome, *not* why it's like everything else.

12. Your Default State Is a State of Rejection

You're going to get a lot of rejection. From agents, from publishers. It's par for the course. Rejections are good. Treat them like battle scars, proof you fought the good fight and didn't just piss around on the sidelines. My book *Blackbirds* was lucky to get picked up by an agent after one month but not before a handful of rejections and a lot of no-shows. Then it took a year and a half to get published. Dozens of rejections. All of them arrows to my heart. But where each arrow punctures, the heart grows scar tissue and gets tougher as a result.

13. Your Best Bet Is a Book That Doesn't Suck

Everybody's got tips and tricks to get published. *It's who you know. Get a good blurb. Get a rockstar agent. Consume the heart of a stillborn goat in a ritual circle made of shattered AOL CDs.* The biggest and best chance you have to get published is to write something that not only doesn't suck *but is actually pretty goddamn good.* Go figure.

14. Even So, a Good Book Isn't Enough

I'd be a naive douchematron (a robot that sprays vinegar and water from his face nozzle) if I sat here and told you, "The only thing you need is a great book. Write it, stick it in your drawer, and the publishing fairy will come and sprinkle his magical discharge all over it." You do have to know how to market the book. How to put it out there. How to get it in front of agents, publishers, and readers.

15. Grim Taxonomy

You may not be concerned about genre, but the publishing industry is. They want to know on what shelf it belongs and under what Amazon category. So that means you need to know, too. Though, let me be clear: This is not a precise equation. These are not well-defined margins. Get close enough for horseshoes and hand grenades. I know many authors whose books were one thing but then were labeled as something entirely different for marketing purposes. Just make a stab at it. Don't freak out.

16. Never Give Someone Money to Get You Published

The old saying is, "The money flows to the writer, not *away from* the writer." This is still true, though self-publishing has complicated this snidbit of advice (snidbit = snippet + tidbit). In DIY publishing, you may have to shell out the capital for an editor, a book cover, or an e-book design. But that's not you spending money on getting published. You're not placing cash in the hands of some charlatan. You're spending money on the book in order to get it ready for publication. You're still the one putting it out there. And money should still flow toward you once that occurs. If you're just a writer, money flows to you. If you are *also* the publisher, money will be spent.

17. Dudes With Guns, Chicks With Swords

If you are a traditionally published fantasy author, you have a 17 percent chance of ending up with a book cover featuring some badass holding a gun or some hot chick holding a sword. Or maybe a battle-axe. She's probably facing away from you and showing you one, maybe both, buttocks. Those buttocks are probably in very tight pants. Your book may be retitled to something like *Demon Slut* or *The Edge Of Steel*. This is why we fight for better covers and gender rights in writing and publishing.

18. Trends Move Faster Than You, So Run the Other Way

You know what's hot right now? Frankenstein strippers. You know what'll be hot next week? Occult epistolaries. The week after that? Pterodactyl erotica. You don't know what's going to be hot by the time you finish that book and get an agent and the agent starts shopping that book around. So just write what you want to write, and make it the best damn book anybody's ever read.

19. Yeah, a Sock Full of Quarters, Bitch! Woo!

What I'm saying is, you won't automatically get rich in publishing. But you can make a passable living or better. Feed your kids. Pay your mortgage. As long as you're willing to write like your fingers are on fire. If you think you can live on one book a year, then you clearly believe your name rhymes with K. J. Schmowling. And I bet it doesn't.

20. The Midlands of the Midlist

Midlist isn't a dirty word. They may not be bestsellers, but they justify their existence. Midlist is a sign of a working author. An author who puts herself out there. Respect to the midlist. *pours toner ink on the curb for my homies*

21. All About Maneuverability

Small publishers don't necessarily move faster than big publishers—but they can turn on a goddamn dime. The same way a little boat can drive circles around a steamship. This is worth considering. Of course, some smaller publishers don't have the infrastructure or cash flow to keep that boat afloat, too. This is also worth considering.

22. Publishing Is Just the Beginning

You get published, and you're not done. You've got more books to write. Promo to do. Interviews. Book signings. That's just the start of it. That's a good thing, though. Makes sure you do more than sit in your cave and bleed words from your eyeholes. That said, you still need to get back in that cave and cry out more words. Otherwise, who are you? Harper Lee?

23. If You Stare Too Long Into the Publishing Abyss, the Publishing Abyss Pees in Your Eye

The publishing industry is the lava eye of Sauron, the sucking, sandy mouth of the Sarlacc pit. If you gaze too long or get too close, it'll suck you in. At the end of the day, your job isn't to be distracted by the industry because that will start to eat your soul. Your primary identifier is still *storyteller*, so that's what you do. I mean, unless you're that guy who sells *One Million E-Books*, because that guy's not a storyteller; he's a human spam-bot.

24. What I'm Trying to Say Is, Shut Up and Write

Your job is to write. Write like you don't give a damn about the publishing industry. Write like that—write like you *goddamn mean it*—and you'll find success. Love what you write and write what you want, and you'll find the words come easy and the story comes correct. Don't worry right now so much with the publishing. Worry about writing. The other part will always come after, but by god, the writing has to come first.

25. Oh, and One Last Thing: Never Give Up

Publishing won't happen overnight. Self-publishing *could* (but probably shouldn't) happen that fast, but the epic sales you're after don't happen overnight. Embrace patience, perseverance, stick-to-itiveness. Gotta have a head like a wrecking ball, a spirit like one of them punching clown dummies that always weeble-wobbles back up to standing. This takes time. Stories need to find the right home, the right audience. Stick with it. Push like you're pooping. Quitting is for sad pandas. And this jar of bees is for quitters only.

25 THINGS WRITERS SHOULD KNOW ABOUT AGENTS

1. No, You Don't Need an Agent

Let's just get that out of the way right now. You do not *require* an agent to survive or be successful in this business. If you are without an agent, you will not be shot in the streets by roving gangs of publisher-thugs. It is a myth that you cannot get published or produced without an agent to get you there. You may *want* an agent. (I have one, and I'm happy I do.) But you do not, strictly speaking, require one.

2. Do Some Due Diligence

Heh. Doo-doo. Ahem. What I mean is, do your goddamn homework. Agents get a rap for being elitists or gatekeepers or snobs of the publishing literati, but you have to have some sympathy for what they do:

They open their digital doors to whatever anybody wants to send them. An agent says, "I represent literary fiction," and just the same they get flooded with sci-fi and screenplays and kids' books and long-lost Tesla blueprints and insane schizoid scrawls written in crayon and possum vomit. The agent's job half the time is to pick through the mud-glop slurry to try to find the few potential pearls hidden deep in the mire. If every writer did research and learned to target the right agents for their manuscripts, the whole thing would probably run a lot more cleanly. So do your research. Don't run off half-cocked.

3. Put the "Social" in "Social Media"

Many agents are on social media. (And one might wonder why you'd want an agent who isn't on social media.) Follow them. Find out what they're looking for. Discover whether or not they're closed to submissions. See if they have any pet peeves (like, say, you snail mailing a query filled with glitter and a "mysterious white powder"). You can even— gasp—ask them questions.

4. (But Please Don't Stalk Them)

The rules of our polite society still apply. Don't be crazy. Don't be an asshole. Act like a professional. Do not hide in an agent's shrubs or sneak onto her fire escape. C'mon. We talked about this. Don't be weird.

5. If They Say Jump, You Ask,
"Can I Do a Karate Kick to Show You My Moves?"

Individual agents ask for individual things. This one wants the first chapter. That one wants the first five pages. A third doesn't want any part of your manuscript until requested. A fourth asks that you send him a query while the moon's in Sagittarius and then only via snail mail and using a query letter scented with the musk glands of a pubescent ermine. (Though why you'd want an agent who still only accepts queries via the Pony Express is between you and your Penmonkey Jesus.) If you're going to query a specific agent, perform the particular tasks that agent requires. Your mother thinks you're a rare and beautiful bird. An agent just thinks you're another cuckoo.

6. Repeat After Me: "Money In, Not Money Out"

You do not pay an agent. If an agent asks for money to look at your submission or anything like that, you can be sure he's either a) a scam artist or b) *really* bad at his job. You want neither of these things. Your relationship with an agent is the same as it is with a publisher: money in, not money out. They help *you* get paid, and an agent takes a cut of that. Easy-peasy, stung-by-beesy.

7. My Query Formula

I split my query into three portions: the Hook, the Pitch, and the Bio. All bookended by the usual pleasantries, greetings, and gratitude. The Hook is a single-sentence logline that is meant to grab the agent by the short-and-curlies. The Pitch is a subsequent paragraph exploding out the Hook (synopsizing in a single paragraph as opposed to a single sentence). The Bio is a *very short* closing paragraph about you. You want to keep the whole thing contained on a single page, which means around 350–400 words max. You want to write with confidence but not ego. You do not want to presume to tell the agent how to do the agent's job. Simple. Direct. Clear. Confident. And again, blah blah blah, don't be a dick, don't be crazy, this is a professional document, etcetera, and whatever. Oh, QueryShark, and AgentQuery. Google them. Love them.

8. Agents Are Trained to Smell Your Flopsweat

Another note about "confidence:" Agents have powerful sniffers and can smell the stink of your desperation from three blocks away. I've read too many queries that possess this wishy-washy vibe, queries that come spackled with fear and uncertainty and bring this sense of laying prostrate before the pedestal and hoping to be allowed to make with the slobbery ring-kisses. If you think your work is good enough to query, then write the query with that kind of authority. If you don't think that it's good enough to query? Then it probably isn't, so don't waste their time. Or, more importantly, your own.

9. Agents Have Seen Everything, but They Haven't Seen You

Agents have seen it all. They are the first line of defense in the war against Bad Books and Shitty Storytelling. It's a wonder that some of them don't just snap and try to take out half of New York City with a dirty bomb made of radioactive stink-fist query letters and cat-turd manuscripts. That's a scary thought: *They've seen everything already.* But the one thing they haven't seen is you. Just as I exhort authors to put themselves on the page of their stories, I say the same regarding your communication with potential agents. To put it more directly, you have a voice, so use it.

10. The Polite Reminder

You will, at times, send out a query and hear nothing. Many agents will suggest a response time on their agency websites or social media pages, and most are reasonable (though every once in a while you read a whopper: "You will receive a response to your query sometime after the year when we first settle on Mars and start flying to work with jetpacks"). If you pass this window of time and have not heard anything, a very short, polite, and totally not-crazy reminder is entirely appropriate. If you don't hear anything after that, well—maybe it's time to write that agent off and concentrate your fire on another star destroyer.

11. You Manuscript Is Not a Half-Eaten Cupcake

Do not try to query an incomplete and unedited manuscript. Don't. Don't. Seriously. Behold my steely gaze and my all caps: DON'T. You wouldn't try to sell somebody a half-eaten cupcake. If you're fortunate enough that the agent requests a full manuscript, you best be ready to deliver on that delightful demand. Oh, and make sure it's formatted correctly, okay? I don't know that an agent will toss your shit in a trash can just because the manuscript font is Times New Roman instead of Courier (I think mine *was* in TNR, actually), but they *will* ditch it if the formatting makes reading it feel like you're burning your eyes with lit cigarettes.

12. Agents Are Readers

It's easy to imagine agents as iron-hearted gatekeepers guarding the gates of Publishing Eden with their swords of fire, marketing angels serving the God of the Almighty Dollar. Most of the agents I know and have met are readers first. They do this because they love this, not because it pays them in private jets and Jacuzzis filled with forty-year Macallan Scotch. They like to read. They love books. Which is awesome.

13. That Said, This Is a Business

Agents are called upon to make business decisions, too. That's the sad fact of the penmonkey existence: Your wordsmithy may be top notch; your storytelling may be the bee's pajamas, but if doesn't seem like it'll survive in the marketplace, then that's just how the dung-ball rolls. They make these decisions based on what one assumes is past experience, current trends and a dollop of gut instinct. Just the same, it doesn't mean they're right—it's not like they run your manuscript through a Publi-Bot 9009 and BEEP BOOP BEEP he computes the chances of your manuscript being a success or failure. Rejections from agents that suggest the story and writing are solid but are unsure whether the story will sell is a sign to do one of three things: keep querying, try out some smaller publishers, or self-publish.

14. Your Heartbreak Is Their Heartbreak

Agents understand rejection. They have to—they go through it, same as you do. They rep authors and those authors' books, and they write pitch letters the same as you write query letters. They send those letters out to editors and they go through rejection same as you. They may be one step removed (as in, an agent did not write the book), but they've invested time and patience and blood and sweat into it, too. A book they rep that gets rejected is sad for them same as it's sad for you—and not just as lost money.

15. Hot Author-on-Author Action

Author referrals matter. They are not the end-all, be-all of everything, but I know of many authors who ended up with agents when another author recommended them. That said, don't cozy up to authors on the sole hope they'll refer you to an agent—that's a little sleazy. You gotta at least buy them drinks and dinner first. Me, I demand nothing less than a Tijuana panther show. What? You don't know about panther shows! Pssh. Donkey shows are so...*passé.*

16. A Deal in Hand Is Better Than
a Bird in Hand Because, Y'know, Bird Poop

This is one of those paradoxical conundrums like, "Every job requires experience, but a job is the only way to get experience." The story goes that it's easier to get an agent if you already have a deal, but of course a lot of publishers don't offer deals to unagented authors. (Further twisting the nipple are these stories that pop up: "I had a deal in hand, went to agents, and they still turned me down.") If you can get a deal pre-agent, then it's a good time to get an agent—but, just the same, don't believe anybody who tells you that it's a necessary component. I, among many authors, did not have a deal in hand and yet still found an agent.

17. The Bones of Literary Agents and Dodo Birds

Are literary agents going to go extinct in the New Publishing Media Regime? Hell if I know. What am I, an oracle? Sure, I sometimes huff printer ink and decipher the secret hidden meanings in coffee grounds and mouse scat, but that doesn't mean I have a good answer here. My guess is that agents aren't going anywhere, just as the whole of the publishing industry isn't going anywhere. It may slim down. It may cull those who are not forward thinking. It may force them to adopt new roles. But I do not believe literary agents are on the endangered list. Now pass the printer ink. DADDY NEEDS TO GET GOOFY.

18. Some Agents Are Total Jerkpants

Rant time. Some agents get a reputation as cold and callous rainmaking gatekeepers because they act like it. Not every agent is the shining embodiment of good-hearted, book-reading, do-it-'cause-we-love-it folk. Some agents won't write you back. Some will snark off about authors on social media (agents, seriously, please don't do this—just as you wouldn't want an author to do this to you, you shouldn't do this to an author). Some will string you along. When I went out to agents with my first book, *Blackbirds*, I was a little amazed that while agents demand professional behavior, several chose not to be professional in return—and we're talking agents who belong to big agencies, not talking about some sleazy bookmonger from Detroit. Some strung me along. Some requested full manuscripts while at the same time forgetting I ever existed. Some responded six, even eight months after I already had an agent. I'd say between 10–20 percent of my total experience with agents was negative. The occasional agent is an unprofessional prick.

19. (But That's Just the Way People Are)

One bad agent doesn't make all agents bad. I've seen reprehensible actions by publishers. I've seen asshole authors and woefully unprofessional self-publishers. I've seen bad janitors and terrible teachers, and I'm sure you could find a handful of astronaut jerks, too. Don't let bad examples be representative of the whole.

20. Pick Proper

Just gonna put this out there: A bad agent will do more harm to your career than no agent at all. You must find the right match. Find an agent with whom you get along. Consult your intestinal flora.

21. A Good Agent Cultivates the Author

A good agent cares about the author, not just about the author as a delivery system for a single book (or, perhaps, a single book that comes inconveniently paired with the author). The right agent has your career in mind. The right agent buys you liquor and puppies. Okay, maybe not so much with the liquor and puppies. But if any agents are reading this, I'm just saying: Let's all get on board the liquor-and-puppies train.

22. A Good Agent Defends the Writer Against the System

I don't mean to get all Rage-Against-The-Machiney on you, but the traditional publishing system can, at times, be a bit predatory. This is by no means universal, but once in a while you hear a real horror story about an author who ends up signing a contract that basically guarantees that if his book makes it into print, they're allowed to pay him in Doritos and, oh, by the way, they get a first look deal on his next 152 books. An agent defends the author against such predation. An agent helps the author not just get a good deal but the best deal. An agent makes sure the author doesn't get screwed over.

23. A Good Agent Is Savvy Toward the Future

Agents who look down on new media? BZZT. Agents who look down on self-publishing? BZZT. Agents who are afraid of digital? BZZT. Authors need to be much more versatile and media savvy in this day and age to survive, and agents have to do the same. Don't sign on with a backward-looking agent. You want an agent who knows how to duck and roll, not stand there and get punched.

24. Sometimes You Need to Break Up

If your agent isn't working for you or you're not simpatico with the agent, maybe it's time for an old-fashioned breakup. It happens. It has to be hard to do (I've never done it and have no reason to do so), but why stay in a business relationship that isn't serving either of your needs? Just don't send a drunken text at 3:30 in the morning. Have some class. Go there in person and throw a potted plant through their window! (Okay, maybe don't do that either. What do I know? I'm drunk right now!) Be professional is what I'm saying.

25. One Word: Symbiosis

The relationship between writer and agent is a two-way street. While it's true that the agent works for you and you don't work for the agent, this is still a relationship based on mutual gain—neither is the other's bitch, but both should listen to and respect the other, even if it is the author who has final say (as it is the author's life and career). I'm not suggesting that the author is *crocodile* and the agent is *little bird who picks the croc's teeth*, but I am suggesting that each feeds off the relationship in positive ways. If you find that the relationship isn't symbiotic, then maybe it's time to take another look at #24, dontcha think?

25 THINGS YOU SHOULD KNOW ABOUT QUERIES, SYNOPSES, AND TREATMENTS

1. Everyone Hates It (and Nobody's Great at It)

Writing a summary of any creative endeavor makes every writer feel like he's wearing a tuxedo made of bumblebees. It's a very uncomfortable process, and any writer who tells you how much she enjoys writing synopses should be immediately shoved in a bag and burned because she is a robot from the future sent here to destroy all writers' self-esteem. Why would we enjoy the process? We just wrote a whole screenplay or an entire novel. And now we're supposed to compress it down until it fits in the palms of our hands? *Goddammit.* It blows. It's difficult. Nobody does it 100 percent. But you gotta suck it up and do the work.

2. Put This Pig in That Bucket

A one hundred-pound pig will not fit in a five-pound bucket, yet that is your task. You must identify all the parts of the pig that you cannot live without. The rest? Chainsawed into bloody gobbets and left on the abattoir floor. You're not here to explore the whole pig. You're here to give a sampling of the beast—a *taste of pigness*. The hoof, snout, squeal, and tail are for later. For now you need to deliver a packet of *prime cuts* only.

3. Excuse Me While I Whip This Out

Length matters. A query letter is never more than a page. A synopsis or treatment is maybe two to ten pages, though some treatments are as long as sixty. A beat sheet for a script is maybe 10 percent of the total document (or six pages/hour). Identify the length, and stick to it. Though, like with a certain *dangling male organ*, it's not just how long it is, but what you do with it. For instance, my dangling male organ kills hooded cobras, like a mongoose.

4. The Shallowest Reader in the World

You know how if you're writing epic fantasy it helps sometimes to read epic fantasy? Well, what do you think this is? You're trying to summarize your work, so read summaries of other works. And book jackets and DVD cases are exactly that. True story: The book jacket for my novel *Double Dead* features text pulled straight from my synopsis. The text on a book jacket or DVD case (or video game case or Amazon description) is meant to entice. Which is also your job when writing a query, synopsis, or treatment.

5. Egg Samples

You need to find examples of good—meaning, *successful*—treatments, queries, and synopses. Grab them from writer friends. Dig them up online. Discover what feels successful about them. Mine and mimic.

6. Get Goofy on Rainforest Drugs, and Explore Core Truths

I often phrase this as, *What the hell is it about, maaaan?* As in, if you were sitting around a drum circle or some shit and you were stoned out of your gourd on some weird powder made from pulverized elk bezoar and someone grabbed you by the collar of your ratty tie-dyed robe and they asked you that question, what would you say? Not the basic plot but dig deep for what it's *really* about, what it *means to you*. The essence of that answer must be present in your truncated treatment. Because it matters. It's one of the things that elevates it from a rote recitation of plot to an exploration of story.

7. Bottle All the Lightning

Another fun exercise: Go through your novel or script, and start identifying all the things that you think are—caps necessary—GODDAMN AWESOME. The knees of the bees, the hat of the cat. Action scenes, plot turns, character foibles. Any of that. Call it out. Write it down. It won't all go into your synopsis, but it helps to have an arsenal of Awesome Things to call out, don't you think?

8. We Come for the Character ...

That sounds dirty, doesn't it? Well, go towel off, we have things to discuss. What's true for your overall story is true for any synopses of that story: Character matters most. Good characters serve as our vehicle through the story, so it must in part be our vehicle through any treatment. Distill those characters down, and make sure we know who they are and what arcs they travel.

9. ... We Stay for the Conflict

Readers are dicks. We want to read about bad shit. We don't want to read about how Sally didn't study and got an A on her test. We want to see sad li'l Sally put through her paces. "She's poor and her textbook was eaten by coyotes and the teacher hates her because he's dating Sally's mother. *How will she ever get an A on her test*?" Conflict is the food that feeds the reader. Any query, treatment, or synopsis must showcase conflict.

10. Heh Heh Heh, He Said "Tentpole"

You will want to include in any synopsis the tentpole plot points—those plot points that hold up the story. Plot points that, were they not included, would bring the whole story ("the tent") down around your ears.

11. Talk That Shit Out

Before you write, vocalize. Sit down with somebody you trust—friend, family member, agent, basement-dwelling cannibalistic hobo—and babble out your synopsis. Have a few drinks. Figure out how you'd sell a buddy (or a man-eating hobo) on your story. Keep pitching it to them. Hone your approach. Write it down. Harness what you learned, and incorporate it into any synopses you must write.

12. Act Structures and Outlines

Maybe you did an outline before you wrote. Maybe you didn't. Doesn't matter now because you need to grasp the architecture of this thing. Act structures and outlines help you get your hands around a story in terms of summarizing and—behold my brand-new made-up word—*succinctifying*. I always exhort writers to grow cozy with writing outlines because, trust me when I tell you, someone's going to ask for one. And when they do, you don't want to be left wide eyed and whimpering.

13. The Logline Is Your Best Friend

Wait, you don't know what a logline is? Take your story. Summarize it in a single-sentence pitch. But it's more than that, too—you're trying to sell the story, trying to give an aura of mystery and possibility. A good logline hits at around fifty words. Go to one hundred words and it's likely too long. Learning to write a logline is important. Take the logline. Hold it close. Nuzzle it to your neck like a cuddly ferret. If you treat it right, it'll coo and burble. If you treat it wrong, it'll spray piss in your mouth and bite off your earlobe.

14. Sharpen That Hook

A bad hook makes for a bad query, treatment, or synopsis. Every molecule in your marrow resists this: Your script or novel is not built on so flimsy a foundation as a single line of marketing text, but I am sad to remind you that life is not fair. Puppies are not immortal, rivers don't run foamy with ice cream, and you don't get free porn every time you pay your taxes. Life is tough. So learn to whet the hook to an eye-gouging point. The hook must be the promise of the premise—the core thing that's awesome about the idea. The thing that *grabs* people. *The Sixth Sense* has an easy hook: A kid has the ability to see ghosts and help them move onto the other side.

15. The "Explode It Out" Method

Summarize your story in one sentence. Then one paragraph. Then one page. Or do it in reverse: page, paragraph, sentence. Imagine someone's got a gun to your private parts. You gotta do this, or they'll blow your nibbly bits into the carpet. You'll soon see what is essential and what is not. Learn to pare down until only its heart remains.

16. Embrace the Holy Trinity: Hook, Body, Climax

Open with a hook: a real juicy logline. Then move into the body: your story laid bare. Sum up the ending in the same way you wrote the hook: A single sentence that delivers the final kidney-rupturing punch. I've seen some advice that says some agents or producers don't want to hear the ending. Unless you know this for sure, I'd say make sure you give it to them—or at least suggest what happens. It's a significant piece of the story puzzle.

17. The Saggy, Fatty Middle

The danger of a novel or a script is the same danger you run into with a synopsis: the saggy, soggy middle. Tighten that shit up. Find the boring parts, and cut them out *or* rewrite so they're a dose of meth instead of a mist of sinister sleep gas. Be advised: Writing a synopsis can suddenly highlight secret problems in your story. Don't let that freak you out. Embrace the opportunity to go back and do some repair work.

18. Stick That Landing

The ending in the synopsis should be as lean and mean as the hook. Maybe fifty words. Maybe one hundred. If the hook is the promise of the premise, then summarizing the ending is the fulfillment of that promise pistoned through the reader's brainpan.

19. Still True: "Show, Don't Tell"

You're not standing in front of your intended audience (editor, agent, producer, executive) and reading a menu of options. You're grabbing their hand, kicking down the door to your storyworld, and showing them what you've built. Always write your synopses from a place of wonder and potential, not from a podium where you deliver a sullen reiteration of your work. You want to excite them! You do not want to bore them.

20. Your Voice Matters

What's going to elevate your synopsis from being as dull as regurgitated cardboard? Your voice. Specifically, the same voice used to write the novel in the first place. Your synopsis is not the place for a dry recitation of plot points (*and then, and then, and then, and then*), but rather, a place for your words to bring the story to life in a different context. Put yourself into the synopsis just as you put your heart into the story.

21. Beware Strip Mining

You've taken your pig, blown him apart with a hand grenade, and fit what you could in the bucket. Suddenly you realize that the value of in *this* pig isn't the loin chops but rather in the squeal. Writing a synopsis sometimes reveals that you've gone the wrong direction. You've taken the best parts out. You've chosen to embody the wrong emotions. You've strip mined the soul out of the thing, and now it's just a hollow exercise. Time to go back and rewrite the synopsis so that you make it engaging and emotionally compelling.

22. Go Back Over It With a Magnifying Glass and a Scalpel

Always re-read your queries, treatments, and synopses again and again. It is your warhorse leading the charge, and if it's an out-of-shape nag with a herniated disc and a bad case of Bell's palsy, then it's not going to survive the coming battle. Read and edit, and read and edit. Then give it to someone else, and let them read and edit, read and edit. Compress that lump of coal until it is a throat-cutting diamond.

23. You Are Not a Pretty Pony

Different recipients want different things. If an agent specifies that she doesn't want an author bio, then do not include an author bio. If guide-lines say, "A ten-page synopsis," then it's your job to give ten pages of straight-up synopsizing. You're not the only pretty peacock in the room. Don't stand out by giving your middle finger to the rules. Stand out by writing a kick-ass query for an even kick-assier story.

24. Vaporlock Is Your Enemy

Paralysis of the analysis: Writing synopses will freeze a writer's brain. You can try all manner of thought exercise, but in the end the only way to the other side is the same as it is with any project: Write your way through the swamp no matter how stridently the mire sucks at your boots. Stomp forth sloppily. Remember that it's okay for your first synopsis to suck. You aren't beholden to just one draft. You get as many at-bats as you need, slugger.

25. In the End, It's About Making People Want More

This is really where writers buck at their chains: For the purposes of this list, a query, synopsis, or treatment is a sales tool. You're trying to get people to buy what you're selling. It is enticement. It is *tantalization*. You're dangling lush grapes, trying to lure someone to take a bite. In the end you think, *this is not what I do, this is a distillation of my work and isn't what I signed up for.* Only problem? It *is* what you signed up for. Storytelling is always an act of enticement and, furthermore, is frequently an act of whittling and winnowing until the best of the story remains and the worst is burned to ash. Sometimes it just takes a reconfiguration of thought. Look at your query as just a smaller version of what you already do, which is to say: Look at it as yet another act of storytelling. Because that's what a synopsis is—it's you telling your story. Except instead of three hundred pages you get, say, ten. Or five. Or one. Hey, nobody said it was going to be easy.

25 THINGS YOU SHOULD KNOW ABOUT SELF-PUBLISHING

1. A Sane and Reasonable Part of the Ecosystem
Self-publishing has become a real contender. Major authors are self-publishing now (and some authors have become major *through* self-publishing). It is now a very real part of the written word's ecosystem. Some truly excellent self-published storytelling is at work. Anybody who turns up their nose at the practice should be kicked in the junk drawer.

2. Not Better, Not Worse, Just Different
Publishing your own work is no magic bullet; it guarantees nothing and is not a "better" or "smarter" way to go than the more traditional route. It's also not a worse path. Each path has its own thorns and rocks, just as each path offers its own staggering vistas and exhilarating hikes.

Self-publishing gets you out there faster and tends to give you a better return on every copy sold. But it's also a more self-reliant path, putting a lot of work onto your shoulders. The self-published author dances for every dinner.

3. Self-Publishers Can't Just Be Writers
This is true of all writers, really: These days, every author must contribute a deeper share of editing and promotion. But the self-published penmonkey does even more. You're a carnival barker, web designer, customer service agent, CEO, porn fluffer—wait, maybe not that last one. The point is, you're now a publisher, with all the responsibilities that come in the package. Don't want those responsibilities? Don't self-publish.

4. Some Doors Are Presently Shut
Media reviews? Major and not-so-major awards? Foreign and film rights? Libraries? Book signings? *Sexy book-signing groupies*? Not so much. Self-published inkslingers will find that many of these things are not necessarily opportunities that exist for them. Not yet at least. Those doors only open right now to those who sell a great deal.

5. This Is Not the Path Toward Credibility and Respect
You will not find a great deal of credibility and respect in self-publishing your work. Part of this is due to old prejudices. Part of this is due to the fact that self-publishing still represents a vibrant and virulent catalog of glurge and slush. Of course, if you were looking for credibility, you wouldn't be a writer in the first place, would you? If you want respect, go be a zookeeper or a sex worker.

6. Most Self-Published Books Suck
This bears special mention: You'll still find that a lot of self-published books are basically canker sores on the prolapsed anus of good writing, good storytelling, and good publishing. Contrary to what some will

say, this crap *can* and *does* sometimes float: I will from time to time peruse the Kindle Charts and gape in amazement at how superheroically buoyant some garbage can be. And yes, I acknowledge that legacy publishing offers some real stinkers, too. But I thought the goal was to be better than that, yes? And for the record, I have every confidence that every shit-ass celebrity book at *least* meets minimal standards compared to some of the piles of midden that pass for books amongst some self-published authors.

7. Your Book Is a Boat Which Must Ride Upon Sewage

Those ass-tastic self-published books are your competition. But they're the competition of any author. It just bears mentioning that, whether traditionally published or whether you DIY, come to the field with the most kick-ass book you can bring. Don't half-ass it. You're here to tell stories, not pleasure your ego. Let your book rise above all the effluence.

8. Pinocchio Wants to Be a Real Boy, Goddamnit

Treat your book like a real book. Not like it's some part-human, mutant hybrid, some stumbling thing with half a brain and a bison's heart. Send out review copies. Get blurbs. Make it look nice. Sound nice. *Read nice.* Force the book to command the credibility and respect that others of its ilk are lacking. It should look like the best book on the shelves at your local bookstore.

9. Two-Fisted Team-Ups

A good self-published book does not need to be the product of some lone weirdo in a closet discharging his foul-skinned word babies onto the Smashwords marketplace. It comes to fruition with the help of a good cover designer, editor, beta readers, and others within the self-published community. It's why I don't like the phrase *self*-published—you should rely on others beyond yourself to bring your book to life.

10. Money Out Before Money In

For the record, that might mean spending some money. It's worth it. The reward of having a professional-grade product and not the remnant of some amateur-hour karaoke will earn out. Though also be aware that you have no guarantee of recouping those expenses. That's how opening a business works. And being a self-publisher is, in a sense, opening a small business.

11. Please Don't Let Your Cover Look Like
A Three-Fingered Smear Of Dog Shit

So many ugly covers. *So many ugly covers.* Once more for the cheap seats: SO MANY UGLY COVERS. Listen, I know—a cover does not make a book. But it's the first line of offense at a place like Amazon, where I'm almost universally seeing the cover before I'm seeing the description. I will click a kick-ass cover because, I dunno, I'm an attention-deficit raccoon who likes shiny trinkets? A great cover shall be your standard-bearer. If you use Comic Sans or Papyrus on your cover, you should be drowned in a washtub.

12. The Value of an E-Book Designer

A novel may not require much in the way of actual e-book design, and it's easy to get DIY with it. Mobipocket Creator does a nice job creating e-books for Kindle. Caliber does the work, too. Scrivener saves to ePub. Amazon and B&N will both autoformat. That said, more complex books—books with lots of hyperlinks or graphics or any kind of coding—may require that you hire an e-book designer in order to avoid soul-squishing agony.

13. Editors Are Your Bestest Friends

Get a good editor. Can you self-edit? Sure. Is it a good idea? Not usually. Bare minimum: Seek the advice of people you trust, and implement their advice in some way, shape, or form. Give them wine, chocolate, hookers, four-wheelers, and kites made from the skin of their enemies and anything else they ask for. Pay their price, whatever it is. A good editor is your best friend.

14. Traditional Legacy Publishing Is Not Your Enemy

You will find little value in slagging those in traditional publishing, particularly authors, agents, and editors. They're not your enemy. We're all part of the same ecosystem, swimming around in the pond where we a) tell stories and b) hope to not starve and die in the process. Most of us are here because we love what we do, so hold hands, kiss each other on the cheek, and stop casting aspersions. (Same goes for you cats in trad-pub: self-publishers are not peeing in your Wheaties, so relax.)

15. Agents and Gatekeepers Are Still Your Friends

Iconoclasts love to hate on those that keep the gate, but those that keep the gate aren't universally bad people. Furthermore, they're trained to a certain standard. Agents in particular don't deserve scorn, and can, in fact, still help the self-published author. They may know when a book is right for a published market. They may be of aid in selling rights (print, foreign, film) that you otherwise might not have had access to. And let's not mince words: Many self-published authors would jump like a cricket at the chance to have a book on bookshelves with a big publisher. For that, you will find an agent potentially quite helpful.

16. Amazon Is the Eight Hundred- Pound Gorilla (and He's Got a Gun)

If you sell anywhere, you're going to sell at Amazon. Start there. Talking to other self-pubbed authors, the majority of their sales come through Amazon. And since we're talking, if Amazon is the big-ass gorilla in the room, I suppose that makes Smashwords the anemic marmoset who keeps scratching his balls and falling asleep in his own waste. I might not be a fan of Smashwords.

17. The Term "Indie" Makes Some People Vomit Fire

Indie has been a term used in publishing for a while now, meaning a publisher who is not beholden to a Big Faceless Corporation. There is some scorn for those who would use the term—"indie"—to describe self-pubbers. Of course, everybody just needs to pop some quaaludes and calm down. Language changes for better or for worse: The definition of "indie" is a moving target and has been in film, music, and now publishing. We can all share the language. If we can't agree to share, you'll have to fight in the arena with poison-tipped fountain pens. (Besides, a self-publisher happens to be a very small, very independent publisher. What's the problem?)

18. Beware the Insidious Whispers of Froth-Lipped Zealots

Eschew false dichotomies. Avoid loaded promises. Spurn those self-proclaimed oracles who claim to know the future. Nobody knows what the truth is regarding self-publishing or traditional publishing, and anybody who thinks you need to jump one way and not the other may not have your best interests at heart. You have a supercomputer inside your head called a "brain." Use it.

19. This Is the Time for Bold-Faced, Brave-Ass Experimentation

So much of self-publishing is doing what's been done. (Another *Twilight* rip-off? *Tell me more!*) But the advantage of DIY publishing is that you are beholden to no one but an audience—so why not go big? Screw the rules. The hell with the genres. Experiment. Play around with storytelling. Do something different instead of traipsing the same paths. Got a picaresque cyberpunk novel loaded with ciphers and clues in your head that links up to some kind of bizarre geocaching transmedia experiment? Why not? You want to write penguin erotica? *Bible II: Son of Bible*? Go for it. Find those things that no major publisher will touch but you have a passion for, and put them out there.

20. A Future Found in Format

The future of self-publishing isn't merely in storytelling. It's in the format. The format now is a clumsy foal stumbling around on wobbly legs. Find ways to break free from that. It'll be up to the DIY authors to find new formats—transmedia initiatives, app-novels, stories told across social media. Do not be constrained by the formats that exist. Story does not begin and end with a physical book. It doesn't stop at e-books, either.

21. You Are Not a Spam-Bot

Self-publishers have a lot of their own promotional work to do. That means it's very easy to accidentally become naught but a megaphone hawking your wares. While you should never be afraid to ask for sales or market, you need to market as a human being. Connect. Be funny. A lot of this is going to succeed based on that most ephemeral of market drivers: *word-of-mouth*. The way you generate that? Nobody knows. But it starts with writing a kick-ass book. Well, that and human sacrifice. But you can't make an omelet without killing lots of innocent people in the name of dark literary entities living beneath the earth.

22. The Power of Data

Self-publishers need data. But not many vendors are willing to offer it. The best thing you can do for yourself and your fellow self-publishers is seek data and share what you find. Be like Johnny-Five: NEED MORE INPUT.

23. Embrace a Vibrant and Active Community

The self-publishing community is a helpful place, for the most part. It can be quite exuberant and vocal in its support. Discover through this community the best practices. Return the favor. Communicate and converse.

24. But Don't Be a Cheerleader for Crappiness

On the other hand, some elements of the community can be toxic and can act as cheerleaders for self-publishing's own worst instincts. Don't champion a novel just because it's self-published. How it got there is irrelevant to the end result. If it's a good book, then talk about it. If it's shit, then forget it. You have the freedom to self-publish; there's no need to vociferously defend that right. But if you want self-publishing to be real, to earn the respect and credibility you think it deserves, then it needs fewer cheerleaders and more police—people who will call a rat turd a rat turd and not pretend it's a Rice Krispies treat. Self-publishing *also* needs more sexy groupies, since we're talking. Call me.

25. The Nature of Risk

You have to understand the nature of risk when it comes to the two publishing paths. In traditional publishing, you risk time but no money. In self-publishing, time is on your side but you're likely to risk money. Traditional publishing offers (upon acceptance) at least a guarantee of an advance; self-publishing offers only the guarantee of control. Understand the pros and cons of each. I will continue to give the same advice when it comes to the fake bullshit battle between self-publishing and legacy publishing: do both. Write books for each—plant a foot in each world so you may reap the harvest of each.

25 THINGS WRITERS SHOULD KNOW ABOUT BLOGGING

1. Your Digital Penmonkey HQ

Your blog is your authorial headquarters on the web—it is your evil mountaintop lair, your underwater submarine base, your fortress of non-solitude. Everything should spring forth from your blog, and everything should lead to your blog. Think of it as the hub of a wheel, with all other social-media extensions being spokes radiating from that wheel. And then you can throw that wheel like a ninja star and put out your enemies' eyes. Okay, maybe not so much with that last part.

2. Write About What Energizes You

Certainly you, as an author, have Things You Enjoy. Or on the other end of the spectrum, Things That Chafe Your Nuts With The Abrasive Power

Of A Cheese Grater. Point is, you get worked up about stuff both good and bad, so that's what you blog about. Blog about whatever makes your heart aflutter or whatever chaps your sensitive nipples. Everyone will tell you that there exist rules for what a writer should and should not blog about—no religion, no politics—but whoever made those rules thinks the best face an author can give is a blank and harmless stare. The hell with that. Be a person. Have opinions. Blog about what makes you happy, angry, or sad. Just be yourself.

3. Oh, Unless You're a Total Shitbird

Because if you are, maybe it's time to put a false face forward and placate the world with artificial niceties. If you cannot present strong opinions without acting like a dick, then please reevaluate your online strategy.

4. Yes, You Can Write About Writing

One of the supposed cardinal rules is that writers shouldn't have writing blogs, which is absurd on a number of levels. Of *course* you can have a writing blog. Do you think the Blog Police are going to come down to your house and crack you over the head with their Batons of Content Adjustment? (By the way, Batons of Content Adjustment is either the name of my new band or the nickname I give my penis. YOU DECIDE.) Write about writing if you want. Who cares?

5. It's Your Blog, and You Can Cry If You Want To

Use your blog to rant. It's okay. But it helps to learn the fine art of ranting with eloquence so you don't sound like a loon. Another fine art is the magic of self-deprecation. A little bit of self-deprecation goes a long way during any froth-mouthed online rage fest! If bloggers weren't allowed to rant, I don't think we'd have any blogs at all. We'd just have cat videos. An endless armada of cat videos. Which is like that old T.S. Eliot poem says: "This is the way the world ends / this is the way the world ends / this is the way the world ends / not with a bang but with Little Whiskers hiding in the cookie jar being all cute LOL Grumpy Cat yay."

6. Fiber Leads to Regular Blog Movements

Blog regularly. Doesn't have to be every day. Doesn't have to be on a set schedule. But if you want a dynamic online space that serves as an effective Penmonkey Head Office, it helps to circulate fresh content with regularity to keep the hummingbirds coming back to your sugarhole. Also, "Sugarhole" was my nickname in prison.

7. My God, "Blog" Is a Horrible Word

I just need to take a moment and note that, while the word has plainly ensconced itself in our parlance in much the same way that a spiky fish can lodge itself in your pee hole, "blog" is a truly awful word. It calls to mind the sound one makes while purging gurgling beer vomit from your gastrointestinal cauldron. BLOOOOOOG. *sploosh* I really wish we had a better word than "blog." And don't even get me started on "vlog." Sounds like some techno-vampire. "I'm Vlog the Impaler! I vant to pirate your e-books! ONE PIRATED E-BOOK! TWOOOO PIRATED E-BOOKS! THREEEEEEE PIRATED E-BOOKS! AH AH AH."

8. Put Yourself Front and Center

You are your blog, and your blog is a reflection of you. Don't hide that. I get tired of looking at blogs and having no idea who the author is. Crazier still is when they're using an online nickname. "This is the writer journal of Corvid DarkDreaymFyre." Okay, can I buy your books under that name? Then stop it. Be a grown-up. Real names—or, at least, real *author* names—please.

9. Own That Space

I don't mean "own that space" as in, "work it, work it, sashay your bootay all over the place, mmm, yeah, *you own that web-log*, honey."

No, I mean—actually own it. Like, monetarily. Own the content and the shell. Have access to your FTP directory. Control as much of it as you can. Other web services—Tumblr, Blogger, Livejournal—could go south at any time, taking your content with it. Own your content, and back it up regularly.

10. Wordpress Is Nice

I'm just putting that out there. Wordpress installations are very versatile and have lots of free and cheap themes and plug-ins available. I'm not a shill for them or anything. Ignore the fact that my racecar has WORD-PRESS emblazoned upon the side. And by "racecar" I mean "racecar bed." Vroom, vroom! Time to nap my way to the finish line!

11. Spend a Tiny Bit of Money

I spent $40 to get a premium theme from Themeforest, and it really paid off. Site looks nice, I get better access to updates and troubleshooting, and pro-themes tend to be highly customizable. Plus, you're going to have to pay for hosting and such. The great thing is that all this is tax deductible if you're a professional writer.

12. Learn Some Minimal Coding

It helps to know how to modify CSS and HTML, even if only at a minimal level. At first you'll crack open the code behind the blog, and your face will melt—it feels like staring into the green, squiggly rain of The Matrix. But it doesn't take long to read some tutorials and figure out where you're going. Just, uhhh, seriously, back your stuff up before you go smearing your poopy hands all over the code. That's a pro tip from me to you.

13. Or Get Yourself a Codemonkey Cohort

Penmonkeys sometimes have codemonkeys. It is a symbiotic relationship, like those little birds that pick the teeth of alligators for food. Consider getting a "web dude" or a "code mistress." Someone who lives under your desk or in your ceiling panels and can emerge when you ring a little bell.

14. Repeat After Me: Reliable Hosting

Unreliable hosts will make you shit fire. When your site yo-yos up and down and you can't get in touch with anybody and then Neil Gaiman links to your site that one time and your entire hosting company implodes thanks to the classic #NeilWebFail, you'll wish you found a more stable host for your site.

15. Please Don't Make My Eyes Bleed

You're an author. Your goal is to be read. Your blog is therefore to be read. Which means that when I go to read it, it should not feel as if you're assaulting my eyes with lasers and fire ants. Clean typography. Dark text on light backgrounds. Text on highly textured backgrounds makes Web Jesus turn all our wine into weasel urine. Tiny text makes me want to punch my monitor. Cut the noise. Aim for elegance and clarity. Simplicity is better than complexity. Think of a book page and how unadorned but perfect it is. That is your goal.

16. Single Soapbox or Community Center?

Design-wise, it helps to know if you're going to be a lone dude standing on his soapbox screaming to the masses or if it's going to be more of a community where everybody gathers around and gets to add their two cents. The latter demands more social elements in play, for instance. The former just means you need effective broadcast.

17. You Don't Need Comments

Wise penmonkey Tobias Buckell removed the ability to comment from his entire blog. And, by all reports, he hasn't looked back. You do not violate some sacred precept by removing comments. Consider it as a way to remove noise and to ensure that the space is yours and yours alone.

18. Don't Let It Gobble Up Your Writing Time

If blogging kills your writing, then that kinda dicks over the entire purpose of having an author's blog. Fix that straightaways and rearrange your priorities. Write first. Blog later.

19. Blog Like Nobody's Listening

This may seem like odd advice, but it is in part how I approach blogging: I blog like nobody's there. I blog for me, to me, about me. That sounds narcissistic (so what if I stare at myself in the mirror and lick my beard for hours on end? DON'T JUDGE ME), but it allows you to be yourself and not feel like you need to constantly perform for an audience. You're not getting paid to blog, so you might as well do it with abandon and blog how you want to blog before worrying about your readership.

20. The Audience Doesn't Just Appear

It takes time to cultivate an audience. They don't just swarm like flies. The Internet is home to—*checks some quick math*—a bajillionty blogs. Be yourself, say some interesting shit, spread your word seed around, and eventually the readers will come.

21. Bring Your A-Game

Write well. Write with roughly the same skill you'd bring to all your professional work. None of this "i saw the newest borne identity movie matt damon has sexxxy pecs lolololololol" if you want to be taken seriously as an author. Why look like a ruddy-cheeked rube? Bring your A-game. Show us your prettiest face.

22. Not Just a Marketing Joint

If your blog is just a self-promotion zone, it might as well be cordoned off, labeled SPAM CITY, and nuked from orbit. If it's a blog—and not just a regular author site—then talk to us. Say things. Communicate. Put the "social" in "social media." You're not just an insane, out-of-control, self-promotional spam-bot. Stop that.

23. Worry About Content Above SEO

The big thing is Search Engine Optimization, which is a phrase so lacking in soul and spirit that it actually just robbed seven hours of my life merely by typing those words. Focus on great content and communication before you start worrying about how to game the search-engine system so as to appear in the top links.

24. Nobody's Making You Do It

Some authors feel pressure to blog, but screw that right in the undercarriage. Nobody's putting a gun to your head. If you don't want to do it, then don't sweat it. Hell, be a weird author recluse if you want. Grow a big beard. Live in a tree. Try to procreate with various species of bears. Whatever works for you.

25. Have Fun, Will You?

If you're not having fun blogging, we're all going to feel it. We've all read those rote blog posts, those entries that feel *ironclad* and somehow *oppressive*—as if they're a chore to do. No more of that. Open up the liquor cabinet inside your brain, and drain whatever bottles you find there— then go blog. Blog with heart. Blog with madness. Blog by going off the script, off the cuff, out of the box—*right over the edge of the cliff*. If it's something you're going to take the time to do, you might as well enjoy it. If you don't like it, don't do it. Who wants to read the blog of someone who doesn't want to be blogging?

25 THINGS YOU SHOULD KNOW ABOUT SOCIAL MEDIA

1. The Devil's Trident
Social media has three essential prongs of activity: broadcast, rebroadcast, and conversation. This is true for everybody, not just writers, but it's worth noting just the same. I say something or repeat something someone else said (broadcast/rebroadcast), and from that social seedbed, conversation may arise.

2. Be the Best Version of Yourself
Writers and other creative types often seem to believe that they need to become someone different online, that they cannot be *themselves* lest they not find a publisher, not get work, not sell their book, not collect sexy groupies, etc. To that I say, bullshit! And poppycock! And piddling

piss-wafers! Be yourself. That's who we want. We just want the *best version* of you. Scrape the barnacles off. Sit up straight. Smile once in a while. But you can still be you. Uhh, unless "you" happens to be some kind of Nazi-sympathizing donkey toucher. In which case, please back slowly away from the social media.

3. Put "Brand" and "Platform" Out of Your Fool Head

You are not a brand. Social media is not your platform. The world has enough brands. You are not a logo, a marketing agenda, a mouthpiece, or a spam-bot. Approach social media not as a writer-specific tool (keyword: tool) catered only toward your penmonkey self, and see it instead as a place where you can bring all the crazy and compelling facets of your personality to bear on your audience. People want to follow other people. People don't want to follow brands. They don't want to hear about your platform.

4. Communicate With Other Human Beings
(and the Occasional Spam-Bot)

Put the "social" in "social media." Social media needn't be a one-way street. A real connection goes both ways. Talk to people. Chat. Converse. Discuss. Share ideas. Don't be one of those writers who uses their social-media channel as a bulletin board announcing naught but their next signing, book release, or $0.99 bowel movement. Don't aim only to be heard but to open your ears as well. (Oh, and I'm totally kidding about the spam-bots thing. Don't talk to spam-bots. Eradicate them with extreme prejudice. Perform the "honey-pot" maneuver—draw them to you with keywords like "real estate" or "ipad," and then EXTERMI-NATE, EXTERMINATE, EXTERMINATE with the vim and vigor of the Daleks.)

5. Guide Them Toward Your Sticky Embrace

Having a blog, website, or online space where you establish an authorial "base camp" is a great thing. It allows you to own your content, track stats, post long-form material, and be whatever it is you need it to be. I use my own website (ahem, terribleminds.com) for talking about writing, toddlers, cocktails, recipes, and pagan Lithuanian pornography. Can't see the porn? You haven't unlocked the special content. Enter Konami code. Password is: "ByTheDampened-BallsOfVilnius123."

6. Determine the Tools in Your Toolbox

Find different uses for different social media. Facebook is pretty light on writer stuff, to my eye. Google+ is good for longer-form discussions. Twitter is really where it's at for me—it's where I get the most conversation and connection. Then the blog is the central tentpole to the whole goddamn circus. Maybe you use Tumblr. Or some as-yet-unknown social network, like Wordhole or iPalaver or Friendhammer. Anything except LinkedIn. I mean, c'mon. LinkedIn is the scabby venereal disease of social media.

7. Breed Positivity, and Share What You Love

Writers are content creators, so it behooves us to share what we love. You're generally better off showing positivity than sowing the seeds of negativity. For the most part, the Internet is a monster that thrives on the rage of countless disaffected white people, so I don't know how it does a writer good to be a part of that noise. Your audience cares more about what you're *into* than what you're *not*. After all, I don't particularly care for a lot of things. Most things, really. If I spent all my time talking about them, I'd be little more than a septic social fountain spewing my bitter froth into the world.

8. Show the World You're Not a Raging Bonerhead

The Internet is like hot dogs: made of lips and assholes. A writer does well to set himself aside from all that and use social media to reveal that he is, indeed, *not* a giant bucket of non-contributing human syphilis.

9. Kill Them With Kindness

Connection, not conflict. Communication, not combat. *Don't get into fights online.* I mean, it's one thing if you're getting into an argument with a Nazi-sympathizing donkey toucher. Because, seriously? What an asshole. But nine times out of ten, getting into a snit-spat-tiff-miff-feud-fuss-or-fracas online doesn't make you look like a shining prince of social media. It just makes you look cranky. Note the difference between "friendly, chummy disagreement" and "pissy Internet rumpus." The former? Fine. The latter? Not so much.

10. Variety Is the Spice Melange of Life

And is essential to the creation of the sandworms, as well as the diet of the wandering Fremen. Wait, what? This isn't Frank Herbert's *Dune*? My bad! What I'm saying is, divvy up your social media existence. Don't talk about any one thing. It may not be critical to chop everything up into neat percentages, but vary the content of your broadcast. Ensure that you do more than share links. Contribute original thoughts. Add conversation. Say something. Just keep the commercials—i.e., self-promotion—to a necessary minimum.

11. Be an Escort, Not a Whore

Speaking of self-promo ... the reality of the modern writer's existence is that self-promotion is inescapable. Whether you're published by the Big Six or published by your buddy Steve out of his mother's basement, you're going to have to serve up some self-promo. Social media is your online channel for this. It has to be. And it isn't a dirty word—if I follow a writer, I want to know that their new book is out because I may have missed that news. I just don't want to hear it seventy-two times a day. And there's the key to self-promotion—like with all things (sodomy, gin, reality TV), everything in moderation.

12. Just Say No to Quid Pro Quo
Controversial notion: Do not reshare something purely as a favor to someone else. I know—it's an easy favor to do. "You shared my link, now I share your link. In this way, we tickle each other's pink parts." The thing is, if one is to assume you are a writer to trust, then those who listen to your social-media broadcasts want to know that the information you share is, in a way, *pure*. If they believe that the things you're saying are motivated only by mutual social-media back scratching, then you've ruined that. Share things you think your audience wants to hear or things you believe are worth sharing. If all you're doing is echoing links endlessly, what separates you from just another spam-bot?

13. You Don't Build an Audience, You Earn It
Lots of writers look at their follower tallies like they're experience points in a role-playing game, like with every MilliWheaton earned, you hear a "ding" and then gain +4 against 4chan or a new Save Versus PublishAmerica roll. Your audience isn't just a number. It's a whole bunch of actual human beings. Humans who don't just want to be sold stuff or yelled at, but who want to interact and be amused and enlightened—and who want to amuse and enlighten in turn. Earn your audience, don't build it. They're not dollar signs. They're not credit you can spend buying vintage porn on eBay.

14. Followers Are Not Fans
It's easy to believe that, pound for pound, those who follow you and read your broadcasts and interact with you online are automatically the same people who are going to buy your books, pimp your stuff, and

become superfans. Bzzt. Wrongo. A retweet or Facebook "like" or "Re-G" on Google+ (that's what I'm calling the reshare feature over there) is free. The investment to procure your wordsmithy is a whole different level of commitment. That said, these people are all potential fans. It's your job to make that happen.

15. As a Storytelling Medium

Use social media to tell stories. Real stories or fictional ones. Hey, if my infant has an epic diaper breach and manages to defy gravity and shit up his own back and into his hair, I'm gonna tell you about it. Talk about your life. Or use Twitter to write microfiction. Or empower your blog to experiment with telling old stories in new ways. Experiment! Do what you're bred to do: Write.

16. My God, It's Full of Words

Social media is, as noted, full of words. Words that must be written. You're a writer, so tackle social media—from tweets to blog posts to Friendhammer Epistles—with all the grace and aplomb you would give to any of your writing. In other words, let social media demonstrate your abilities as a writer. Use punctuation. Capitalize. Write well. Learn to engage in brief spaces. This will help you be a better writer.

17. The Self-Correcting Hive Mind

Social media self-corrects. Many find this uncomfortable, but it's an excellent memetic Darwinism. If I tweet about, say, my three-month-old's poosplosion, inevitably I'm going to come across people who don't want to hear about that. Eventually they may say, "This guy talks a lot about poop," or "Boy, he sure says 'shit' a lot," and then they stop following me on Twitter or stop going to my blog. It's regrettable, but that's the nature of life. Social media is a frequency that people can tune into or turn away from. That's normal. Let that happen. Don't get mad at it. Embrace that kind of course correction.

18. Dip Your Ladle Into the Brain Broth of Social Media

Writers need to know things. So ask those in your social-media world. Say, "I need a good book on wombat husbandry for a novel I'm writing," or, "Can anyone recommend good writing music?" or, "If I were to write a stage play based on the Twitter stream of Kanye West, would anybody beta read it for me?" Don't be afraid to ask for things. And don't be afraid to answer when others ask. Again, communicate.

19. The Water Cooler for Writers

I believe it was game designer and writer Jeff Tidball who said he sees Twitter as a water cooler for stay-at-home freelancers, and I think he nailed it. Writers don't have the ability to hover around a water cooler and talk to other writers most of the time, so social media fills that function. It's a great way to connect with other penmonkeys and creative types and engage, interact, and amuse. It's important for writers to know other writers. It's how we get book blurbs or find out what bottle of bourbon we should try. It used to be you had to travel to conventions and conferences to do it. Now you can do it at home. Without pants.

20. Gaze Into the Whirring Gears of Industry Machinery

You can use social media to do more than connect with writers. The entire industry is out there. So go and watch. And then partake. Follow agents. Ping publishers. You can watch trends unfold and see what agents are looking for (or what mistakes people are making in their queries). It's a great place to interact with the industry as a person-who-is-a-writer, not merely a writer-shopping-a-product. However, I must pass along a critical warning: Gazing too long into the publishing industry is like dropping a fistful of acid and then staring into a backed-up toilet for days. You will starve and go mad. Don't ask how I know this.

21. Behold Zen Serendipity

Open yourself to the social-media experience. Don't be one of those walled-garden scrod-boats who follows like ten people but has ten thousand followers. Put your ear to the ground like Tonto. Listen to shit. Pay attention. Let the sweet serendipity and weird waves of connection wash over you. People are each their own little rabbit hole: Grab a thread, and follow it down into the dark. Just as you might use Pandora to discover new music or Amazon to discover new books, use social media to discover new people. Without people and their thoughts and stories, writers are just lonely weirdos screaming into an empty closet.

22. Appreciate Your Audience

Your audience follows you and rebroadcasts you, and that's a very nice thing. So appreciate them. Interact with them. Respond to them. I don't mean to say you should act as God from on high, acknowledging the little people—I mean that you're them and they're you and social media is a powerful equalizer. Appreciate that they take the time to listen to your nonsense day in and day out. That's pretty cool of them, innit?

23. Crucify Gurus and Stab Them With Your Mighty Spears

Anybody who wants to charge you a bunch of money to "optimize" your "social-media skills" is selling fool's gold. This stuff isn't hard. It ain't goddamn math. At its core, social media is really "Talk to people, and try not to be a dick." That's as true for writers as it is for everybody else.

24. Go Old School

Every once in a while you need to unplug and embrace some old school social media: *Go outside and talk to people.* Go to a bar, a book signing, a game store, whatever. Engage with fleshy 3-D meatbags!

25. Remember That You Need to Escape Its Gravity

In the end, social media has uses for the writer. But it also runs the risk of becoming the Sarlacc Pit: a giant evil desert orifice that draws you in with its tentacle dongs and slowly digests you over the course of many millennia, not allowing you to make any progress on that screenplay you've been writing for the last sixteen years. Your priority is to write stories, not to fritter away hours on Facebook or LinkedIn or Booty-finder or CatHarmony. (I kid—nobody uses LinkedIn!) The most important thing a writer should know about social media is that it is not the crux of the penmonkey's existence. What matters most of all is that you write great stories. The social media must follow that.

25 THINGS YOU SHOULD KNOW ABOUT CROWDFUNDING YOUR WRITING

1. Wait, What the Hell Is Crowdfunding?

Crowdfunding is when you go to a large group of people and say, "If you all give me a little bit of money collectively, I will be able to write and/or publish my new novel, *The Orangutan's Revenge*." Different models of crowdfunding offer variations on this theme, but that's how it shakes out.

2. Reversing Crowdsurfing

In music, the musician leaps off the stage and, ideally, his audience catches him and they surf him around (and probably steal what's in his pockets). Not so ideally, they drop him and he shatters a hip and spends the rest of the concert wailing like a lovestruck cat. Crowdfunding is a little like that, but with one significant twist: You're not leaping *from* the stage into the crowd, you're leaping up from the crowd in the hopes that the audience will carry you to the stage. If they do, your project gets funded. If they don't, well—see earlier comment re: hip shatter, wailing cat.

3. Kickstarter Is Not a Publisher

Worth noting: None of the crowdfunding platforms are publishers. I've heard this from time to time: "I'm publishing on Kickstarter." No, you are not. Kickstarter is a mechanism. It *facilitates* publication, but it's still all up to you to make all of the fiddly parts of publishing happen: writing, editing, marketing, cover design, three-martini lunches, crushing ennui, writer's block, distribution, and so on.

4. Kickstarter Versus IndieGoGo Versus Pubslush Versus?

At the time of this writing, three primary crowdfunding mechanisms exist for authors, with several secondary platforms up and coming. Kickstarter and Indiegogo are likely the biggest. The former runs projects that only succeed if 100 percent or more of the funding is secured. The latter runs campaigns that succeed the moment you start them, and whatever money rolls in (from $1.00 up!) is what you get. Pubslush deserves special mention as a crowdfunding platform specific to books. They won't help you crowdfund a new watch or an artisanal yogurt boutique or a line of bow ties made from recycled wombats. They only help fund books so the tools tend to be a bit more author specific.

5. A Product-Driven Life

The process is all well and good, but generally speaking, crowdfunding (and Kickstarter in particular) is geared toward an end product. They don't want "fund-my-life" projects, and they don't want "help me feed myself with ramen and squirt cheese" projects. They want an end result: "I'm funding a book, or an app, an injectable transmedia cocktail."

6. Pledge Versus Preorder

Crowdfunding presents two philosophical approaches to any campaign: The first is that money coming in is akin to a pledge, like the kind you'd give to, say, your favorite public broadcast station. If you give $50 to PBS, you're not so much buying the umbrella that comes with the pledge but the peace of mind that you're helping to fund content and creators that you love. The other side of the coin is that the money coming in is akin to a preorder. This means that people aren't here to support the creator so much as they're here to secure purchase of the resultant product. Which approach the campaign takes is up to the creator of the campaign, though you'll attract types who support projects in both ways. The ideal approach is perhaps to offer reward tiers for both types of customer.

7. Your Lovable Mug

You're going to have to make a video. Okay, you don't have to—but campaigns with videos, particularly good-looking and/or earnest videos—tend to be more successful. Maybe it's you talking into the camera, explaining the book. Maybe it's you putting together some high-octane, super-produced video featuring art, animation, and voiceover. Whatever it is, just keep your pants on. *It's not that kind of video.* Though, now I wonder, is there a site used for crowdfunding porn? *runs to Google*

8. The Person and the Profession

Crowdfunding often demands that the author walk a middle ground between *I'm a professional* and *I'm just a person, like you*! *No I'm totally not a doom-bot hell-bent on the eradication of humankind*! You have to look like you know what you're doing (clear, professional language, correct spelling, strong grammar, compelling writing) while at the same time offering that same kind of confessional connecting language you find present on social media. And that's not just a "sales tactic"—it really helps to connect with the audience on a personal level so they will invest in you and your work.

9. No Audience, No Reach
Remember what I said about crowdsurfing? If you have no crowd, you will not surf. (I think that's an apocryphal Harlan Ellison short story.) This is where crowdfunding gets tricky—if you step into the arena without anybody in the stands, your project may land with a dull thud in the dust. You might get a couple bucks from your mother and a few drunken friends, but you need to connect to a larger audience to get your work funded. Kickstarter has some mechanisms by which it promotes interesting projects, but it's imperfect. The rest is all on you.

10. Make Damn Sure They Get the Damn Book
I've seen author campaigns where the pledgers don't get the book at low tiers or at any tier at all. That's absurd. Whatever it is you're crowdfunding (short story collection, novel, travel journal, weepy teenage diary), make sure at some tier the pledgers receive a copy. Otherwise, what's the damn point?

11. Something Right Out of the Gate
We are reward-driven creatures. We are monkeys who want to press a button and receive an immediate treat (or, for a certain subset of us, a *delicious electric shock to our naughty parts*). A crowdfunding campaign to write and publish a book is likely to have a long lead time to write, administrate, and publish the book. Still, at the conclusion of the campaign it'd be great to be able to give backers something immediately: a short story set in that storyworld, the first chapter of the book, another unrelated book or story. A pony ride, maybe!

12. Variety of Pledge Tiers

The way a crowdfunding campaign works is that the project creator offers up a series of varying pledge tiers where backers get different rewards based on their level of financial investment. The goal is to offer a variety of tiers so that people will have inceptived to pledge $5, $25, or even $500, and this way they feel rewarded properly for the money put forth. Putting in $5 might get them a short story or a thank you in the back of the book. Putting in $500 better get them a whole lot more—an elite edition of the book, dinner with the author, etc. (Maybe time to revisit that "pony ride" concept?) The trick is also not to overwhelm with choices. A tier structure with ten tier levels is probably good. If you exceed that then the choices start to all blur together. Some choice is good. Too much choice makes backers want to just lay down and take a nap.

13. The $25 Tier Is the Magic Tier

Most pledges come in at $25—this, then, is the sweet spot, the golden ticket, the magic kiss. Make sure this tier exists and that they get something for it. Usually this tier at least ensures a copy (digital and maybe even print) of the book itself.

14. More Time Doesn't Mean a Better Chance

Long campaigns are the pits. They drag on and on. You have to keep talking about them. You have to keep uploading videos, and by the seventh week, the video is just you weeping into the camera, a snot bubble popping while you gamely gnaw on a handful of stale popcorn. The average length of a campaign is thirty days. Any longer than that and you're going to want to punch yourself right in the no-no spot. And others may want to punch you there, too.

15. The Mushy Middle of a Kickstarter Campaign

Just as a novel can drag on in the middle of its writing and reading, so too can a crowdfunding campaign drag on in the middle. The first and last weeks tend to be a whiz-bang-boom of activity, and then the middle two to three weeks are as flat as old soda. You can try to keep the campaign shorter, or you can endeavor to make that middle interesting (just as you would a novel). Add new stretch goals! New videos! Make it interesting. Add a little drama.

16. Wait, What the Hell Are 'Stretch Goals?'
Great campaigns go over 100 percent funding. Which means you want to continue to incentivize backers beyond that point. After all, the race is finished, so why the hell would folks keep running it? Because, voila, stretch goals. If you asked for a thousand dollars and got it, then maybe at $1500, they unlock a new short story collection. At $2000, a new novella. At $3000, all backers receive a free chimpanzee. (Call me, I know a guy who sells good discount chimps.)

17. 33 percent = 100 percent
One of the rules of thumb per crowdfunding is that if you manage to secure 33 percent of your funding at any point in the campaign, you're likely to fund to 100 percent. I have no idea if this remains true by the time you read this. I have no idea what foul wizardry has been used to achieve this number—I assume something-something dove guts and salamander bile. The idea behind this is, I think, if you have enough momentum to get a third of the necessary funding, you likely will manifest the audience and energy to get you to the final funding marker. There might also be a cat in a box that's also dead and alive at the same time, I dunno.

18. Little Krill and Giant Whales
"AS SOON AS STEPHEN KING FINDS KICKSTARTER, WE'RE ALL SCREWED." So goes the fear of what happens when crowdfunding becomes dominated by celebrities or bestsellers, pushing the little guys to the margins. At present, it just isn't true. Kickstarter did a study and showed that after high-profile Kickstarter campaigns (topping a mil-

lion or more funded), new people came to the site and began supporting campaigns left and right. Bigger projects tend to give a boost to small ones. Stephen King will not steal your Kickstarter mojo.

19. What the Book Needs

Some folks ask, "Well, what the hell does a book need in terms of investment? Don't you just write the damn thing in Microsoft Word, then print it out, doodle a cover on the front, and mail it to all your friends and loved ones?" Turns out, that is not actually how it works. A crowdfunding campaign for a book tends to pay for the very real and sometimes costly essentials of getting that book birthed from your literary womb, which means: writing, editing, cover art, book design, physical output, and potential distribution.

20. What the Book Needs II: Electric Bookaloo

Other things your campaign may deem it necessary to pay for as part of the original total or as part of the stretch goals? Book tours! Merchandise! Limited editions! Alternate versions! Literary magazine! An app! An audio version! An injectable nanite version of the book so it always lives inside the reader forever! A pony ride!

21. Overpromising, Underdelivering, Miscalculating

Crowdfunding campaigns sometimes fly high and then face-plant in the dust. Folks overpromise and underdeliver, or they simply miscalculate the costs going into things (if you're printing physical copies, get your costs beforehand. By the Trident of Poseidon—*do not forget shipping costs*). You are obligated to complete your campaign. If you promise a book in people's hands—that's what you owe them by the end of it. Which is also a tip to offer realistic timeframes for the completion of various reward tiers. "Tomorrow" is probably not realistic, eff-why-eye.

22. Think of Your Campaign as Having a Narrative Arc

A crowdfunding campaign has all the beats of a story. Inciting incident (the campaign begins!), the conflict (will I raise the money and will the project ever happen?), the ups and downs along the way (holy crap, stretch goals!), the climax (will the campaign reach its final goal or falter at the finish line?). It's good to treat it that way, too—try to keep the campaign exciting and interesting by adding new updates, new challenges, new successes, and new goals.

23. Energy Begets Energy; Tension Creates Action

Fortune favors the underdog. Creating stretch goals or offering tension—er, real tension, not the made-up kind—can give your campaign that sense of watch-and-contribute needed to keep it going. You also don't want to just fall off the map during the mushy middle of the campaign—the creator (er, you) should feel active and interested all the time. (Which is why crowdfunding campaigns tend to be more work and as a result more tiring than expected.)

24. But Please, Hammer, Don't Spam 'Em

People who spam other people about their crowdfunding campaigns have a special place in Hell where demons crowdfund your very own lava enemas.

25. Bubble or Biosphere, We Don't Know

Is crowdfunding here to stay? Or is this a bubble that will pop? It remains as yet unseen, but *at present* it is a viable, fascinating way to help bring your book or other storytelling project to fruition. What might pop the bubble? Too many campaigns. Too many campaigns that fund but don't deliver. Too much spam about too many campaigns. Not enough pony rides.

25 WAYS TO EARN YOUR AUDIENCE

1. It's All About the Story

Normally, this is the type of thing I'd put as the capstone #25 entry—
"Oh, duh, by the way, none of this matters if you write a real turd bomb
of a book"—but it's too important to put last because for all I know you
people will fall asleep around #14. So, let's deal with it here and now:
Your best and most noble path to audience earning is by having something awesome (or many awesome somethings) to give them. Tell the
best story you can tell. Above all the social-media posturing and bullshit
brand building and stabs at outreach, you need a great "thing" (book,
movie, comic, whatever) to be the core of your authorial ecosystem. Tell
a great story. Achieve optimal awesomeness. Build audience on the back
of your skill, talent, and devotion. You can ignore everything else on
this list. Do NOT ignore this one.

2. Swift Cellular Division

The days of writing One Single Thing every year and standing on that single thing as if it were a mighty marble pedestal are long gone. (And, if you ask me, have been gone for a lot longer than everybody says—unless, of course, you're a best-selling author.) Nowadays, it pays to write a lot. Spackle shut the gaps in your resume. Bridge any chasm in your schedule. This doesn't mean write *badly*. It doesn't mean "churn out endless strings of talentless sputum." It just means to be generative. ABW: Always Be Writing. Take more shots at the goal for greater likelihood of hitting the goal. One book is less likely to find an audience than three. *Put that coffee down.* Coffee is for generative penmonkeys only.

3. Painting With Shotguns

The power of creative diversity will serve you well. The audience doesn't come to you. You go to the audience. "One book is less likely to find an audience than three?" Correction: "One book is less likely to find an audience than two books, a comic, a blog, a short story collection, a porn movie, various napkin doodles, a celebrity chef trading card set, and hip anonymous graffiti." Joss Whedon didn't just write *Buffy*. He wrote films. And comics. And a webseries. The guy is all over the map. Diversity in nature helps a species survive. So too will it help the tribe of storytellers survive.

4. Sharing Is Caring, or Some Bullshit Like That

Make your work easy to share. This is triply true for newer storytellers: Don't hide your work behind a wall. Make sure your work is widely available. Don't make it difficult to pass around. I have little doubt that there's a strategy wherein making your story a truly rare bird can serve you—scarcity suggests value and mystery, after all—but the smart play for creative types just setting out is to get your work into as many hands as possible with as little trouble as you can offer. This is true for veteran storytellers, too. Comedian Louis C.K. made it *very easy* to get his new comedy special on the web. And that served him well both financially *and* in terms of earning him a new audience while rewarding the existing audience.

5. Value at Multiple Tiers

Your nascent audience doesn't want to have to take out a home equity loan to try your untested work. If you're a new author and your first book comes out and the e-book is $12.99, well, good luck to you. Now, that might not be in your control, so here's what you do: Have multiple expressions of your awesomeness available at a variety of value tiers. Have something free. Have something out there for a buck or three. Make sure folks can sample your work and still support you, should they choose to do so. Be like the drug dealer: The first taste is cheap or free, baby.

6. Build the Sandbox

I think I hate the "sandbox" metaphor because, I gotta say, I did not like sandboxes as a kid. What, like I want gritty sand in my asscrack? Hey, great, my Yoda figure's limbs don't move well now because he's got sand in his plastic armpits. Oh, look, Tootsie roll! *nom nom nom* OH GOD, CATSHIT. Anyway, as a *metaphor* I suppose it holds up, so let's stick with it—these days the audience has a greater percentage of prime movers and participants, people who want to be more involved, who don't want to just be baby birds waiting for Momma Bird to regurgitate new content into their open gullets. They want some participation in … well, something. The story. The characters. The creation. The author. Needn't be all of the above, but something is better than nothing. Let them in. Let them invest emotionally and intellectually.

7. Sometimes It's Just About Not Discouraging

Even if you don't want to encourage—damn sure don't discourage. Authors who bristle against fan fiction are authors who don't appreciate how wonderful it is to have an active and engaged audience.

8. Be You

(Ignore the fact that the title rhymes with "pee yoo!") The best audience isn't just an audience that exists around a single work, but rather, an ecosystem that connects to the creator. The audience that hangs with a creator will follow said creator from work to work. That means who you are as a storyteller matters—this is not to suggest that you need to be the center of a cult of personality. Just be humble creator of many things. You're the hub of your creative life, with spokes leading to many creative expressions rather than just one. Put yourself out there. And be you. Be authentic. Don't just be a "creator." You're not a marketing mouthpiece. You're a human. For all the good and the bad.

9. Um, Unless "You" Are a "Total Dick"

If you're a total dick, then it might be wise to sew your mouth shut and instead just … make up a persona. Or have a computer do it for you. Maybe an AI? Hell, hire a person to be the public non-jackass face of you. This is probably bad advice because I can name a handful of total dick writers who do really well. They are true to themselves and are, in fact, totally authentic bastards who happen to sell a lot of books. I'm just trying to prevent there from being more jerks and jackasses in the world, thanks. Is that so wrong?

10. Be a Fountain, Not a Drain

Put differently, be a fountain, not a drain. Take all that negative shit, throw it in a picnic basket, duct-tape it shut, and feed it to a starving bear. The world is home to enough rank and rancid human flatulence that you don't need to add to it. An audience is likely to respond to negativity in a negative way—is that who you want to be? Screw that. Go positive. Talk about the things you love rather than the things you hate. Voicing your insecurities, fears, and sorrows is okay from time to time, but as soon as it starts to overwhelm, you're just going to start bumming people out. Who wants to engage with a sad, simpering panda?

11. Have Opinions

Some authors are afraid of having opinions. They feat that by saying they vote Democrat or go to church every Sunday or prefer Carolina barbecue over Texas barbecue, that their delicate little author platform (which are clearly made of fragile bird bones) and they will end up alienating the audience. I urinate on the head of that idea. Your audience is way tougher than you think. And if they're willing to abandon you because you're going to vote for Ron Paul or didn't like *The Avengers*, then they were probably going to ditch you anyway. Opinions are fine. They make you human. Why sterilize yourself and your beliefs? The key to having an opinion is obeying Wheaton's Law: Don't be a dick. A corollary, Wendig's Tenet, cautions against having and/ or offering crazy-person opinions. "I think all the Jews should be sent to the moon" is not a sane position, so maybe you just want to button that one up and go away.

12. The Passion of the Penmonkey

To add to that last point, reveal your passion to the world. Be passionate about your story. About other stories. About … well, whatever the hell it is that makes your grapefruit squirt. That energy is infectious. And don't you want to infect the audience with your own special brand of syphil … uhhh, "passion?"

13. Engagement and Interaction

Very simply: Talk to people. Social media—though I'm starting to hate that phrase and think we should call it something like the "digital conversation matrix" or maybe just "THE CYBERORGY" (all caps necessary)—is a great place in which to be you and interact with folks and be more than just a mouthpiece for your work. The audience wants to feel connected to you. Like with those freaky tentacular hair braids in *Avatar*. Get out there. Hang out. Be you. Interact. Engage. Get sloppy in THE CYBERORGY.

14. Head's Up: Social Media Is Not Your Priority

Special attention must be paid: Social media is a *side dish*; it is not your main burrito. See #1 on this list.

15. Hell With the Numbers

Just as I exhort you to be a human being and not an author carved out of marble, I suggest you look at all those with whom you interact on social media as people, too. They're not resources. They're not a number. They're not "followers"—yes, fine, they might be called that, but (excepting a few camouflaged spam-bots hell-bent on dissecting your life and, one day, your actual body) they're people. Sure, as you gaze out over an audience, the heads and faces start to blur together like the subjects of a pointillist painting, but remember that the audience is made up of people. AND PEOPLE ARE DELICIOUS. Uhh. I mean, people are really cool.

16. Don't Be Afraid to Ask for Help

An earnest plea to your existing audience to help you find and earn a new audience would not be remiss, provided you're not a total jackass about it.

17. Share Knowledge

As you learn things about the process, share them with others. Free exchange of information is awesome. If I may toot the horn of one of my publishers, this is why the game (and now fiction) publisher Evil Hat gets a lot of love and continues to find new fans. Evil Hat shares all the data they can manage. It's insightful, compelling, and human. This doesn't mean being a pedant about it—"Here are my experiences" is a lot different than "YOU'RE WRONG AND HERE'S WHY, LACK-WIT." It just means being open and honest. It means being useful. We like useful people.

18. Shake Hands, Kiss Babies

The real world is awesome. They call it "meatspace" because you can go out there and eat meat. You can even hunt and kill your own sources of meat. And, while out there, you are encouraged to share meat with other human beings. Kiss some hands and shake some babies. Face-to-face interaction is probably worth more than that you get over social media.

19. Embrace Feedback

Reviews, critiques, commentary, conversation—feedback is good even when it's bad. When it's bad, all you have to do is ignore it. Or politely say, "I'll consider that!" and in the privacy of your own home, print out the feedback and urinate on it with wanton disregard. When it's good, it's stellar and connects you all the more deeply to the audience. The audience is now a part of your feedback loop, like it or not.

20. Do Set Boundaries

That feedback loop is not absolute. I'm not a strong believer in creative integrity as an indestructible, indefatigable "thing"—but, I recognize that being a single-minded creator requires some ego. Further, the reality is that once something is "out there", it is what it is and there ain't poop-squat you can do about it. So you have to know when to turn off comments, back away from social media, or just set personal and unspoken boundaries for yourself. Just because we interact with our audience doesn't mean we are subject to their stompy boots and groping hands. I mean, unless you're into that sort of thing.

21. Be Generous With Time and Tale

Put yourself and your work out there. To reviewers. To interviewers. To that hobo on the street who will run up to bike messengers and beat them about the head and neck with your book.

22. Foster Other Creative Types

You're not a lone author batting back the tides with his magnum opus novel. You're not the only creator who's ever wanted to write a movie or ink a comic book. Other creative types are out there. And you love them. They're why you do what you do—I'm a writer because other writers have given me so much and shown me the way. Like that time Stephen King and I went fishing down by the creek and he taught me how to bait a hook and then afterward we made out under the willow tree and we both fought a giant spider in the sewers. Or something. I may be misremembering. Point is, you have peers in the creative realm and you're also the audience yourself—so, forge the community, and foster other creators. Don't just bring people to your tent. Point them to other tents, too.

23. Don't Wrassle Gators If You're Not a Good Gator Wrassler

What I mean is, don't try to be something you're not. If you're not good in public, don't go out in public. If writing guest blogs is not your thing … well, maybe don't write a guest blog. Again, this isn't a list where you need to check off every box. These are just options. Avoid those that plunge you into a churning pool of discomfort. You don't want to lose more audience than you earn.

24. Take Your Time

Earning your audience won't happen overnight. You don't plant a single seed and expect to see a lush garden grown up by morning. This takes time, work, patience, and, y'know, earning the attention of other fine humans one set of eyeballs at a time. It's why you put yourself out there again and again.

25. Have Fun, Goddammit

If it feels like what you're doing is some kind of onerous, odious chore, I'm going to tune out. OMG A THOUSAND SISYPHEAN MISERIES, you cry, wailing and gnashing your teeth with every grumpy tweet and every miserably written short story. Hey. Relax. Enjoy yourself. This isn't supposed to be torture. You should have fun for two reasons: First, because people can sense when you're just phoning it in, or worse, when you're just a mope. Second, because *fun* is *fun*. Do you hate fun? Why? I like writing. I like putting my work out there. I like interacting with people in person and online. If you don't like these things? Don't do them! Why would you punish yourself like that? It's like watching you stand there stuffing your face full of candy you hate. "Mmmphh these Swedish fish are so gross grrpphmble oh God, stupid, gross Necco wafers mmmphhchewchewchew I hate myself so bad right now." Don't put yourself through that. And don't put your (potential) audience through that, either.

25 THINGS YOU SHOULD KNOW ABOUT HYBRID AUTHORS

1. We Do It All, Baby

The hybrid author embraces many (or all) forms, modes, and mechanisms of publishing that lie between the extremes of traditional publishing (i.e. signing with a publisher) and self-publishing (i.e. publishing and distributing one's own work).

2. No, We Weren't Made in a Lab

"Hybrid author" sounds like we were grown in a lab. Our DNA mutated by beams of radiation, and the books of hundreds, even *thousands* of authors piped into our genetic helices so that we can become BIGGER, FASTER, STRONGER. Don't be scared. We aren't mutants pressed up against the too-fragile walls of our Plexiglas enclosures. This isn't *Ju-*

rassic Park. Even if we do sometimes like to eat a goat or three. (And no, we also don't get "really good gas mileage.")

3. Diversity Is Your Bestest Friend

Diversity is necessary in ecology. It's crucial in establishing an investment portfolio. It's character building when there's diversity among our friends and family. Diversity ensures that if one part of a thing fails, the rest is there to pick up the slack. So why shouldn't we have diversity in our publishing models? There are too many ways and means nowadays to choose only one method of storytelling.

4. For Every Story, a Different Choice

The great thing about being a hybrid author is that no story need sit in a drawer, gathering dust. Provided a story is of requisite quality, the hybrid author is equipped with a variety of trebuchets with which to launch that tale into the hands of whatever audience awaits. One story goes this way. Another story goes that way. Some genres do very well in self-published spaces (romance, for instance), where others, like literary work, will do better in the traditional space. Lots of options and avenues to feed the beast.

5. The Value of Traditional Publishing

You get a lot of things out of traditional publishing: print distribution to bookstore shelves, some marketing support, a pro-grade editor, pro-grade cover design, a greater access to foreign rights, film rights, reviews, money up front (which mitigates risk), and some prestige.

6. The Problem With Traditional Publishing

Traditional publishing is also rife with problems: weak royalties, slower than cold honey dripping off a tauntaun's no-no pole, potentially damning contract clauses, and no control over cover design, editing, or certain aspects of marketing, and the you may still have to do a lot of marketing (because screw you, that's why).

7. The Value of Self-Publishing

Self-publishing gives you: a generally excellent percentage on "royalties;" control over cover design, editing, and marketing; speed, since you can publish with the click of a button and have your work sent across the digital ether within twenty-four hours; ability to publish whatever the hell you want whenever the hell you want it.

8. The Problem With Self-Publishing

The downsides of self-publishing are: minimal print distribution, lots of work on your part (you're no longer just a writer and are, in fact, a small publisher); difficulty accessing to film rights, foreign rights, other licensed rights, or reviews; still the occasional person looking down their nose at you because you're not "really published," and larger financial risk going in with no guarantee of recouping expenses.

9. The Hybrid Author Sees Opportunity Everywhere

Where other authors see difficulty in transitioning, the hybrid author looks at all the models new and old as an *opportunistic challenge*. These are doors to open, not walls impeding us. Hybrid authors are the tripped-out, mind-boggled shamans of the tribe: We wander away from the firelight illuminating known paths, find our own way through the darkness, and then eventually report back. Somewhere in there we also fight the Jaguar Queen and free the Machine Elves from her reign of terror. Or maybe that's just me.

10. How to Choose? The Three Axes

Each project will go its own way. How does one choose? Consider these three axes of possibility—money, exposure, and rights management. First, let's talk about …

11. Cash Money, Honey Bunny

Money matters. I have a family. A mortgage. A couple of dogs. A raging pop culture addiction. I NEED CASH. Money is a major consideration for how to publish, so you want to take a look at which path maximizes your cash flow for a given project. But it isn't *all about* the money, either. And what seems like a guarantee for cash may not be: 70 percent is a great rate for a self-pub book, but if the book isn't likely to sell a lot in that space, then traditional publishing will be a stronger buy-in. (Consider that 70 percent of $1,000 is less than 25 percent of $5,000. The percentage rate there isn't the end-all, be-all of the discussion.)

12. Audience Exposure

Sometimes it's not about how much money you can make but how much audience you can earn from a given release: Diversity across publishing models and genres can offer you access to different audience makeups, so early on you may be more focused on gaining an audience than earning money. (Though be aware, too, that writers, like hikers, can die from exposure.)

13. Rights and Control

Some authors are control freaks—you may know that a certain book of yours won't get the treatment you feel it deserves in the hands of a publisher, so you choose to control everything yourself. On the other hand, maybe you've heard rumors that right now, Hollywood and foreign markets are buying the hell out of Urban Extraterrestrial Erotica, so you decide to go to a more traditional market in the hopes of selling ancillary rights, thus ceding some control for a larger distribution.

14. Hybrid Authors Need Hybrid Agents

If you want to do everything, you need to have an agent that supports you doing everything. Note that this doesn't mean having an agent who is also your publisher (for there lies squicky, sticky territory). It does mean having a forward-looking agent who recognizes the value of your hybridity.

15. Leverage One Form Against the Other
Strong sales in self-publishing can transition into a traditional deal (perhaps even one for print only); a strong audience built via traditional release may then be more likely to buy into a self-published offering even if they were before unlikely to do so.

16. Allies on All Sides
Publishing lends itself to all manner of tribal war: The traditional publishers in their hovering doom-craft sweep over the guerilla cave-hackers of self-publishing, and the war for the hearts and minds of readers everywhere goes on. But if you trod all the paths, you're like some mythic warrior out of an epic fantasy novel born with a mother and father from both sides of the warring peoples. You'll have allies—and audience—on both sides of the divide.

17. From Self to Trad (AKA, "Doin' the Howey")
Some authors begin in self-publishing, make bank, get attention, and secure a traditional deal as a result. In the case of Hugh Howey (author of the Wool series), his deal was purely for print—he maintains his own digital rights.

18. From Trad to Self (AKA, "Pulling an Eisler")
Barry Eisler (author of the John Rain novels), on the other hand, established himself with a best-selling series of thrillers (traditionally published) and moved most of his work into the DIY "indie" space, controlling his work and embracing the higher royalties found in self-publishing.

19. All of It at Once (AKA, "The Wendig Twist")

If I may honk my own boobies on this one, I began by doing it all at once. Not particularly strategic so much as it was both *eager* and *fortunate* that it paid off—I published a series of self-published writing books and a short story collection at the same time I became traditionally published, the loose and uncertain goal being to have as much available for people at one time. If they find one of my releases and like it, they'll have something else to pick up right away. Furthermore, I was able to take self-published releases and turn them into traditionally published ones. My YA "teen detective" novel *Bait Dog* will now be published by Skyscape, and my self-published writing advice became (drum roll, please) this very book you're holding right now.

20. King Kong

Amazon is the skyscraper-climbing gorilla here for hybrid authors: Most of our published books are run through their digital bowels and excreted onto reader's laps or upon their Kindles. If Amazon ever goes tits-up, we're going to see tremors in the industry like we've never seen before. The good news is that self-published authors can distribute directly, though not yet to as far-reaching an audience.

21. Hybrid Authors Make More Money

At least, so says a recent *Writer's Digest* survey. I'd also like to think the survey says that hybrid writers are happier and that they don't get fat when they eat tons of cupcakes, they don't bald, and they have the finest liquors. I might be making all of that up, though.

22. It's Quite a Lot of Work

Traditional publishing is a lot of work. Self-publishing is a lot of work in a different direction. The hybrid author does *all of this work*. It's a veritable work-a-palooza. A *worksplosion* of *workpocalyptic proportions*. But you reap what you sow, right?

23. Power and Choice Now With Authors

Here's what's awesome about hybrid authors: They represent a power shift away from larger entities (publishers) and toward authors. And at the same time, it's still a win for publishers, too—because in many cases they're getting material by authors who have been vetted by the audience and who in fact already have an audience.

24. Not Everybody Needs to Be a Hybrid Author

You don't have to be a hybrid author, by the way. Success isn't guaranteed by becoming one, nor is it withheld by not being one. You may never want to go into traditional spaces, or you may have a grim distaste for self-publishing. Find your own mojo, young penmonkey.

25. No One True Way

The takeaway here is that we have many paths up the mountain: traditional, DIY, crowdsourcing, crowdfunding, small presses, transmedia, whatever. Nobody can tell you what the true way is. They have their way; you find yours. Look for advocates, not for preachers. Seek those who wish to share knowledge, not espouse an agenda. And in the meantime? Try everything. See what works for you.

CODA: ONCE YOU HAVE KICKED ASS...

So, you just had your book published.

And you want to know what's going to happen now.

Here is—roughly, potentially, *maybe*—one scenario.

For a variable amount of time—let's call it a week—you're going to be *flying high*. Hell, flying high doesn't even cover it. You're going to be flitting around the big blue heavens with a pair of magical laser dolphins as shoes. You're going to be *past the moon*. You're going to feel like you're snorting comet dust and making sweet love to asteroids.

Because you wrote a thing.

And now that thing is really for real a really real *thing*.

Like, holy shitsharks, *it's a book*. That you wrote. That people can buy!

This is the best feeling ever … and it is not going to last. Your first high is always your best high.

But when you're not vibrating through floors and walls, you will do things in support of your books. You will write guest blogs. And you'll go to bookstores to sign books. You'll tweet about it or say things on Facebook. Maybe you'll make a book trailer. Maybe you'll do some interviews. It's still exciting! You wrote a book! You birthed it out of your head womb! This squally word baby needs your love and the love of everyone around you!

But the feedback loop isn't as robust as you'd like.

The guest blogs you wrote maybe don't get as many comments as you would have imagined. Or the tweets about your book haven't been retweeted as far and as wide as you might have hoped. You did a book reading and only three people came. Or hell, thirteen. Or *thirty*. Is it enough? You don't know. You don't even know if this stuff has an effect. Is it just you belching into the abyss? Throwing words into the void? Again you ask: *Is any of this enough?*

And you start to wonder: *Well, shit, what is enough?* You don't know.

How's the book doing? Is it selling? You literally can't tell. You don't have enough information. So you start trying to suss out information. You go to the bookstore. Maybe they have plenty of copies on the shelves, which is good, until you realize that maybe it means they haven't sold any. Or maybe they have *no* copies, which could also be *yay* but could also be *oh shit they never ordered any in the first goddamn place.*

So, you go and look at your Amazon ranking. Which is a number that has almost no discernible meaning, yet you stare at like it's a Magic Eye painting where eventually you'll see the image bleed through the chaos. You try flicking the number on the screen with your finger like maybe you can make the number jump up—tap tap tap—until you realize you want it to jump *down*, not up, and then you wonder if you'd be better off sacrificing a pigeon or a lamb or at the very least attempting to divine some news about your book from the guts of said pigeon or said lamb. You know people are buying the book, so you do another promotional salvo. Three hours later the number *increases*, it gets *bigger*, which means it's going the wrong damn way, and in three hours it gets *bigger again* like it's a snake that just ate a heavy meal.

Then you see there's an Amazon Author Ranking, which is a number that may not be hooked up to anything at all, but it purports to place you in some kind of Penmonkey Hierarchy, some Authorial Thunderdome where you aren't a champion, where you aren't within a thousand miles of a champion, and where you are in fact sandwiched between the author of *How to Avoid Huge Ships* and some algorithmic spam-bot biography of the guy who played Potsie on *Happy Days*.

Ah, so, time instead to look at reviews, because even if you don't know how many copies you're selling, you can at least see what people think. And the reviews might be glorious—readers have written epic paeans to your wonderful book and authorial presence and for one fleeting moment it's like you're back huffing comet dust and banging meteors with those magical laser-dolphin shoes until—until!—you see that someone has written a one-star review, or worse, a completely milquetoast, mediocre review where they say awful things about your book. They take to task your voice, your characters, your plot, your face, your fashion sense, your very existence, and it's like someone flung a booger into a perfectly good bowl of ice cream. Because no matter how good that ice cream was, *now it is utterly booger-doomed.*

After a few weeks, you can at least start to see Bookscan numbers through Author Central at Amazon. And the numbers are, you know, not great. You've at least sold some! So that's good. Though they're reportedly way inaccurate. And they don't show Kindle numbers. And they don't show Amazon's own sales numbers for physical copies because while Amazon is happy to give you other people's numbers, *their* numbers are a trade secret. HA HA HA STUPID AUTHOR!!!

The news isn't helping. Barnes & Noble has decided that the only thing the Nook is good for is to sell to North Koreans to control the nuclear missiles that will eventually irradiate the Californian coast. J.K. Rowling published under a pseudonym and only sold like four hundred copies, which sounds bad except then you realize it's really good and you haven't sold four hundred copies and oh … shit.

And then you start to look to see how *other* authors are selling compared to you, and screw-me-sideways-with-a-set-of-horsehead-bookends if that is not a good idea. Even if you're selling well, somebody's always doing better. They have more reviews, more fans, and more "to-be-reads" at Goodreads. Then you're gonna find that one self-published author with the ugly book cover and the misspelled book description who's probably outselling you by a margin of 137 to 1, so that night you soothe yourself by reading a good book and suddenly you're all like o*h shit this book is way better than mine I'm screwed my book is screwed we're all screwed this is the goddamn bookpocalypse for me shit shit shit SHIT!!!*

But you calm down. You got an advance. You have money. Book money, as a matter of fact, which is money you made from selling books and you used it to buy dinner or pay some bills. And that's exciting! Okay, it's not as much money as you once thought it would or could be—hell, even a low six-figure book deal on three books (one book per year) is like, barely cutting it financially. But you *made money.* On your writing. You breathe. You scrub the panic urine spots out of your office chair. And then maybe some other good news trickles in: An agent just sold foreign rights for your book to some distant country—Libya, Ancient Hyperborea, or Canada. Maybe there's an audio-rights sale. Or an options sale for some guy who wants to write the script so it'll be an episodic YouTube smash sensation.

And you start to get emails here and there. People have read the book, and they liked it. Some people have *loved it.* Those emails are kite string and a strong wind. They lift you, buoy you, send your spirits maybe not quite as cosmically high as they were, but you're still doing barrel rolls and loop-de-loops in the clouds now and again.

So you do what you must. You do what you're made to do.

You sit back down, and you start writing the next book.

And you love it. And you hate it. And the days come where you want to throw it all on top of a giant garbage fire. And the nights come where you secretly remember why you love what you're writing, and your heart pinballs around the bumpers and flippers inside your soul.

You soon are reminded that you can edit a bad page, but you can't edit a blank one.

And you realize that you can't manufacture luck, but you can maximize your chances.

You write the next book. And the next after that. And the one after that.

Somewhere along the way you realize that the happiness of publication is fleeting. The second published book isn't quite as exciting as the first, maybe. It's chasing the dragon. The first high remains the craziest and best high. But what happens is that you get to be okay with that.

Because at some point you recognize that a fleeting high or profits isn't why you write.

That isn't why you tell stories. You tell stories because you like to tell stories, not because you like to sell books. That's what gets you through. You marvel at the craft. You drown in the art. You roll around in it like a dog covering himself in sweet, sweet stink. It's not that you don't care about being published. It's not that the money is meaningless. The money is a lifeline. The money lets you do this in a bigger, more real way. But all the publishing piffle—the Amazon rankings, the guest blogs, the tweets and marketing and Kirkus reviews and drinking and existential dread—it's all *out there*. It's extra. That stuff is connected to it, but that's not it.

You do it because you love it.

You do it because you want to be read.

You tell stories because you're a storyteller. And because stories matter.

And so whether you sell four million copies or whether you sell forty, you keep going. You keep taking your shot. You keep writing your books, your comics, your movies. You write shorts and novellas and you publish some stuff traditionally and you publish other stuff directly and you find satisfaction not in the high of putting out books but in the power of doing what you do, day in and day out. It is the work that sustains you: the work of taking a dream and making it real.

You don't write to be published, but rather, you write to write and to be read.

Because that, for really real, is the truly best thing of all.

INDEX

action, 41–42, 93, 98, 168, 169, 178
act structures, 220
agents, 203, 208–16, 229, 269–70
Amazon, 229, 271, 274–75
antagonist, 136
archetypes, 92–93
arcs, 125
argument, 157–58
atmosphere, 145
audience, 18–19, 23–24, 137, 238, 244, 247, 269
   earning, 257–65
   and theme, 163
authenticity, 47, 52, 145–46, 260
   and dialogue, 178–79, 179–80
authors. *See* writers

backstory, 26
beats, 80, 90–91, 117, 118, 123, 124, 126, 134, 256
beginnings, 27, 79
blocks, writing, 18
blogging, 50, 233–39, 242
brand, 241

cause and effect, 128
change of state, 122, 134, 168
chapters, 81
character agency, 122
character arc, 81, 134
characters, 15, 26, 27, 42, 86–93, 219
   beats, 90–91
   and dialogue, 177–78
   and endings, 187
   flaws of, 138, 154
   main. *See* protagonists
   and plot, 115–16
   and scene, 166
   and setting, 17, 141–42
   supporting, 91
   and tension, 152–53
clarity, 10, 107, 197

clauses, 104
clichés, 100
climax, 79, 170, 182–83
coding, 236–37
collage, 82–83
complexity, 26–27, 91, 92, 123–24, 146
conflict, 16, 24, 79, 113, 114, 122, 138, 144, 167, 219–20
   and dialogue, 179
   and setting, 17
consistency, 135, 144, 160, 197, 198
control, 57–58, 95
covers, book, 205, 228
creativity, 51, 76, 196
criticism, 9, 35, 49, 263
crowdfunding, 249–56

danger, 151
death, 65
denouement, 79, 183–84
description, 42, 93, 94–102, 142, 143
detail, 94–95, 95–96, 98, 142–43, 145
dialogue, 41–42, 81, 93, 98, 168, 169, 173–81
distractions, 17, 75
diversity, 58, 258, 267, 269
drafts, 38–39, 80, 191–98
dramatic irony, 151

e-books, 228
editing, 9, 10–11, 48, 191–98
editors, 48, 194, 203, 228–29
emotions, 22, 139
endings, 79, 120, 182–90, 221, 222
entertainment, 21–22
episodic narrative, 128
escalation, 24, 79, 113, 125, 150, 153
expletive construction, 110
exposition, 119, 175

Facebook, 242
failure, 155
falling action, 183
fear, 60, 63, 114, 155, 156, 166
feedback, 263
feelings, 17, 22

risk, 57, 232
role-playing, 72–73
rule of three, 90–91, 95–96, 124, 142

sadness, 138–39
scenes, 16, 118, 165–72
screenplays, 101–2
script writing, 74, 81, 96
search engine optimization, 239
self-care, 56
self-promotion, 239, 243–44
self-publishing, 34, 54, 201–3, 205, 225–32, 268, 270–72. *See also* publishing
senses, 101, 143–44
sentences, 103–11
sequences, 23, 76, 79, 118
setting, 17, 28, 140–48, 166
sex, 65
simplicity, 92, 105
social media, 209, 240–48, 261–62
spreadsheets, 83, 196
stereotypes, 146–47
story bible, 83
story boards, 84
storytelling, 7–8, 10, 21–28, 123
  as art, 28, 29, 31, 47
stream of consciousness, 83–84
structure, 23, 121–30
struggle, 24
subplot, 113, 118–19
subtext, 28, 169–70
suspense, 64, 89, 149–56, 177
synopses, 82, 217–24

templates, 83
tension, 24–25, 63, 64, 89, 115, 117–18, 149–56, 177
tentpole moments, 79, 117, 220, 242
theme, 137, 144, 157–64
  and dialogue, 178
  and endings, 184–85
  identifying, 13
Themeforest, 236
tragedy, 62
treatments, 217–24

trends, 58, 206
Tumblr, 242
Twitter, 242

urban legends, 62

villains, 26
voice, 8, 14, 51, 54, 177–78, 222

wants, 114
white board, 82
word count, 18, 20
Wordpress, 236
worry, 54
writers, 5–12. *See also* writing
  and agents, 215, 216
  aspiring, 29–36
  as bridge to audience, 23–24
  how to be better, 45–52
  hybrid, 266–72
  and reading, 32
  things to stop doing, 53–60
writer's block, 70–77
writing, 13–20. *See also* writers
  basics, 5–6
  commerce of, 32–33, 58, 59
  as craft, 28, 31, 47
  degree in, 6, 32
  finishing, 31
  groups, 48, 50
  horror, 61–69
  importance of practice, 45
  organizing the story, 78–84
  as process, 6–7
  reading it aloud, 49
  reasons for, 14
  rules for, 31
  saving, 19
  selling, 274–76
  skill vs. talent, 6
  technical skills, 47–48
  value of, 8
  and writer's block, 70–77